CRY WOLF:

The Psychology of False Alarms

CRY WOLF:

The Psychology of False Alarms

Shlomo Breznitz
University of Haifa

LEA LAWRENCE ERLBAUM ASSOCIATES, PUBLISHERS
1984 Hillsdale, New Jersey   London

Copyright © 1984 by Lawrence Erlbaum Associates, Inc.
All rights reserved. No part of this book may be reproduced in
any form, by photostat, microform, retrieval system, or any other
means, without the prior written permission of the publisher.

Lawrence Erlbaum Associates, Inc., Publishers
365 Broadway
Hillsdale, New Jersey 07642

BF
789
.F29
B73
1984

Library of Congress Cataloging in Publication Data

Breznitz, Shlomo.
  Cry wolf.

  Bibliography: p.
  Includes index.
  1. False alarms—Psychological aspects. 2. Warnings—
Psychological aspects. 3. Threat (Psychology)
4. Fear. I. Title.
BF789.F29B73   1984   155.9   83-16456
ISBN 0-89859-296-8

Printed in the United States of America
10 9 8 7 6 5 4 3 2 1

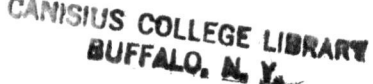

TO THE MEMORY OF MY MOTHER

Contents

Acknowledgments   xi
Introduction   xiii

1. WARNING SYSTEMS   1
   Threat as a Psychological Variable   3
   Parameters of Threat   5
   Functional Warning Systems   6

2. THE FALSE ALARM EFFECT   9
   The False Alarm Effect   11
   False Alarm Effect as an Instrument for Achieving
       Surprise   14

3. NAIVE VERSUS CYNICAL DANGERS   17
   Naive Dangers   18
   Cynical Dangers   18
   Accidents   20

4. RESEARCH METHOD: STRATEGY AND TACTICS   23
   General Considerations   23
   An Intellectual Exercise with Parameters of
       Threat   25
   Basic Threat   27
   Indexes of the False Alarm Effect   39

5. PACING OF WARNINGS AND THE FALSE ALARM EFFECT   40
   Experimental Design   41
   Results   46

6. PROBABILITY OF THREAT AND THE FALSE ALARM
   EFFECT 61
       Effect of Probability of Threat on Fear   63
       Experimental Design   64
       Results   66

7. PROTECTIVE BEHAVIOR AND THE FALSE ALARM
   EFFECT 77
       Behavioral Measures of the False Alarm Effect   77
       Methodological Considerations   79
       Laboratory Setting and Instructions   80
       Results   82
       Much Ado About Nothing   98
       Typology of Threat Reactions   100

8. IT'S NOW OR NEVER: PROTECTIVE BEHAVIOR
   UNDER TIME PRESSURE 103
       Results   104
       Summary   112

9. ATTEMPTS TO RESTORE CREDIBILITY BY EXPLAINING
   THE CAUSES OF FALSE ALARMS 114
       Methods   117
       Results   120

10. PERFORMANCE, TRAINING, AND PROTECTIVE
    BEHAVIOR 128
        Task Orientation Versus Danger Orientation   129
        Part One: Task Performance and Training   133
        Results   138
        Part Two: Training of Protective Behavior   154
        Method   154
        Results   155

11. THE ROLE OF PERSONALITY DIFFERENCES IN
    THE FALSE ALARM SITUATION 160
        Method   163
        Results   164

12. THE THREE SYSTEMS ANALYSIS OF FEAR
    RECONSIDERED 177
        Desynchrony as a Goal   178
        Desynchrony and the False Alarm Effect   184
        Four Systems Analysis of Fear   194

13. SOME CLINICAL AND THEORETICAL ISSUES   195
        Avoidance and Protective Behavior   195
        Fear of Danger Versus Fear of Fear   198
        False Alarm Effect: Habituation,
            Extinction, or What?   200

14. TOWARD A THEORY OF CREDIBILITY
    OF WARNING SYSTEMS   204
        The Law of Initial Credibility   206
        A Possible Explanation of the Law of Initial
            Credibility   212
        The Law of Interwarning Similarity   214
        Positive Aspects of False Alarms   217
        The Psychology of False Promises   217

15. DEFENSE AGAINST FALSE ALARMS:
    PRACTICAL IMPLICATIONS   219
        Preventive Measures by Information-Management
            Subsystems   220
        Corrective Measures by Information-Management
            Subsystems   223
        Selecting Individuals Resistant to the False Alarm
            Effect   225
        Training Against the False Alarm Effect   226
        Social Norms in Defense Against the False Alarm
            Effect   226
        Institutional Support in Defense Against False
            Alarms   227
        Natural Disasters   229
        Military Dangers   230
        Warning Systems in the Area of Health   232

Appendix A
        Post-Experimental Questionnaire   234

Appendix B
        Ordered Display   236

Appendix C
        Instructions for the Number Search Task   237

Appendix D   239

Appendix E
>   Means, Standard Deviations and Analyses of Variance of Task Performance   241

Appendix F
>   Instructions for Intolerance of Ambiguity Task   250

Appendix G
>   Instructions for Risk-Taking Test   251

References   253

Author Index   259

Subject Index   263

Acknowledgments

The research reported in this volume has been made possible by Contract number DAERO-75-G-055 from the U.S. Army Research Institute for the Behavioral and Social Sciences through its European Liaison Office at the European Research Office of the U.S. Army, London, England. The opinions expressed are those of the author and do not necessarily represent those of the U.S. Army.

The personal support I received from the leading staff of that institute is immeasurable. I owe special thanks to Drs. Zeidner, Uhlaner, Helme, Drucker, and Sasmor. It was, however, only through the active interest, encouragement, and good counsel of Dr. Michael Kaplan that this work could be accomplished.

The staff of the Ray D. Wolfe Centre for Study of Psychological Stress at the University of Haifa provided invaluable help. I am particularly indebt to H. Ben-Zur, who was irreplaceable at all stages of the research. R. Maos, D. Katz, and E. Baksi did marvels with the manuscript and the figures.

This book could not, however, have been completed without the helpful pressures from my family and the patience and understanding of my publisher. Larry Erlbaum gave me all the time I needed, which was all for the better.

Introduction

The story of "the shepherd who cried wolf" appears in Aesop's Fables, and in some minor variations it can be found in the folklore of many different cultures. The psychological effects of false alarms have been widely recognized and even put to use. Thus, according to Liddell Hart (1962), Alexander the Great in the battle against Porus (331 B.C.) produced deliberate false alarms: "Repeated noisy marches and counter-marches of Alexander's cavalry kept Porus on tenterhooks, and then, through repetition, dulled his reaction [p. 41]."

False alarms play a major role in any warning system, whether manufactured or natural. It is thus surprising that they have not been studied systematically. This volume reports an experimental program that attempted to provide such systematic analysis of what appears to be a highly prevalent phenomenon.

With the rise of sophisticated early warning systems, false alarms are inevitably on the increase, and their psychological impact may well turn out to be the most vulnerable link of many warning systems. It is my hope that this volume provides some answers to these new challenges.

1 Warning Systems

"Coming events cast their shadows before them."
—Thomas Campbell: *Lochiel's Warning*, 1802.

The human ability to anticipate the future is one of our most cherished possessions. No longer bound to the immediate sensory experience, individuals can plan ahead and prepare themselves for things to come. Sometimes, if it is in their power, people might even try to use this foresight to turn the course of events to their liking.

However, this competence to leap beyond the here and the now has its cost. Remote dangers often become part of the present, and by virtue of symbolic representation in thought, we are masters as well as slaves of future events. Thus, the knowledge that death is inevitable is in a sense the kernel of the "human condition." In the extreme form, through fear and anxiety—those cornerstones of anticipatory knowledge—a person dies a thousand deaths before his or her time. The idea of inevitable personal death is, however, too overpowering to be psychologically acceptable as a constant facet of the present. "Memento Mori" became a slogan just because of the tendency of humans to deny death the status of an omnipresent companion. Closer dangers, even though less important, are much more difficult to deny.

Consider a woman waiting to undergo surgery. The real and imaginary dangers would be relevant only during the operation proper, let us say a day, a week, or a month from now. But through anticipation, these dangers exist in the woman's present right now, and might stay there until the operation is over.

Consider a student about to take an important examination in a week's time. He can prepare himself by studying the material. But to the degree that the examination becomes anticipated, he would also ponder upon its negative aspects. He might fail, and failure has certain consequences. These in turn have other additional consequences. Thus, during the week preceding the examination, some unpleasant possibilities lie in store.

Many other examples come to mind. For instance, what happens to a soldier who is told in advance of a dangerous mission?

It would be a great asset if it were possible to extract from the future only the positive components and let the negative ones take care of themselves when the time finally arrives. How good if the student's knowledge of the impending examination made him study without at the same time causing him to worry. How peaceful the last days prior to surgery can be with the comforting knowledge that one is in good hands and nothing can go wrong.

Anticipation, however, is a package deal, and the knowledge that something dangerous, painful, or unpleasant is going to happen in the future is bound to be threatening. And yet, this is a price we are willing to pay to avoid that archenemy—surprise. Surprise is a major blow to human intelligence and dignity. Homo sapiens prides itself in fighting ignorance. It is our forte, our domain, but at times, our undoing.

What is the driving force behind this concentrated attempt to reduce uncertainty? Why this major effort to penetrate the mysteries of things to come? Are uncertain threats more frightening than certain ones? Is ambiguity always a major source of distress? Or, perhaps, Freud was right after all, and man is driven to explore the external world by displacing his overriding anxiety of discovering his inner uncharted territory.

The behavioral pragmatist would laugh this off, pointing out the functional elements in anticipation of future events, particularly negative events. One might utilize the time between a threat and its materialization to his or her advantage. One can learn to prepare for the danger or, if possible, even to avoid it. Such effective coping would surely reinforce the tendency to study the warning signals of future dangers. In other words, so goes the argument, we invest in predicting the future because it pays off.

A "pleasant surprise" is pleasant, whereas an "unpleasant surprise" is not. Thus, it is not "surprise" as such that we abhor, only its negative variety. In an article discussing all available evidence on choosing between predictable and unpredictable shock conditions, Badia and Harsh (1979) conclude that animals: "prefer predictable conditions whether shock is avoidable, escapable, or inescapable [p. 1107]." They also note that most of the evidence favors the theoretical explanations stressing notions such as "preparation" and "safety." The human animal is presumably no exception to this rule.

But a word of caution is in order. Not all futures provide sufficient warnings, not all of those that do can be actively coped with, and not all people seem to take advantage of those that can. The intricate complexity of these issues becomes more evident as our discussion unfolds. The point should be made, however, that neither behavioral prgamatists nor their dynamic counterparts can hope to furnish a coherent answer to this set of questions. The interactions between the situational determinants and personality predispositions are the crux of the matter, and they defy any simple formulation at this point.

THREAT AS A PSYCHOLOGICAL VARIABLE

In order to anticipate impending negative events, certain warning signals must precede them. The existence of such warnings is an essential feature of psychological stress. The central concept here is *threat*, which students of stress seem to agree is the key concept when dealing with psychological rather than physical stress. In his illuminating analysis, Lazarus (1966) states:

> It is not the present damage or harm that constitutes the threat, but rather the harmful events provide cues about future consequences. In effect, threat arises from present cues about future harms. This is one of the distinctions between physiological and psychological stress. The former is a response to physical damage already incurred. The latter refers to the psychological harm anticipated from cues which are interpreted as portending that harm [p. 32].

The same point was made by Withey (1962):

> The notion of threat specifically implies that the noxious stimuli are not actually present. Only the cues heralding their coming are involved. In some cases these cues themselves may have physiologically stressful characteristics, but we are not interested here in purely physiological adaptations to an extremely stressful condition but rather in reactions mediated by psychological processes such as conditioning, perception, thinking, defense mechanism, etc., that are triggered off by various available cues signifying impending stress [p. 94].

Accepting the anticipatory nature of psychological stress, the centrality of the threat concept must also be granted. After all, the word itself denotes some harm in the future, which becomes relevant to the present only through mediating psychological processes.

When the whole course of a stressful episode is analyzed, as for instance in disaster studies, threat becomes central to the initial preimpact period. This is well illustrated in the works of Powell and Rayner (1952), Wallace (1956), Chapman (1962), as well as in the interesting analyses of Janis (1954, 1962).

The importance of the concept of threat makes its exact definition a tempting, though frustrating, exercise. Various researchers have attempted to define threat in their own special way best suited to their particular theoretical and empirical interests. As in many other areas of psychological inquiry, there is no single accepted definition, with all that this implies for comparability of the various analytic frameworks. Thus, for instance, Withey (1962) defines threat by its consequences:

> The presence of threat will be regarded as a form of stress in which the severity of the possible impending event, its probability of occurrence, and the ability of the person to cope with the eventuality and the present tension result in various degrees of apprehension, worry, fear or anxiety [p. 94–95].

A somewhat different approach is advocated by Lazarus (1966). Being interested in the various cognitive processes that mediate the reaction to stress, he chooses to highlight the individual's appraisal of the situation:

> For threat to occur, an evaluation must be made of the situation, to the effect that a harm is signified. The individual's knowledge and beliefs contribute to this. The appraisal of threat is not a simple perception of the elements of the situation, but a judgment, an inference in which the data are assimilated to a constellation of ideas and expectations [p. 44].

Ours is yet a different kind of bias, and the studies to be reported in this volume all assume a situationally based definition of threat. In order to save an additional degree of freedom, the response to threat is never used as a definiens, nor are the beliefs and expectations of the threatened individuals used in this manner. Both of these are used as dependent variables only, whereas threat is conceived primarily as an independent variable. There is obviously nothing definitive in taking a position on a particular definition. It should be viewed as a preference for a particular research strategy rather than as a statement of well-documented conclusion. For the purposes of the research presented here the following should suffice: *A stimulus conveying information about a future event with which a negative affect is associated is termed a threat.*

Being a stimulus, in order to exist psychologically the threat must be perceived by the individual. In other words, like any stimulus, it must be above a threshold level on some relevant sensory dimension. In order to insure that a particular stimulus is indeed threatening, it is the task of the researcher to choose such stimuli that leave no doubt about the affective implication of their message. As an ardent believer in utilizing powerful experimental manipulations, this requirement is in my view a major asset of the proposed definition. In other words, as long as the threats are sufficiently intense, we might be better off assuming them a priori rather than attempting to detect them on the basis of our subjects' behavior.

PARAMETERS OF THREAT

Threats are essentially messages about the future. The information they convey typically contains the following parameters:

1. The probability of the impending danger to actually materialize.
2. The qualitative nature of the danger.
3. The intensity or magnitude of the potential harm.
4. The extent to which active coping is possible.
5. The imminence of the danger.
6. The extent to which similar dangers have been experienced before.
7. The level of clarity or ambiguity of the message.

All these parameters have both objective and subjective values which need not overlap. Such discrepancies are among the most fascinating issues of stress research. At the same time, they also pose a major obstacle to our understanding of threats and their effects on behavior. Although there is a growing interest in providing the clues to subjective estimates of objective probabilities (e.g., Slovic, Fishoff, & Lichtenstein, 1980; Slovic & Lichtenstein, 1971; Tversky & Kahneman, 1974), the process is still very much a mystery. The same is true of subjective versus objective helplessness (e.g., Seligman, 1975; Seligman & Groves, 1970).

The information concerning some of the foregoing parameters of threat need not always be explicit. When implicit or when inferred from other available cues, it can be just as influential in controlling the threat reaction as when directly stated.

From the point of view of warning systems, the two most important features of threats are: (1) the objective ability to cope with the impending danger and (2) their imminence. The logic is simple: The raison d'etre of a warning system is to provide the opportunity for coping. Thus, if the situation is one of objective helplessness, there is not much to gain by an early warning system. Alternatively, if there is objective control over a danger, which is already so close that there is not time to engage in the effective behavior, the warning system is once again futile. It follows that in order for a warning system to have any effectiveness at all, there must be some objective control over the danger and sufficient time to carry out the necessary actions.

Both conditions are necessary. Having one without the other is not just ineffective, but may actually be detrimental to adjustment. Thus, the availability of long warning time in objectively helpless situations was found to increase the fear reaction due to a process called "incubation of threat." Breznitz (1967, 1968, 1971) reported studies indicating that the longer the duration of helpless anticipation, the stronger the fear and worry demonstrated by human subjects.

Similar results were obtained by Nomikos, Opton, Averill, and Lazarus (1968), Folkins (1970), Mansueto and Desiderato (1971), and others. It is conceivable that incubation of threat is particularly potent in situations that do not allow subjects to distract their minds from the impending danger.

Dangers that are objectively escapable but in which time is too short to insure safety likewise have the potential of being extremely stressful. These are the situations that best fit the prototype of panic behavior, with all its dire consequences (e.g., Kelley, Condry, Dahlke, & Hill, 1965; Mintz, 1951; Smelser, 1963).

Objectively controllable dangers can be subjectively perceived by the threatened person as situations of helplessness, leading to incubation of threat or, at best, to coping by "palliation" (Lazarus, 1966) of the emotional reaction rather than acting upon the environment itself. This can happen for a variety of personal reasons beyond the scope of this discussion. Similar causes can make a particular person perceive the danger as more imminent than it actually is and "freeze" due to the implication of such an interpretation of the threatening information. Such a response in turn clearly leads to waste of precious coping time, turning the person's initial subjective interpretation into a self-fulfilling prophecy.

It is obvious that we cannot escape the complexities of the objective/subjective dilemma. At most, we can claim that objective control and sufficient coping time are the necessary conditions for warning systems to be functional. Sometimes, but clearly not always, they are also sufficient conditions.

To complicate matters further, the decision as to what constitutes active coping is not a simple one. Dangers have many facets, some more explicit than others. Thus, when a cancer patient is told that his chances to stay alive beyond a limited time are minimal, there is clearly not much he can do to control the danger of death itself. And yet, his is not a case of total helplessness. He may utilize the remaining time to put his finances in order, to prepare his will, and by managing his priorities, to concentrate on doing just that which is most precious to him. All this is active coping, even though the main threat remains unaffected. Real-life situations are just too complex to fit our classification systems, which have been developed in the protected environment of the research laboratory.

FUNCTIONAL WARNING SYSTEMS

Functional warning systems provide the opportunity for protective behavior to occur before a threat materializes. The variety of warning systems defies any attempt to enumerate them. They appear in finished forms as products of the long experimentation of biological evolution. They may develop as a consequence of a learning history with dangers or as systems protecting inanimate objects. Warning systems can be part of a biological system, a sociocultural system, or an artificial technical system. They can be inborn or acquired, intentional or unintentional, automatic or intelligent.

For example, one of the most intricate biological warning systems is *the immune system* of mammals. It consists of continuous surveillance of the internal environment of the organism, on the lookout for potential intruders. When a danger is apprehended, the immune system calls the alarm and starts mobilizing vast resources to cope with it. Early detection insures that in most instances the alarm is sounded before the danger is too serious to handle. To enhance its effectiveness further, the immune system possesses a remarkable ability to learn and to sensitize the body's defenses to previously encountered threats. This facilitates dealing with similar threats in the future, as is best demonstrated by the principle of biological inoculation. When the initial attempts to combat the danger prove insufficient, other levels of organization such as inflammation, rise in temperature, and so one, register the warning. These cues can lead to further mobilization of defensive resources. In the case of humans, consulting a physician and taking medication are important additional cultural components of a basically inborn warning system. For people to consult a physician, they must first apprehend the threat, utilizing symptoms as warnings.

A much simpler biological warning system is illustrated by the pain produced when a sharp pointed object touches the skin. The pain serves as an early warning of the potential danger of tissue damage, and the automatic response is one of removing the organ from contact with the danger. If time permits, such action will suffice to escape before the damage is serious. In the absence of sufficient time (i.e., when the sharp object immediately penetrates the tissue), the pain, though not instrumental in avoiding the danger, can yet alert the organism to the need for help.

Biological warning systems are particularly multileveled and versatile, taking into account the possibility that one section of the warning system might prove ineffective, enhancing the need for alternative lines of defense. By contrast, many artificial warning systems are quite simple. Consider, for example, the function of a smoke detector, a sign stating DANGER—EXPLOSIVES, the symbol of a human skull warning of high electric voltage or poison, or the red light on the control panel switching on when a car engine overheats. These are all functional warning systems conveying information of a potentially dangerous event before it actually takes place. If the recipient of the threat heeds it and acts upon it, the danger is reduced or even avoided entirely.

Another different class of warning systems deals with large-scale dangers, such as natural disasters, military disasters, or major industrial disasters. Warning time can be essential if an entire population has to be evacuated from a target area. Thus, floods, hurricanes, spillage of poisonous chemicals or atomic radiation, or for that matter, an enemy attack, should all be apprehended as soon as possible to allow the carrying out of measures to protect life and property. There do not exist functional warning systems of impending earthquakes as yet, but they might be forthcoming in the not too distant future. When that happens, all major natural dangers could, in principle, be apprehended before they strike.

Let us not forget the forest for the trees. The interesting variety of warning systems should not keep us from seeing the basic common properties they all share. Chief among those is the distinction between two subsystems—one dealing with *the detection of information* and the other with *the management of that information*. The detection subsystem utilizes specific sensors to pick up cues of dangers, which are the input to that subsystem. Its output consists of threats, that is, information concerning impending dangers. This output is in turn the input of the information-management subsystem. Its function is to release and disseminate the information according to certain principles. It should be noted that the rules of operation of the information-management subsystem are largely independent of the detection subsystem. In other words, the way some particular threatening information is released and disseminated is not a direct function of the way it was derived in the first place. Whereas detection sensors can have biological, chemical, or electrical properties, the management of the information always has a psychological aspect to its modus operandi.

The analysis of warning systems in our research, therefore, concentrates on the information-management subsystems and assumes the detection component as a given input. The existence of a warning system, even of a functional one, does not always necessarily imply reduced danger. As the research shows, there is an imminent weakness in most warning systems. The exploration of that weakness is the main subject of this book.

2 The False Alarm Effect

Day 1: A tropical storm is forming somewhere in the Atlantic, far from any coast. Its development is slow but persistent, and on Day 6 the winds reach hurricane force. The hurricane travels northwest, in the general direction of the Caribbean. On Day 10 it slightly alters its course taking a more northerly route. It is now just a few hundred miles off Florida. On Day 11 the eye of the storm is almost stationary, and then it starts moving due north. The winds are subsiding, and on Day 13 what remains of the original weather system is quickly dissipating on its northeastern route toward the vast open spaces of the Atlantic.

The year is 1900, long before the advent of satellite photography or radar screens. Nobody in Florida, or for that matter in the entire United States, heard about the hurricane. With the exception of a small fishing vessel, which ventured too far and failed to return, the birth and death of a terrible storm was never detected, never noticed. Were it not for the change in the winds during the night between Day 10 and Day 11, it would have been an entirely different story. During the early morning hours, the hurricane would have been barely 40 miles from Miami, and everybody who cared to look would have seen its unmistakable signs. Being that close, close enough for eye contact, there would have been no time left for a miracle change in its course. The people of Miami would have looked seawards and, realizing that the storm was almost upon them, would have taken whatever protective action they could. But that is not what happened on that summer morning. Instead, the winds changed, and Miami went about its daily business as usual.

But imagine the same storm in the year 1980. Day 1: The National Hurricane Center in Miami releases to the media satellite pictures of the tropical storm forming in mid-Atlantic. Millions of Americans see the pictures on television.

2. THE FALSE ALARM EFFECT

During the coming days, the storm becomes a familiar feature of the news broadcasts. On Day 6 a hurricane watch is issued for the entire Gulf of Mexico. At this point the hurricane can hit any of the Gulf areas. On Day 10 southern Florida is on a hurricane alert, and all the low-lying areas are being evacuated. On Day 11 the alert is called off. Toward evening, citizens are returning to their homes. This time it was a false alarm.

Between 1900 and 1980, the warning system for tropical storms was entirely revolutionized, particularly its detection subsystem. As a consequence, there is now a much longer warning time. Practically no detection time is lost, and the potential danger is apprehended almost immediately. A longer warning time inevitably implies less accuracy.

In the year 1900 there were fewer false alarms than today. People learned about the danger when they actually saw it. They had only a short time to prepare for it, but it was always credible. Their preparations were always necessary, and those who made them were invariably vindicated by the events. In the event of a false alarm, they never knew about it, and thus, from their point of view it did not exist.

By contrast, any attempt to utilize longer warning times takes the risk of massive false alarms. When the storm is 5 days away from the coast, even the most minute change in its direction will bring it far from its presently anticipated point of impact. Consequently, in our hypothetical story, the entire Gulf of Mexico must be alerted, though even in the event of a true impact only a small fraction of that entire area would be affected. The sooner the alert, the larger the number people who subsequently find out that it was unnecessary.

Because the future can only rarely be entirely deduced from the present, and because an element of uncertainty is inevitable, all warning systems, particularly sensitive ones, trade off accuracy for warning time. The more sensitive a warning system is, the greater the uncertainty under which it operates and the more frequent the false alarms it produces. There are two main reasons for this:

1. The more sensitive a warning system, the weaker are the signals it detects. The signal-to-noise ratio of sensitive warning systems is smaller than that of crude warning systems. This in turn implies a high frequency of false alarms (Green & Swets, 1966).
2. The more sensitive a warning system, the less imminent is the danger. Consequently, there is more time available for changes. There are more opportunities for changes in the situation, and even minor changes have time to develop their impact.

Thus, attempts to reduce surprise necessarily lead to more alarms, particularly, more false alarms.

THE FALSE ALARM EFFECT

The effectiveness of a warning system depends significantly on its credibility. To what extent does a person take a threat seriously enough to engage in protective behavior? Is the warning system credible? What is its record of "hits"?

Each false alarm reduces the credibility of a warning system. The credibility loss following a false alarm episode has serious ramifications to behavior in a variety of response channels. Thus, future similar alerts may receive less attention. They may elicit weaker fear reactions. The threat may be perceived as less intense or less probable. People may overestimate their ability to cope with the danger if and when it materializes. Or, most important, they may reduce their willingness to engage in protective behavior.

The credibility loss due to a false alarm can be labeled the *false alarm effect* (FAE). It is assumed that the FAE is an automatic consequence of a false alarm episode. It is particularly strong in warning systems in which the recipient of the information is an intelligent being. The reason for this is that the FAE indicates learning from experience. On the basis of a false alarm experience, the recipient of the threatening information draws some conclusion about the credibility of the warning system. Thus, the more developed the learning capacity of the alerted unit, the stronger the FAE. On the basis of our analysis of sensitive early warning systems, we may now posit that the more sensitive a warning system, the greater the FAE it suffers through repeated false alarms.

There is something essentially realistic about this, because such warning systems are truly less credible. FAEs are the psychological mechanism through which the credibility level is ascertained.

What Is Learned by False Alarms?

The observable indicators of FAE are behaviors implying that the threatening information is taken less seriously than before. However, the diagnostic value of these behaviors is somewhat limited due to the fact that credibility loss can indicate two quite different learning processes. To explicate them, we must first consider the flow of information in a given warning system. This is schematically presented in Fig. 2.1.

Intrinsic information is the information supplied by the warning system proper. By contrast, extrinsic information about both the danger and the warning system itself is supplied by other channels. It is worth noting that in the anticipatory phase, information about the danger proper is often exclusively intrinsic (i.e., it is supplied by the warning system). In the extreme case where there is no extrinsic information available, receivers are entirely dependent on the warning system. Following a false alarm episode, receivers might change their beliefs about the effectiveness of the warning system to provide credible information;

2. THE FALSE ALARM EFFECT

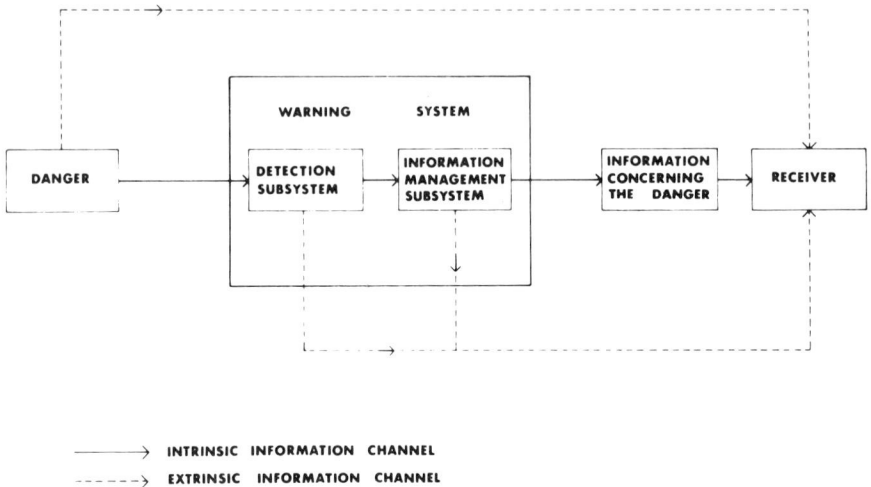

FIG. 2.1 Information flow in a warning system.

after all, the initial threat proved to be unwarranted. They might, however, also change their beliefs about the danger itself and perceive it as more benign than prior to the FAE. Phenotypically, both of these changes will result in behaviors indicating credibility loss in the advent of a similar subsequent threat. Because in both situations the immediate overt symptoms of a FAE will be the same, a more sensitive probe is needed to distinguish between those two entirely different phenomena. Let us have a closer look at what is involved.

Upon learning that a previously announced threat was canceled by the warning system and thus the danger is over, people attempt to assimilate this new information cognitively. Why did the threat turn out to be a false alarm? They may attribute it entirely to the ineffectiveness of the detection function of the warning system. In such a case there is no need to change the view of the particular danger involved. As a consequence, the warning system loses credibility, and the concept of the danger remains unaltered. This can be further enhanced by extrinsic information supporting the notion of the warning system's ineffectiveness or of the seriousness of the danger.

Alternatively, receivers may keep their belief in the credibility of the warning system intact and change their perception of the danger proper. Such a cognitive process can in turn be facilitated by independent extrinsic evidence.

Attributing the false alarm exclusively to either one of these factors protects the other one from change. In attributing the "blame" for a false alarm the receiver need not have a clear choice between the two, thus the FAE may affect both to a different degree. Logically, however, their respective vulnerability is mutually exclusive. The greater the change in beliefs concerning the one, the smaller is the need to change beliefs concerning the other. The particular outcome following a given false alarm episode will be greatly influenced by extrinsic information as well as by previous experience with the warning system and with similar dangers in the past.

Because the main function of warning systems is to reduce the chances of a danger striking by surprise, if a warning system indeed fails to alert the receiver to an impending danger, it often becomes totally discredited. And yet, such a major blow to the warning system at the same time increases the credibility of the danger itself. This once again illustrates indirectly the negative relationship between these two factors.

It ought to be stressed that if the FAE primarily affects the credibility of warning systems, leaving that of the danger intact, this is the less damaging of the two. A warning system can be corrected or replaced, whereas the dangers as such only rarely lend themselves to direct manipulation by the receiver. This implies a fascinating paradox: In conditions of uncertainty, the higher the initial credibility of a warning system, the greater danger it poses to the credibility of the danger it is monitoring.

An obvious, legitimate argument to the contrary is that a highly credible warning system is less likely to fail in the first place. However, in the case of sensitive early warning systems, the foregoing argument is true only in relation to one kind of mistake, namely, failure to alert in case of actual danger. The other kind of mistakes (e.g., false alarms) are actually more frequent in the case of such warning systems. Thus, the paradoxical weakness of a highly credible warning system lies of course in the FAE.

The hypothetical 1980 hurricane illustrates this point quite well. The credibility of the warning system in this case is greatly enhanced by the fact that receivers can actually see for themselves the satellite pictures of the storm. There is no doubt that it exists and that it is approaching. Thus, when the threat is eventually called off, the main lesson learned by the receiver relates to the nature of hurricanes themselves rather than their detectors.

There is an interesting asymmetry between true alarms and false alarms. Whereas true alarms (i.e., threats which materialize) increase the credibility of both the danger and the warning system, false alarms may reduce the credibility of only one of these two.

True alarms, particularly if they follow a long period of false alarms, significantly restore the lost credibility. At any given time, the credibility status of warning systems is a function of the ratio of recent true alarms to recent false alarms. Sensitive warning systems typically go through cycles starting with a phase of high credibility, which is gradually reduced by FAEs, restored by true alarms, and so on. The effectiveness of such credibility restoration of true alarms depends on the magnitude of loss caused by the dangerous event and by the degree of protection that could have been achieved if the warnings were heeded.

This is the main reason a true alarm is more effective in restoring credibility if it follows a series of false alarms. It sets the stage for an unpleasant surprise and thus augments the impact of a true alarm.

The inherent weakness of sensitive warning systems is particularly critical when dealing with very rare dangers that can cause potentially serious damage. When the potential damage is prohibitive and the chance of a surprise cannot be taken, there are often many false alarms, and *only* false alarms. A surprise nuclear attack is a good illustration of such a case. Realizing the fact that as of today a true alarm has not yet occurred and that a surprise is prohibitive, false alarms rule supreme. This in turn makes it imperative that there is as little "learning from experience" as possible or that certain routines protect the warning system in spite of a massive FAE.

FALSE ALARM EFFECT AS AN INSTRUMENT FOR ACHIEVING SURPRISE

Sophisticated early warning systems and surveillance make it practically impossible to hide large-scale preparations for attack. The detection subsystems are well equipped to provide intelligence concerning redeployment and major movements of forces. Thus, at least in principle, surprise attack is ruled out. And yet the very sensitivity of warning systems poses the greatest modern danger of achieving surprise. This time, however, it is not a surprise due to hidden secret preparations, but rather in spite of, or perhaps because of explicit warnings. The following variation on the "cry wolf" story illustrates how it works.

> There was once a very hungry and very frightened wolf. All he wanted was to enter the stockade and kill some sheep, but that seemed to be an impossible task to accomplish. For as soon as he approached the fence, the shepherd sounded the alarm for all the villagers to come and defend their animals. He would make his approach, but the cries of the shepherd always frightened him off back to his hiding place. He was so afraid of the villagers that by the time they came he was already safely far away. Then, one day, something strange happened. From his hiding place he watched the stockade, but in spite of repeated alarms by the shepherd, nobody seemed to come to his help. On that day he made his move.

The villagers never saw the wolf, and thus, what to the shepherd was a series of true alarms was for them a repetition of false alarms. Their willingness to heed the warnings was gradually exhausted, hence the surprise attack. The key to its success lies in the fact that the shepherd could see the wolf. It is a surprise based on the FAE. The monitoring of the 1980 hurricane, which changed its direction in the last hours after a large-scale evacuation already had taken place, likewise increased the danger of a future surprise from that quarter.

FALSE ALARM EFFECT AS AN INSTRUMENT FOR ACHIEVING SURPRISE

There is yet another way the wolf could have achieved his purpose. Through a series of false alarms he could have fooled the shepherd himself. Imagine the wolf emerging from the forest, making a circle approaching the stockade indirectly, and then continuing all the way back to the forest. Better still, imagine that this seemingly harmless excursion is repeated in the same manner and at the same time each day, say just before sunset. On the first few days the shepherd cries for help, but by the time it arrives the wolf is visibly returning to the forest. He does this precisely in the same way, and before long, the shepherd learns to anticipate this predictable behavior. Then, after a few days, seeing the same familiar wolf emerging at sunset from the forest and slowly circling toward the stockade, the shepherd decides that it is just another harmless walk and there is no need to call for help. The rest is by now familiar.

In this second example, the danger is always detected, but on the basis of cumulative experience, it is reinterpreted at some point as benign (e.g., it's just another familiar maneuver or military exercise). What was damaged here was not just the credibility of the warning system, but its very rules of functioning. A clearly detectable danger lost its threatening message due to a systematic desensitization by FAEs. In other words, in this case the FAE did not affect the receiver, but rather it affected the warning system itself. If the warning system possesses learning ability, it too is subject to the same dangers as the receiver.

It should be noted that in neither instance was any assumption made about the wolf operating according to a preconceived plan of action. The FAE poses major hazards even if it is unintentional. Needless to say, an intelligent and cunning wolf can do better still.

Independence of Consecutive Experiences

In many real-life situations, consecutive threats of a similar kind are objectively independent of each other. Their early detection by a warning system implies a certain amount of uncertainty concerning their evolvement in time. In other words, from the earliest signals until the presumed time of impact, there is a lot that can change. With increasing knowledge about certain kinds of dangers, the amount of unexplained variance in their behavior is of course reduced. Taking the point of view of the warning system, there might be an important lesson to learn from each instance of threat, and cumulative experience may increase the predictability of similar future threats. Our viewpoint, however, is not that of the scientist attempting to discover order in the course of development of a particular danger. Rather, it is the viewpoint of the receiver that we must adopt.

Insofar as the receiver is concerned, two threats are similar to the extent that the information provided by the warning system makes them appear as such. The greater the perceived similarity between two threats, the greater the lesson learned about the second by experiencing the first. Hence, if the first turned out to be a false alarm, the amount of FAE on the second will depend on their perceived similarity. This follows the simple notion of learning to predict the future on the basis of prior experience.

The fact that the two threats are objectively independent does not help. There is overwhelming evidence indicating that people operating under uncertainty tend to organize their experiences by resorting to schemata that assume interdependence between any two events having some psychological proximity, whether temporal, spatial, or conceptual (e.g., Heider, 1958; Michotte, 1963; Ross, 1977; Tversky & Kahneman, 1971, 1973, 1974). Intelligent receivers are thus bound to perceive consecutive instances of similar threats as psychologically interrelated. We can safely assume that it is practically inconceivable to go through a false alarm experience without drawing some conclusions from it.

The impact of a false alarm is not reversible. Something has been learned in the process; one cannot wipe out an experience that has registered in a human brain. A subsequent episode, even if objectively independent of a previous case, is automatically altered by the past experience. Because the FAE is essentially reducing the effectiveness of warning systems, the fact that it in principle cannot be avoided or fully reversed is of major importance. The credibility of warning systems having many false alarms is thus bound to be seriously affected, often with very dire consequences to safety. This is one case in which we might have preferred no learning to have occurred.

Even though the FAE cannot be totally avoided or eliminated, its magnitude may depend on certain psychological principles. The central theme of the research to be reported in this volume is the search for psychological principles that will increase a warning system's protection against false alarms.

3 Naive Versus Cynical Dangers

Earlier in our analysis, the two conditions necessary for a warning system to be functional were specified. They consist of the possibility for objective control over the danger through protective behaviors and sufficient warning time to carry them out. The extent to which such a functional warning system succeeds in carrying out its function depends on a variety of factors such as the degree of protection that can be gained in a particular situation, the cost to receivers of engaging in protective behavior, and their willingness to accept that cost. These in turn are substantially influenced by the credibility of the warning system, a credibility based upon its history of performance as well as extrinsic information about its functioning.

The actual damage caused by a particular danger that materializes is the net outcome of its intensity on impact and the protective measures that were taken against it. In some instances the protective measures may reduce the damages to a minimum or even nullify them. In such cases the only negative outcome of the entire episode is the cost of the protective actions themselves. In other instances even the maximal protective measures may be only minimally effective in reducing the damages.

Whatever its effectiveness, this kind of protection is typically passive in the sense that it does not affect the danger itself, just its consequences. Stated differently, utilizing the warning at their disposal, receivers may attempt to combat the forces of the danger by mobilizing defensive counterforces of their own. They do not, however, influence the dangerous forces themselves, at least not prior to their impact. And yet, there are dangers that will respond to protective behaviors even before impact. Because this possibility is for obvious reasons of extreme importance, it ought to be explained more thoroughly. This chapter attempts a preliminary characterization of dangers along these lines.

NAIVE DANGERS

Consider an impending danger of a given probability of impact an anticipated intensity at impact, and an anticipated time of impact. These are parameters of the danger itself, and they do not necessarily correspond to the parameters of the threat of that danger as it is monitored by the warning system. The parameters of threat depend on the ability of the warning system to detect and interpret early signals of the danger. The better the warning system, the smaller the discrepancy between true parameters and the announced ones.

A variety of forces may change these parameters between warning time and impact. If the protective behavior of the receiver cannot be among these forces, the danger is a naive one. Thus, a *naive danger* is one in which protective behavior by the receiver cannot have an effect on its preimpact parameters. Take the by now familiar hurricane. Whether or not it will eventually strike a particular area and, if it does, when and in what force depend on a variety of weather conditions. The citizens of Florida may take the warnings seriously or disregard them—their behavior has no effect upon the storm. If it could learn that extensive precautions were taken against it, it would not change its course or the velocity of its winds. Such knowledge would leave it totally unaffected; it couldn't care less what the people in Florida do about it. It is purely a naive danger, without intelligence or motive. All natural disasters belong to the naive dangers category.

CYNICAL DANGERS

Two neighboring nations, A and B, live in enmity and mutual distrust. One day the central intelligence of A detects signals of an impending, surprise attack by B's military forces. The warning is taken very seriously, and general mobilization follows. The central intelligence of B detects the signals of mobilization and preparedness, and perceving the loss of the element of surprise, B decides to call off the entire operation.

This illustrates the functioning of a danger that is highly responsive to the protective behavior of the receiver. Such a danger continuously monitors its chances of success in achieving its goal. Because its goal is to maximize the damage to the receiver, we call it a *cynical danger*. Cynical dangers are to a great extent controlled by considerations of outcomes. As such, they require "intelligence" and an evaluation function estimating means–goals effectiveness.

The definition of a cynical danger does not, however, rest on those additional characteristics. For a given danger to be cynical, the necessary and sufficient condition is that its preimpact parameters can be affected by the protective behavior of the receiver. It so happens that most cynical dangers do have the additional properties mentioned, but that is not essential to their definition.

Note that the definition does not assume that the parameters of the danger are actually affected by the protective behavior of the receiver. Rather, it requires the property of "capability of such influence." The analysis of any particular danger must therefore establish whether it is in principle capable of being influenced by the receiver's protective behavior. It is a logical-philosophical question or, perhaps, a systems analysis question, not a strictly empirical one.

The proverbial wolf who was so afraid of the shepherd's cries for help that he quickly retreated to his hideout is another example of a cynical danger par excellence. Out of fear, the probability and timing of his attack is affected by the protective behavior of the receiver.

Question. Why is the distinction between naive and cynical dangers important from the particular angle of the credibility of warning systems, which is our primary concern?

Answer. If receivers take protective action against an impending cynical danger and it turns out that the danger does not materialize, they have an inherent difficulty in distinguishing between false alarms and true alarms. In the absence of special extrinsic information about the danger, there is no basis for making such a distinction. On the one hand, the danger might have been a false alarm, in which case there follows a false alarm effect reducing the credibility of the warning system. An obvious outcome will be that receivers will perceive their protective actions as "wasted" and will be less likely to repeat them if a similar threat occurs in the future.

On the other hand, the danger might have been a true alarm, in which case it did not materialize precisely because of the protective action. That is, the cynical danger changed its course after detecting the precaution taken against it. The obvious implication would be to reinforce the protective measures if similar threats occur in the future.

The choice between these two dramatically opposed interpretations of the same event (i.e., the cancellation of the threat) will, whenever possible, rely on extrinsic information about the danger. When such information is unavailable, recent experience with similar situations will become a prominent factor. If there is no relevant experience or if it is equivocal, there is a distinct possibility that for certain dynamic, personal reasons receivers may have a clear bias toward interpretations that are personally more gratifying. Thus, they might cherish the notion of a *deterrent* and lean toward interpreting such events as demonstrating their ability to control the danger. It is of some interest to note that in the absence of extrinsic information to the contrary, cynical dangers are more protected from the FAE than are naive ones.

Whereas a great amount of good empirical research is needed to elaborate this analysis, the necessity to distinguish between the two kinds of dangers is, I hope, clearly established. The relative complexity of cynical dangers in contrast to naive dangers is also self-evident. This issue has a direct bearing on the research strategy that was employed in our work.

Question. Do all dangers clearly fall into one or the other category?

Answer. Yes, but some dangers may contain elements of both, making them particularly difficult to categorize. Thus, cynical dangers almost invariably have a naive component that resists any change in their preimpact parameters. Previous plans, commitments, or considerations of bureaucracy all tend to support the status quo even in the face of highly relevant information concerning the protective actions of the receiver. It follows that in a particular instance, although a danger can in principle react to protective behaviors, other structural and organizational properties may make it highly reluctant to actually do so. According to our definition it is still a cynical danger, but one that might be incorrectly diagnosed as a naive one.

ACCIDENTS

There is yet another reason why in practice it can sometimes be very difficult to decide whether a specific danger is naive or cynical. The problem can be illustrated by considering the danger of an accident (e.g., a traffic accident). The probability of being involved in a traffic accident while driving is to a great extent affected by the protective behaviors of the driver. The more cautious the driver, the smaller are the chances of the danger materializing. Thus, even though there are many additional factors over which the driver has no control whatsoever, which may determine the occurrence of an accident, the principle of being able to have some effect on its preimpact parameters turns them clearly into cynical dangers. So far there appears to be no problem. But the difficulty arises whenever one poses the question about the nature of the threatening stimuli, which presumably lead to the protective action. Although it is sometimes possible to detect the danger of an accident from certain cues in the traffic, this is not always the case. In other words, drivers frequently take precautions and drive carefully even in the absence of clear threats. This, indeed, is what constitutes safe preventive driving. One is simply engaged in continuous protection on the basis of previous learning and training, rather than as a reaction to a specifically detected threat. We should not, however, be confused by this difficulty. As long as the protective measures affect the probability, intensity, or timing of an accident, the accident is a true cynical danger.

Another psychological difficulty with such a label may be based on the anthropomorphic connotation of cynicism. The accident, after all, does not care, and unlike a sophisticated enemy it does not plan to maximize its impact. And yet, objectively, there is no difference, because the probability will dramatically increase with the neglect of precautions. It is as if accidents are omnipresent dangers waiting for the first opportunity to materialize.

Many illnesses follow the same pattern, because their probability of impact depends on the person's defenses, among other things. Bacteria and viruses, just like accidents, are continuously present in our environment, waiting for their chance to strike. When for a variety of reasons (e.g., the impact of other stressors) the defenses of our bodies are weakened, this increases the probability and imminence of infection. This relationship was aptly stated by Hans Selye (e.g., 1956, 1973, 1976) and more recently and most dramatically by Norman Cousins (1979).

It is of some interest to note that many cynical dangers utilize *detection* subsystems of their own to acquire intelligence about the protective measures of the receiver, whereas accidents and some infectious diseases utilize *persistence* instead. Needless to say, this is just a figurative way of describing their particular dependence on protective measures.

At this point in the analysis, the following additional categorization of dangers may prove helpful:

1. Dangers that will materialize irrespective of what the receiver does.
2. Dangers that will materialize unless the receiver acts appropriately.
3. Dangers that will materialize only if the receivers stops acting appropriately.

Type 1 belongs invariably to the naive category. Type 2 can be either naive or cynical. It is naive if the protective behavior totally eliminates the danger by direct means (i.e., without influencing its preimpact parameters). A simple example of such prevention is stopping the car when a warning signal indicates that the engine is overheating. Type 2 is cynical danger wherever there is indirect prevention, indicated by detection of protective measures by the danger itself. The cancellation or postponement of an impending enemy attack is a case in point. Finally, Type 3 dangers are continuously present dangers such as accidents and infections. Here safety is maintained by continuous prevention, in sharp contrast to the discrete prevention initiated by a specific threat.

The objective presence of continuous danger in the absence of psychological threats quickly makes the receiver subjectively unaware of the danger itself. Thus, constant dangers are usually not perceived as such. Routine protective behavior must sooner or later reduce the signaling ability of the danger. In the absence of distinct warning signals, protective behavior operates in a "motivational vacuum," thus increasing the possibility of occasional performance deficit. If the resulting neglect of protective behavior is minute, without any obvious detrimental consequences, it might be interpreted as a false alarm episode leading to a FAE. Such FAE may further reduce the willingness to engage in protection against what may appear to the receiver as "nonevents."

The complex relationship between fear, protective behavior, and false alarms is discussed in detail at a later stage of our analysis. At this point, it is enough to state the possibility that even Type 3 dangers may be susceptible to the FAE.

On first impression, cynical dangers may appear to be more frightening than naive ones, particularly if they have intelligence and operate according to an evaluation function that attempts to maximize their impact. On second thought, however, naive dangers seem to be the more frightening of the two, precisely because they cannot be affected by anything the receiver does. Neither precautions nor counterthreats have any effect on them. The degrees of freedom when confronted by a naive danger are much smaller than in the case of a cynical one. The latter can be tempted, bullied, or accommodated by a compromise, but a naive danger cannot. The frequently documented tendency of people confronted by such naive dangers as natural disasters to evoke religious feelings as a way to achieve subjective control over the danger is quite indicative (e.g., Wolfenstein, 1957). Such an appeal to "higher authority" may reduce the psychological stress when confronted with a threat that holds itself aloof and "incommunicado."

4 Research Method: Strategy and Tactics

GENERAL CONSIDERATIONS

The credibility loss following a false alarm is inevitable in any warning system. That much has already been established. Protecting a warning system from the false alarm effect is therefore bound to be a difficult and arduous task, and complete success is impossible. Our research program, which aims to study ways of reducing the FAE, faces the major obstacle posed by learning from experience. The most that we can hope for is partial success by sufficiently delaying the eventual ineffectiveness of a warning system to encourage protective action. It is a delaying action only—a controlled retreat—never a victory. Indeed, it is a somber thought that the only way to win the battle for credibility is to experience the shattering consequences of a true alarm.

The cost of unpreparedness is, however, too great to accept without trying to defend against the FAE. The question is how to do it and how to find out how to do it. What research strategy ought to be employed? Should one concentrate on real-life situations or prefer the controlled artificial environment of the experimental laboratory? How difficult will it be to generalize whatever principles are discovered in the laboratory to complex life events? And alternatively, what are the chances, if any, to engage in systematic investigation "in the field"? Can the spontaneous whims of nature or the malicious designs of others be trusted to produce sufficient dangers to allow systematic analysis in the field?

On this issue our bias is clear. The phenomenon is too complicated to be adequately studied in its "natural environment." That can be done later, when we become equipped with some knowledge abou the relevant main effects and with some analytic tools to ask good questions. Thus, our research is based entirely upon laboratory experiments. At the same time, however, the analysis of real dangers and real warning systems plays a major role in the actual design of the various experiments. The motive to eventually translate our findings in terms of their potential applicability to complex real-life problems has dictated the choice of our manipulations to some extent. From among the almost infinite number of possible experiments, we attempted to choose the ones which in addition to following a certain logic imminent in the search itself were most conducive to such subsequent extrapolation. As our story unfolds, the way these two determinants actually expressed themselves in experimental design should become more evident. At this point, it is sufficient to keep in mind that ours is a blend of basic research with application constantly in mind.

Having decided to investigate the FAE in the laboratory, how should we proceed? What are the ways to reduce this effect? At this starting point, there were naturally only guesses and speculations, and there was no guarantee that anything at all could protect the warning system from such credibility loss. These guesses and speculations fell into two major categories. On the one hand, the information-management subsystem could be thoroughly probed for practices causing differential levels of FAE. In other words, it is conceivable that if the threatening information is managed in a certain way, it might increase or decrease the FAE itself. Such a claim assumes that the intensity of a FAE is to some extent the psychological outcome of a particular sequence of messages, terminating with the "all clear" message, which cancels the threat and defines the situation as a false alarm. If this is the case, it might be worthwhile to investigate the preceding messages and test whether they can influence the FAE. We are dealing here essentially with attempts to reduce the FAE before the cancellation of the threat.

On the other hand, following a cancellation of a threat, certain measures may restore the credibility of a warning system. These measures are typically based upon information extrinsic to the warning system itself. In other words, prior to the "all clear" message, there may be ways for a warning system to protect itself from a strong FAE, but after it, any help it can get must come from outside.

Our research efforts try to deal systematically with both the precancellation information management and the postcancellation restoration of lost credibility. We do so by moving from the simplest situations to ones of increasing complexity. In so doing, however, we keep the basic experimental paradigm constant, in order to allow comparisons between as well as within experiments. The transition from simple to complex situations advances one step at a time to facilitate the growth of a cumulative body of knowledge in this research area.

Any attempt to maintain essentially the same single experimental paradigm throughout the entire sequence of studies makes the choice of that particular paradigm tremendously important. Inasmuch as the research program will generate consecutive varieties around one central theme, its basic features may well determine the outcome of the whole effort. One can build a most impressive structure only to discover that its foundations are weak. Consequently, we now proceed to analyse the desirable characteristics of the experimental paradigm.

AN INTELLECTUAL EXERCISE WITH PARAMETERS OF THREAT

Some of the more important parameters of threat have been mentioned in Chapter 1. Warning systems often provide explicit or implicit information about the quality of the danger, its probability of materializing, its anticipated intensity, its imminence, the amount of experience with similar dangers in the past, the ability to cope with it, ambiguity of the threatening information, and so forth. Even on a common-sense level of analysis, it is not obvious how the reaction to the threat will be affected by variations in these parameters.

A brief intellectual exercise can help us demonstrate some of the inherent problems involved in any attempt to actually predict the reaction on the basis of a priori analysis of the parameters of threat. Let us assume that we are only concerned with the intensity of the fear reaction produced by a given threat. Let us also assume, for the sake of our exercise, that we have a perfectly reliable single measure of fear reaction. Having made these assumptions, it is relatively simple to assume also that this measure is continuous and linear. We now proceed to test the presumed effects of the various parameters on fear reactions.

Starting with the probability that the danger will materialize, the common-sense level of analysis may suggest that the higher such probability, the stronger the fear reaction. There are however, serious problems involved. We have already discussed the various biases in translating objective probabilities into subjective ones (e.g., Slovic & Lichtenstein, 1971; Tversky & Kahneman, 1974). We may add the problems of linearity and continuity. Conceivably, there is a limited set of codifiable estimates, which are easily assimilated into linguistic concepts. Thus, one can verbally translate quite easily the probabilities of .0, .25, .33, .5, and so on. The question remains, however, whether any meaningful discriminations can be demonstrated in addition to these simple categories. Another issue of some interest would be the testing of the psychological difference between more than .5 and less than .5. To this we can add the question of the psychological difference between .99999 and certainty. There have been some interesting, though inconclusive, attempts to test Berlyne's (1960) notion that uncertainty itself (greatest around the $p = .5$ region) may increase anxiety and produce a curvilinear relationship between probability and fear reaction (e.g., Epstein & Roupenian, 1970; Jennings, Averill, Opton, & Lazarus, 1970; Monat, Averill, & Lazarus, 1972; Niemela, 1969).

Moving now to the intensity of the threatened danger, similar nonlinear difficulties may arise. Thus, one might assume some kind of "adaptation level" principle to operate (Helson, 1948), making intensities relative to the base line upon which they are superimposed. The simple notion that the more intense the future danger, the stronger the fear reaction to it is further shaken by findings such as Janis' (1958) who found no major differences in fear reaction between surgical patients anticipating major surgery and those with minor, almost trivial, problems.

The parameter of previous experience does not lend itself at all to simple prediction about fear reaction. The amount of experience as such is quite meaningless without the additional information concerning the exact quality of that experience: If it was a pleasant surprise, it might reduce the fear reaction to subsequent similar threats, whereas a disappointment, or a psychic trauma, would lead to the opposite.

The amount of subjective fantasy concerning the impending danger is negatively related to amount of experience. Experience—whatever its quality—reduces the degrees of freedom the individual has in trying to envisage the future, because previous occasions serve as a focus. Lazarus (1966) attributed a similar effect to ambiguity: "Ambiguity permits maximum latitude for idiosyncratic interpretations of situations, based on the individual's psychological structure [pp. 117–118]." We submit that ambiguity is directly related to lack of experience with similar situations.

Objective control over the danger does not necessarily lead to lower fear reaction. Averill's (1973) comprehensive review of the research on various kinds of personal control over aversive stimuli indicates that: "Each type of control is related to stress in a complex fashion, sometimes increasing it, sometimes reducing it, and sometimes having no influence at all [p. 286]."

In order to appreciate more fully the complexities involved in any attempt to predict the intensity of fear directly from the parameters of the threat, the various parameters should not just be analyzed separately. Thus, amount of experience may influence the subjective probability of the event, with greater experience increasing the probability. Experience may also influence the sense of control. Intensity and probability may interact negatively with each other on the subjective level. Some dangers may be perceived as too serious to be true or too certain to be serious. Potent psychological mechanisms may operate as an effective defense against information that is threatening beyond the receiver's capacity.

The preceding analysis, in addition to being speculative, is also greatly oversimplified. However, the major point shall be clear: Even when taking only the most obvious parameters and assuming only the most obvious types of effects, the complexities seem to make any prediction of the threat reaction extremely doubtful. It appears that any particular threat can be viewed as a unique configuration of the various parameters and as such cannot be easily compared to other similar threats. This ends our brief intellectual exercise, so where do we go from here?

BASIC THREAT

One possible way to cope with the foregoing research problem is to simplify the situation as much as possible. A promising approach may proceed along the following lines. First, it would attempt to study the effects of threats in which the contribution of most of the parameters would be minimized. If the reaction to such threats is a reliable and specific one, any systematic deviation from the simple threat to a more complicated threat might then be evaluated against such a specific reaction.

We suggest to define a concept of *basic threat* as one having the following characteristics:

1. The probability that it will materialize is 1.0.
2. The amount of experience with it is 0.
3. The ability to control the outcome is 0 (i.e., it is a situation of objective helplessness).
4. The intensity of the danger is high.
5. The exact time of the impact is known to receivers.
6. Receivers have no opportunities to distract their mind from the threat.

To some degree basic threats are obviously ideal types because it is practically impossible to produce in laboratory experiments using human subjects threats with a probability of 1.0, in the sense that the subject can leave the experimental situation.

Characteristic 4 is also problematic because the scale of intensity is always arbitrary. At the same time, however, the ideal type can be closely approximated. The definition poses only very few limitations in terms of content, and almost any type of danger can be a basic threat if it is intense, certain, new, and unaffected by the receiver's behavior. In basic threats the time of impact is fully predictable and distraction is difficult, hence the only thing left to do is attend to the imminence of the danger.

What would people's reaction to such a situation be? How would they respond to this kind of helplessness, and more specifically, what course would the intensity of their fear follow?

In a basic threat any change in fear is probably due to time-related processes. As there is no change in the parameters of probability, experience, intensity, or in the amount of control, the only variable in constant change is the imminence of the danger. Moreover, the change is systematic, that is, the person is aware of the fact that as time goes by the danger is coming closer.

Plotting the intensity of the fear reaction between the onset of the threat and the impact of the threatened event itself, what then can we expect?

If fear reaction is related to imminence, some kind of monotonic positive relationship between imminence and fear can be postulated. However, the actual curve can be either straightly linear, positively accelerating, or negatively accelerating. All these functions satisfy the requirements of monotony and growth with imminence.

In terms of the stimulus situation, there are in basic threat two discrete events that take place: (1) the threat is announced; (2) the threatened danger materializes. It is therefore quite possible that the communication of the threat itself might also have an impact on the intensity of fear. Thus, it can temporarily change the "base line" upon which the effect of imminence is superimposed, it may stay constant throughout the anticipation period, or it can gradually dissipate. The particular function that best describes the relaxation from the effect of the announcement of future danger is interesting in its own right and might well be under the control of other features of the threat configuration. The logic of the basic threat concept makes it imperative that any empirical work studying the outcome of these various components must take double precautions to insure that the subject attends to the information about the passage of time and the proximity of the danger.

Breznitz (1965) tested the fear reaction to a basic threat of an intense, unavoidable electric shock. Sixty subjects were randomly divided among three groups of varying imminence of the shock: 3 minutes, 6 minutes, and 12 minutes, respectively. The danger was dramatized by specific stress instructions and the requirement for health certificates. Subjects never experienced the shock prior to the threat and were requested to observe a clock showing the imminence of the danger. Thus, the conditions for basic threat were approximated reasonably closely.

Heart rate and skin conductance were continuously monitored, and their mean reactions for all three groups for the entire duration of anticipation appear in Figs. 4.1 and 4.2, respectively. The curves show a similar pattern. This reliable finding justifies the simplification implied by the basic threat paradigm. We have here a typical U function, with the two discrete time-locked events (i.e., the threat and its execution) producing the two peaks. Immediately following the threat there is a rise in both indexes of fear reaction, and the heart rate as well as skin conductance show a steep rise from the base line. Next we can see that there is a gradual relaxation from this steep rise, and the fear seems to be reduced for some time. Coming closer to the actual time when the threat is bound to be executed, we find another steep rise in both indicators, with the single exception of the last minute in the conductance channel of the 3-minute group. Subjects differ in their positions on the ordinate and in their rates of change in time, but all have the essential characteristics of the U curve.

Before attempting to analyze some of the theoretical and practical implications of this particular curve, let me attempt a systematic survey of other relevant research material in order to test the generalizability of our findings. It appears

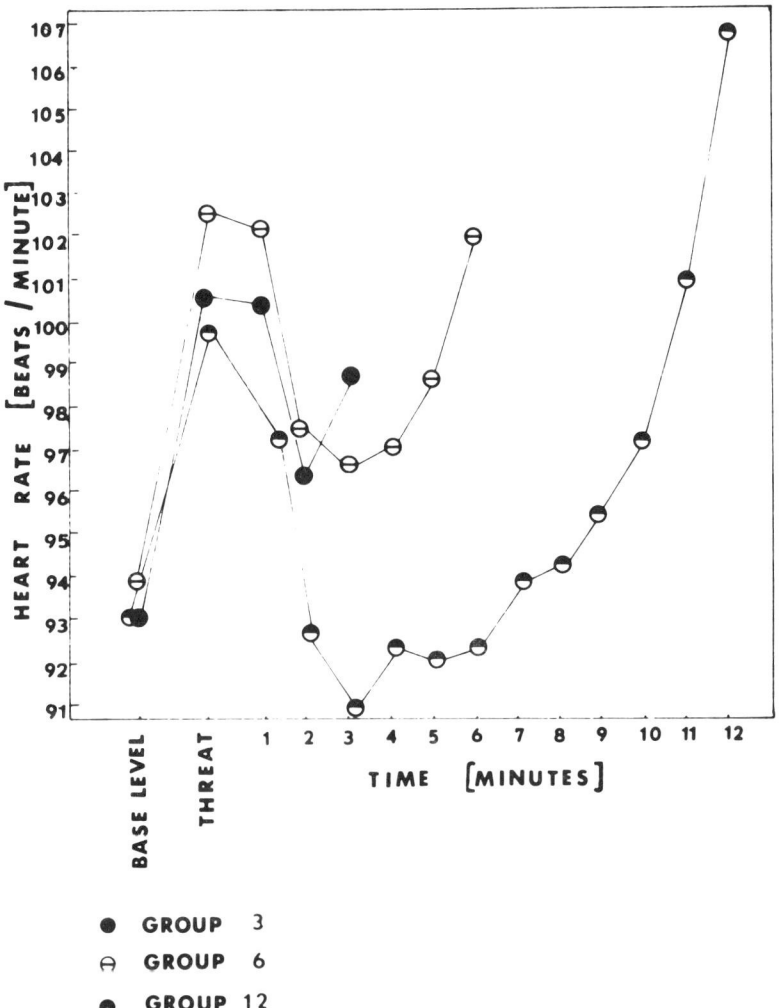

FIG. 4.1 Mean heart-rate reaction during basic threat.

that in various laboratories in the U.S. as well as elsewhere, researchers have been able to replicate this U-shaped curve. Thus, Nomikos et al. (1968), using the technique of vicarious threat and studying shorter time durations, found the U curve to be an appropriate description of their data. Epstein and Roupenian (1970), using a method very similar to ours but varying the parameter of probability that the threat will materialize, also report U-shaped curves. Elliott, and Bankart, and Light (1970) demonstrated the U curve in heart rate using a 30-second interval. Folkins (1970) attempted to study the pattern of fear reaction

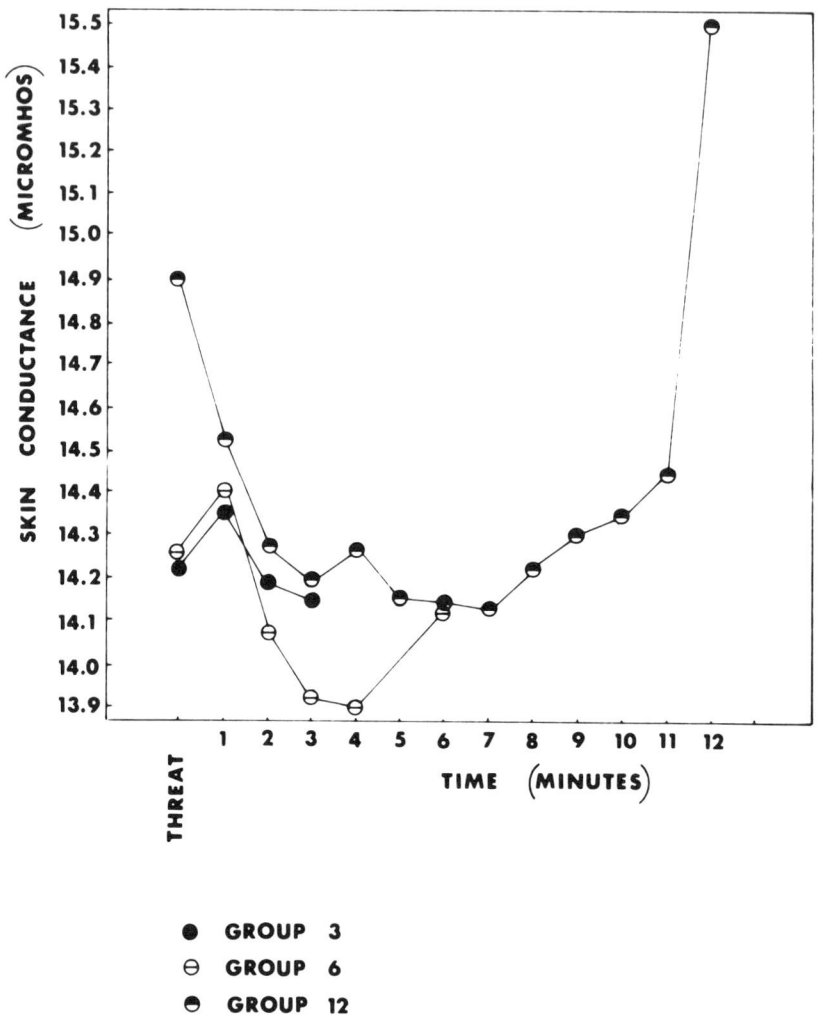

FIG. 4.2 Mean skin-conductance reactions during basic threat.

with varying durations of anticipation; starting from 30 seconds through 1 minute, 3 minutes, 5 minutes, and up to 20 minutes. The heart rate indicated a U-shaped curve, which was clearly demonstrable for durations of 1 minute and more. Mansueto and Desiderato (1971) made a full-scale replication of Breznitz's (1967) study and found essentially the same results. Hess and Breznitz (1971), monitoring only the heart-rate channel, were able to reproduce the exact curve appearing in Fig. 4.1 using a 6-minute interval. Averill and Rosenn (1972), studying the effect of various coping strategies on psychological stress, found that when subjects had knowledge about the imminence of the danger, their responses (skin conductance) indicated the U-type curve. This was especially apparent when the anticipated harm was intense. Monat et al. (1972) used both of our autonomic indexes, as well as the subjective reports of fear, with their subjects waiting for 3 minutes before an electric shock. The U curve was once again replicated in all the indexes that were measured. The fact that the subjective reports indicated the same pattern raises some interesting questions about the kind of feedback mechanisms that might be involved. Thus, one possibility is that the subjects reported their states on the basis of autonomic feedback or, possibly. that the physiological indexes were the outcome rather than the cause of some cognitive processes. In a more recent study, Petry and Desiderato (1978) obtained perfect U curves in the "clock condition," in the heart-rate channel. This U curve seems to be highly reliable, and we submit that within the affective component, it indeed demonstrates the basic threat reaction.

The next step would be an attempt to explore the various mechanisms that might determine this particular shape of the curve. One possible approach would be to view the curve as being a combination of two separate curves. The first part shows the reaction to the announcement of the danger (i.e., the threat), and the second part plots the reaction to the impending danger. Starting with the first part of the U, we see that there is a gradual relaxation from the threat. The relaxation has the pattern of a negatively decelerating function, implying that most of it takes place shortly after the threat. The positive acceleration characteristic in the second part is, however, in some ways more interesting and more difficult to explain. Two possible alternative models can be proposed:

1. It is conceivable that the subjects in our experiment are responding at any time unit in proportion to the total remaining time before the danger is supposed to materialize. A given unit of time reduces the amount of uncertainty about the imminence of the danger. The shorter the total remaining time, the greater the information value in terms of uncertainty reduction of any given time unit. The impact of a time unit (T_u) on fear can be presented algebraically by the simple equation:

$$T_u = \frac{t_i}{T-t_i}$$

where t_i denotes present time and T the time of anticipated impact. The following example illustrates how this kind of model can account for the shape of the curve. Let us assume that the subject has to wait for 5 minutes and that we deal with the time unit of 1 minute. The first minute reduces the total remaining anticipation time by 20%, the second minute by 25%, the third by 33%, the fourth by 50%, and finally the last minute reduces the uncertainty by 100%. This might lead to the particular positively accelerating curve that has been reported by us as well as by others.

2. An alternative approach to the same problem would concentrate on the actual size of a "meaningful psychological unit." It can be argued that as the

danger comes closer, we tend to make better differentiations in terms of time, and our meaningful units become smaller and smaller. This would imply that for a given objective duration of time, the frequency of subjective meaningful units (or JND's, *Just Noticeable Difference*) would grow as the danger comes closer. Assuming that the passage of each such unit adds a "quantum of fear," such a mechanism might well account for the positively accelerating curve.

Any attempt on our part to corroborate one of these models would of course be premature, because a great amount of parametric research is necessary. We do not know enough about our dependent variables, as well as about the subjective processes taking place in the formation of "time perspective." In addition to all these difficulties, we have to keep in mind that the two proposed explanations are not mutually exclusive, and it is quite possible that both operate at the same time.

At this point it might be worth mentioning that Lundberg, Ekman, and Frankenhaeuser (1971), who attempted to investigate the exact shape of the second part of the anticipation curve using a psychophysical method, found an empirical curve very similar to ours.

A different interpretation of the U curve was proposed by Elliott et al. (1970). They asserted that:

> The quadratic function reflects the fact that in a situation in which one is awaiting a certain response instigating event, there are a few responses to prepare and relatively little incentive to prepare them until it is time to do so. Therefore heart rate will be lower in the middle of the waiting period than at the end [p. 171].

We would like to challenge this interpretation in view of the fact that in basic threat there is at no point in time any objective way to cope with the danger. In these conditions any coping attempt is unrealistic anyway, and there is no reason to assume that it should be emitted particularly during the last phase of anticipation, unless at the same time assuming that because of greater fear there is a greater need to engage in such activity. However, such an explanation already assumes the U-shaped curve that it attempts to explain.

Until now we have been dealing primarily with a strictly defined situation of basic threat. Our next endeavor is the analysis of the consequences of gradual relaxation of the various constraints that define basic threat. What happens to the fear reaction if some of the conditions that were put down as necessary for a basic threat to occur are not fulfilled? Fortunately, we already have at our disposal some initial data on this important problem.

Probability of the Danger

The reader should recall that basic threat was defined in terms of certainty that the threat will materialize in the future. The study by Breznitz fulfilled this condition. Some other studies, however, attempted to vary the degree of certainty of the danger. Thus, Epstein and Roupenian (1970) tested the effect of various probabilities (5%, 50%, and 95%) upon fear. Their data show that event uncertainty can produce a U-shaped curve in both heart rate and skin conductance. The same was demonstrated by Monat et al. (1972), as well as by Epstein and Clarke (1970). Therefore, we may surmise that certainty is not a necessary condition for basic threat reaction to occur.

Experience with the Threat

Epstein and Roupenian (1970), as well as Epstein and Clarke (1970), found that the U curve fits the data best on the first trial. Experience with the shock and the procedure tends to change this pattern. This indicates that lack of experience might be a necessary condition for basic threat to occur. This might also explain why the probability need not be high, because if there is no experience with differential probabilities, as indeed is the case on the first trial, the probability as communicated by the experimenter might be psychologically meaningless to subjects. They have no way of telling whether the danger is going to materialize on the first trial or not, irrespective of the numerical probability given to them.

Temporal Uncertainty

Elliott (1969), Mansueto and Desiderato (1971), Monat et al. (1972), and Petry and Desiderato (1978) all attempted to study the effect of threat that does not include any information about the exact time of the danger. In all cases, without exception, subjects under these conditions gradually relax. For the U-shaped curve to occur, therefore, it is necessary that the subject has sufficient information concerning the imminence of the danger. As Mansueto and Desiderato (1971) indicate, the clock that the subject is looking at need not necessarily be a correct one, and the U curve might be obtained irrespective of that. What is necessary, however, is for the subject to know when, according to the clock, the shock is bound to come.

The Discrete Warnings Paradigm

In considering the signaling of imminence, four experimental paradigms have been used:

1. Temporal certainty paradigm.
2. Surprise paradigm.
3. Conditioning paradigm.
4. Discrete warnings paradigm.

The temporal certainty paradigm (sometimes also called the "clock paradigm" or "time-locked" condition) is a central ingredient of basic threat. It leads to the typical U-type curve in arousal.

The surprise paradigm (sometimes called "time-unknown" condition) does not provide information concerning the imminence of a particular threat. It can be seen as a special case of the discrete warnings paradigm, employing a single warning (i.e., the threat itself). Needless to say, if no threat is announced, the warning system is simply inoperative, and a total surprise if achieved. Under such conditions there is, however, no way to study the effectiveness of warning systems, nor is there any anticipatory fear reaction without a threat. Sometimes the surprise paradigm is qualified by giving the time range during which the danger will materialize. Such a situation is another instance of a discrete warnings paradigm employing a single warning.

The conditioning paradigm is the one most frequently used by psychologists. Following the acquisition of the association between the conditioned stimulus (CS) and a subsequent unconditioned stimulus (US) on the basis of experiencing their temporal sequence, the CS becomes the single warning for the US. When the conditioning procedure is carried out in a particularly different environment over more than one session, the environmental cues become the first discrete warning, and the CS becomes the second. Whatever the specific elements of the situation, the conditioning paradigm can always be seen as a special case of the discrete warnings paradigm.

The discrete warnings paradigm is one in which the receiver has partial information about the imminence of the danger. Thus, a warning system may employ three discrete warnings—A, B, and C—so that the receiver knows something about the "distance" of the danger, without at the same time knowing when a transition from one warning to another will take place, or following the last warning, exactly when the danger will materialize.

This analysis indicates that there are actually only two main ways to signal imminence: temporal certainty and discrete warnings. It is between these two that one must choose, and the odds are overwhelmingly in favor of the latter. Here are the the arguments:

1. When there is temporal certainty, the approach of the danger becomes psychologically so overpowering that it reduces the impact of all the other parameters of the threat. This was particularly demonstrated by researchers testing for the effects of probability reactions to threat. The reaction to basic threat is highly reliable, perhaps too reliable in terms of the needs of our experimental program.

2. Psychophysiological indexes of fear reaction are particularly determined by imminence. Perfect knowledge of imminence may almost entirely determine these reactions, leaving little variance for additional experimental manipulation.

3. Temporal certainty allows only minimal information management by the warning system. Besides durations of anticipation, there are no other degrees of freedom. The discrete warnings paradigm is much richer and allows for a variety of manipulations. Thus, one can have warning systems with similar numbers of discrete warnings and yet different durations. The opposite is also possible, that is, having few or many discrete warnings for the same objective duration.

4. Most real-life situations resemble the discrete warnings paradigm. Only rarely is the receiver given exact information about imminence of the impending danger. This is particularly so in situations of uncertainty. Temporal uncertainty is one feature of uncertainty. Thus, if we are interested in maintaining a high practical application potential of our basic research, discrete warnings should be preferred.

5. Last but not least, it is logically possible to reduce the temporal certainty situation to a special case of discrete warnings, with many short warnings. Thus, if a clock is used to signal the danger, each minute (or if needed, each second) can be seen as a discrete warning. The empirical evidence for this is quite convincing and is presented shortly.

On the basis of these arguments the discrete warnings paradigm was chosen for our entire experimental program. We should now briefly discuss what some of its known properties are.

In a series of experiments, Breznitz (1972) systematically explored the effects of frequency and pacing of warnings upon fear reaction to an unavoidable electric shock. One-hundred-twenty subjects were individually tested in four experiments in a laboratory setting which, with the exception of temporal uncertainty, met the requirements of basic threat. The main dependent variables consisted of heart rate and skin conductance. On the basis of these experiments, the following preliminary propositions could be formulated.

Proposition A. Warnings form an ordinal scale starting with the threat and ending with its execution. *Each new warning brings the danger closer and therefore intensifies the fear reaction.* Expected warnings are discrete yardsticks of imminence of the anticipated danger. Each warning constitutes a psychological step closer to the danger. The fear reaction to a warning consists of two components:

- a_1. *Stimulation component.* The effect can be analyzed conceptually as an "orienting reflex" or a "startle response"; it is very brief, and it gradually habituates.
- a_2. *Information component.* The understanding of the implication of a warning conveys information about the proximity of the danger. The effect of this component depends on the content of the information transmitted by the warning.

Proposition B. The information value of a warning depends on the frequency of expected warnings. *The smaller the number of expected warnings, the greater the information value of each warning, and hence the stronger the fear reaction to it.* If one expects to have only one or two warnings before the danger materializes, each warning becomes rather important, whereas if one expects to have tens or hundreds of warnings, every single one is of very limited importance.

Proposition C. The effects of consecutive warnings differ. *The impact of a warning is positively related to its ordinal position.* Imminence is here viewed as a monotonic, but nonlinear, dimension. The closer the danger, the greater the impact of warning. Thus, the last warning has the greatest psychological impact, the penultimate warning has the next greatest impact, and so on. Consequently, the fear reaction follows the course of a positively accelerating curve.

Proposition D. *The psychphysiological effect of a warning is reduced as a function of "empty time."* Whatever the importance of a warning, its impact reaches a peak and then gradually dissipates. In a situation of helplessness, the time between two warnings is regarded as empty. Consequently, a gradual recovery from the fear reaction to a warning is to be expected. The intensity and timing of the peak reaction depends on the information conveyed by the warning. It follows that the onset of the relaxation process would also be a function of these parameters of information. Another implication of Proposition D is that the greater the frequency of warnings, the shorter the empty time. This relaxation process is automatic and does not require any psychological intervention on the part of the subject.

Proposition E. *The relaxation process following each warning is a negatively decelerating function.* It follows that the empty time immediately following the peak of the warning effect contributes more to relaxation than later empty time.

Proposition F. *The relaxation process that takes place between warnings levels off at a new base line higher than that which preceded the threat.* The concept of "base line" is naturally misleading, because there is no true base line, and its estimation is arbitrary. During anticipation of danger, empty time may bring about relaxation, but only up to a certain point. Its influence is limited by the nature of the ongoing threatening situation. This is in contrast with the relaxation that would follow the actual termination of the danger. The actual level of this base line would depend on the exact features of the warning system.

Proposition G. The total duration of "warning time" (as opposed to empty time) affects the level of fear reaction. *The greater the duration of warning time, the stronger the fear reaction that develops.* This is a cumulative effect, and consequently, it is most apparent during the last phases of anticipation. In all important aspects, it is analogous to "incubation of threat," the only difference being the way in which differential durations are produced. Whereas in the incubation of threat studies, the total duration of anticipation is manipulated as a variable, here it is the warning duration that is manipulated with a given total time interval. This cumulative effect is directly opposed to the notion of habituation to warnings and is therefore based entirely on the accumulation of the informative components of warnings (a_2) rather than the stimulation components (a_1).

Proposition H. *Unexpected stimuli that are interpreted by the subject as warnings produce a full warning effect.* The effect of such unexpected warnings is added to the effects of the expected warnings. Being unexpected, such a warning does not reduce the specific information value of the expected warnings. In all other respects an unexpected warning is similar to an expected one. Its reaction reaches a peak and is followed by a relaxation period. Because an unexpected warning has no ordinal position within the sequence of a warning system, its position is estimated by the subject on the basis of the information it conveys. In principle, an unexpected warning may imply a return to earlier stages of anticipation, or it may imply a situation of imminent danger.

Figure 4.3 illustrates the typical course of fear reaction to a warning system employing three discrete expected warnings, issued at the beginning of the first,

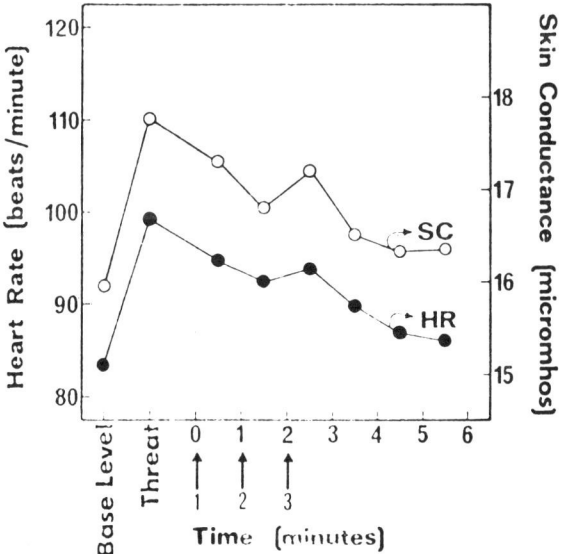

FIG. 4.3 Fear reaction to a warning system with three warnings.

38   4. RESEARCH METHOD: STRATEGY AND TACTICS

second, and third minute of anticipation. Thus, the first two warnings last for 1 minute each, whereas the third and last warning lasts for 4 minutes. Data for heart rate and skin conductance are presented. Figure 4.4 illustrates a more differentiated warning system employing 12 expected warnings, each lasting 30 seconds. The arrows under the X-axis indicate the onset of a warning.

Most of the propositions can be traced in the patterns of these curves. It is of particular interest to note the relaxation during the empty time in the last 3 minutes in Fig. 4.3, even though the last warning was already issued. Figure 4.4 clearly supports our earlier point concerning the reduction of the temporal certainty paradigm to the discrete warnings paradigm. With a discrete warning issues every 30 seconds, the curves clearly resemble the U-type reaction obtained with a clock, as any comparison with Figs. 4.1 and 4.2 strikingly reveals.

Study of FAEs prescribes the need to expose the same subject to at least two consecutive threats in order to measure the credibility loss of the second as a function of calling off the first. The research framework therefore consists of a combination of between-subjects as well as within-subjects designs. The need to repeat the anticipation sequence makes it impractical to use very long durations, and all experiments use either a 3-minute or a 6-minute duration for a single trial.

Many real-life warning systems employ three discrete warning stages, which we found very convenient for our purposes. Consequently, our subjects are told to expect three discrete warnings of imminence—A, B, and C. Warning C is always the last warning of the impending danger.

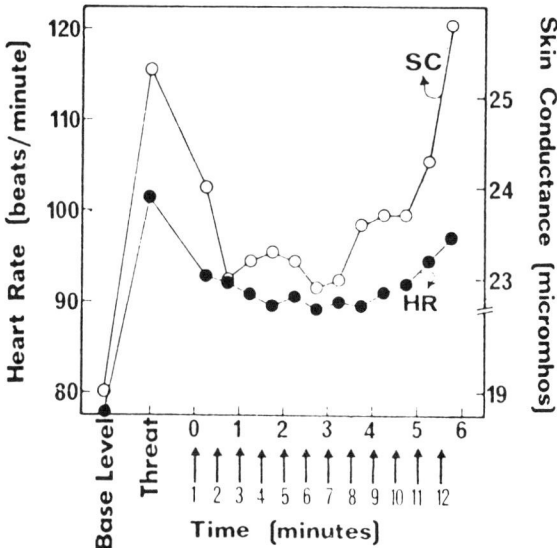

FIG. 4.4 Fear reaction to a warning system with twelve warnings.

INDEXES OF THE FALSE ALARM EFFECT

Within the context of fear reaction, the FAE can be measured by comparing the intensity of fear on the first trial with a subsequent one following a false alarm. Intensity of fear reflects the credibility of the warning system, and it is presumed to decrease with decreased credibility. The fear reaction itself is operationally defined by two separate psychophysiological indexes: heart rate and skin conductance. Our earlier work (Breznitz, 1965, 1967, 1972), as well as other research (e.g., Deane, 1966; Elliott, 1966, 1969; Hodges & Spielberger, 1966; Martin, 1961; Petry & Desiderato, 1978), indicates that intensified fear corresponds to heart-rate acceleration. Heart-rate deceleration was found only when dealing with very short periods of seconds rather than minutes (e.g., Graham & Clifton, 1966; Lacey, Kagan, Lacey, & Moss, 1963; Obrist, 1963). Rise in skin conductance is invariably accepted as an index of autonomic arousal (e.g., Lazarus, 1966; Opton & Lazarus, 1967).

In addition to the continuous monitoring of the psychophysiological indexes of fear reaction, subjective reports concerning fear and credibility were used. However, these measures were tapped only after the stressful part of the experiment was over. The disadvantages of interfering with the effects of the threat during anticipation proper outweighed all other considerations. The FAE is measured by the difference in subjective reports concerning the consecutive trials.

As our research program evolves and achieves higher complexity, another central measure of the FAE is used, namely, the amount of protective action aimed at reducing the impending danger. At an even more advanced stage, performance and performance deficit are also used.

5 Pacing of Warnings and the False Alarm Effect

Our first experiment serves a variety of functions. Foremost among them is the testing of the experimental paradigm which is then maintained throughout the entire research program. More specifically, it is of vital importance to find out to what extent the procedures are effective in inducing a significant threat reaction, and how to measure it in a reliable way. Furthermore, the effect of canceling the threat should also be obvious and easily ascertained. After all, we ought to keep in mind that false alarms have never before been investigated experimentally. Although Breznitz (1967) was able to demonstrate a clear false alarm effect in the clock paradigm, the manipulation used was not one of calling off the danger, but rather postponing it. The psychological impact of the two can be quite different.

In addition to being a probe for the planned procedures, this experiment at the same time attempts to investigate one aspect of the information-management subsystem, namely, that of pacing of warnings. A particular warning system utilizing a fixed number of discrete expected warnings may control the transition points from one stage to the next. Whenever the receiver is fully informed about the number of warnings, each transition from one state to the next implies that the anticipated danger is getting closer. Therefore, the pacing of warnings controls the psychological distance of the impending danger.

The impact of various pacing schedules upon the fear reaction has been studied by Breznitz (1972). But those experiments consisted of only a single trial and consequently cannot provide any information about the potential FAE of threat cancellation. It is an open question as to whether differential pacing of warnings can produce different levels of FAE. We submit that such indeed is the case, and the experiment was designed to test this proposition.

The specific hypothesis is: Warnings issued prior to the cancellation of the threat will all be subjected to the credibility loss. By contrast, those warnings not issued prior to the cancellation of the threat will be less affected by the FAE. Stated differently, stages of warnings that are not experienced by the receiver during an event which eventually turns out to be a false alarm are to some degree sheltered from credibility loss. The rationale for this hypothesis can be phrased in many ways, because it rests on a variety of psychological principles. Thus, for instance, taking the extinction model as our analytic framework, it follows that mainly those signals that are exposed to an extinction trial will reduce their potency to elicit fear reaction on a subsequent similar trial. Those cues that are not present during the extinction trial are protected from extinction.

In terms of the analyses made earlier in this book, the foregoing can be restated as follows: If a receiver experiences Warnings A, B, and C, of the warning system, and yet the danger is called off, the subsequent exposure to these warnings will be essentially identical to the first experience, and thus the credibility of the second threat will be seriously affected by the experience of the first. On the other hand, if the threat is canceled during Warning A, the transition to Warnings B and C in the second instance will produce a new situation, one never before experienced by the receiver. This may lead to a smaller FAE.

Yet another way of analyzing the situation may lead to the same predictions. Thus, later stages of warning imply greater proximity of the danger. When the already close danger is called off, this may be interpreted by the receiver as a greater blunder in terms of the warning system than if it is called off during the initial stages of alert. After all, so runs the argument, "by then they should have known better."

The same hypothesis can be reached from another approach as well. In terms of the fear reaction of the receiver, it will presumably be much more intense when during the first threat the warnings indicate that the danger is imminent rather than still distant. Following the cancellation of the threat, it will become a situation of "much ado about nothing." Those receivers who were made to react strongly to the initial threat, which turned out to be unnecessary, may become more reluctant to trust similar threats in the future.

The list of potential theoretical bases for our prediction is a long and interesting one. It illustrates the complexity and richness of the FAE phenomenon and its potential centrality in fine theoretical arguments. At this point, however, we should concentrate on testing the empirical status of this prediction and leave the theorizing for a more advanced stage of our investigation.

EXPERIMENTAL DESIGN

Two groups of subjects were threatened with a strong electric shock. They were told that there would be three warnings preceding the shock: A, B, and C. After Warning C the shock could come at any time without any additional warning.

Group E (early cancellation) had the following warning system: Warning A was issued immediately after the start signal and lasted for 4 minutes. Warning B lasted for 1 minute, and C lasted an additional 1 minute. The total duration of anticipation was therefore 6 minutes. The warning system for Group L (late cancellation) consisted of Warning A lasting for 1 minute, B for 1 minute, and C lasting for 4 minutes. The total duration of anticipation was again 6 minutes. On the first trial, however, the threat was canceled for both groups after exactly 3 minutes. At that time Group E was still at the stage of the first warning, whereas Group L was already in the last stage of anticipation. Using this design it was possible to keep the total duration of anticipation equal for both groups, and yet vary the psychological imminence of the danger.

Immediately following the cancellation there was a period of base-line recording and a start of a new trial. On the second trial the entire sequence of warnings was issued up to the end of the sixth minute of anticipation. In addition to subjects being their own controls, this design permits the subjects' reactions to be compared to two other control groups (Control E and Control L) having the same kind of warning systems without the first threat and without the cancellation. The data on these groups were taken from Breznitz (1972). The experimental design is schematically presented in Table 5.1.

Independent Variables

In terms of testing the effectiveness of the research procedures, the following manipulations should affect the fear reaction: (1) the first threat; (2) cancellation of the threat; (3) the second threat. If all the manipulations are effective, the FAE can be studied by comparing the reactions to the first threat with those to the

TABLE 5.1
The Experimental Design

Experimental Manipulation	Time in Minutes	Group E	Group L	Control E	Control L
First Threat	Minute 1 Minute 2 Minute 3	Warning A Warning A Warning A	Warning A Warning B Warning C	None	None
Cancellation	2 Minutes	Yes	Yes	None	None
Second Threat	Minute 1 Minute 2 Minute 3 Minute 4 Minute 5 Minute 6	Warning A Warning A Warning A Warning A Warning B Warning C	Warning A Warning B Warning C Warning C Warning C Warning C	Warning A Warning A Warning A Warning A Warning B Warning C	Warning A Warning B Warning C Warning C Warning C Warning C

second threat and reactions to the various warnings during the first threat with those during the second one. Comparisons between Group E and Group L provide the basis for testing the central independent variable of this study (i.e., the differential psychological distance of the danger).

Dependent Variables

As stipulated in the preceding chapter, the central dependent variables were the two autonomic indexes of fear reaction: heart rate and skin conductance. In addition to their major role in most of the experimental treatment of psychological stress, they have the advantage of making a continuous monitoring of the fear reaction possible.

Verbal reports of subjective feelings of tension during the various critical stages of the experiment were also secured through a postexperimental questionnaire. Any attempt to monitor these cognitions "on line" while the experiment was in progress significantly alters the situation of the subject. Among the various effects of such a procedure, alerting the subject to his own feelings may substantially reduce the fear reaction itself. Thus, Petry and Desiderato (1978) found that requesting their subjects to provide verbal reports of their subjective anxiety reduces the fear reaction. Because a strong threat is one of the major ingredients of basic threat, we preferred to postpone the questions until after the experiment proper was over.

In addition to subjective reports of tension, two additional kinds of information were obtained by the postexperimental questionnaire, namely, ratings of credibility of the threats and time estimates of the various segments of the experiment. This last index was included on the basis of earlier findings by Anner (1972) and Breznitz (1972) to the effect that estimated durations were negatively related to the intensity of fear reaction. Appendix A presents the postexperimental questionnaire.

Subjects and Procedure

The basic procedures and instructions in all the experiments were essentially the same, with only minor variations as required by the particular manipulations employed. Thus, in order to give the reader a clear notion concerning these procedures, they ought to be presented in detail at least on this first occasion.

Considering that our experiments are inducing substantial psychological stress, the protection of the subjects was one of our major concerns. The specific steps taken to insure the rights of the subjects adhered to the guidelines of the American Psychological Association, as well as to those of the granting agency, the U.S. Army. For reasons that become evident shortly, the main facets of the specific measures taken in this respect should be mentioned:

1. At no point were electric shocks actually delivered. As the chief concern of this research was in false alarms, this made the execution of the threats unnecessary.

2. All subjects without exception were volunteers.

3. At the time they volunteered, subjects were told that they must be in perfect health and must agree to the actual screening of their medical records.

4. The medical records of all subjects who volunteered to participate in this experiment were screened by the medical authorities of the university. (In the case of the experiment discussed in this chapter, the subjects were students at George Washington University, Washington, D.C.) The nature of the experiment was made explicit to the physician who was then asked to take a strictly conservative approach and disqualify any person who according to his best judgment was not in perfect health

5. Upon coming to the laboratory, subjects were explicitly instructed that they could terminate their participation at will and at any point during the experiment. Furthermore, they were told that such termination, should it occur, would not affect their remuneration. Subjects were asked to read and sign an explicit statement to that effect, stating their willingness to proceed.

6. When the stressful nature of the experiment was made known to them, subjects were reminded of their option to terminate their participation, and they again signed a statement concerning their willingness to go on with the experiment, as well as to keep its details confidential in order not to compromise future subjects.

It is of some interest to note that the very precautions taken to insure the rights and protection of the subjects contributed significantly to the intensity of their fear. By taking all these precautionary measures, the stressful aspect of the experiment was of course perceived by the participants in a rather dramatized form. In view of the importance of inducing a meaningfully intense fear reaction, the significance of these protective steps cannot be overemphasized. They serve two functions simultaneously: (1) they truly insure the well-being of a well-informed volunteer; (2) they augment the potency of the threatening instructions.

All our subjects throughout the entire experimental program were young males, and very few of them chose to terminate the experiment before its completion. This in itself is of some interest to be considered at a later stage of our discussion. Considering the dramatization of the stressful character of the experiments implied by the various protective devices, it is perhaps not surprising that, on the whole, the intensity of fear reactions obtained by these practices is rather high. From the point of view of this study, this is almost a prerequisite for any meaningful investigation of the FAE. After all, the fear reaction should be sufficiently intense to allow a systematic analysis of its subsequent reduction.

In the present experiment 40 subjects were randomly assigned to the two experimental groups. There were 20 subjects in Group E and 20 in Group L.

Each subject was greeted by the experimenter outside the psychophysiological laboratory. He was seated in another room and given the first statement of willingness to participate. Next, the experimenter removed the subject's watch and took his pulse from the wrist. This served two purposes: First, it was thought desirable to have some preliminary reading of pulse rate at this point in the experimental sequence; second, this served as an excuse for removing the subject's watch, which was necessary in order to get his time estimations without prior warning that time is an issue in this experiment.

The subject was then taken into the psychophysiological laboratory and attached to a Beckman, Type S-II Dynograph. Two channels were used: ECG and GSR. The subject was seated alone in a booth and observed through a closed-circuit television camera. All communication was conducted via an intercom system. Following the attachment of the electrodes, there was a 2-minute period of base-line recording. The prerecorded stress instructions followed:

> You are participating in an experiment which aims to study how people behave under stress. There is of course nothing in this experiment which can harm you physically or mentally, but the experiment will not be easy for you. Depending upon the particular experimental group to which you have been allocated you might be given electric shocks or other kinds of difficult tasks. Remember that you may stop the experiment at any moment, although we hope that this will not be necessary. Try to concentrate upon the tasks that will be given to you, and follow the instructions as exactly as possible.

After these instructions the experimenter entered the subject's booth and gave him the second statement to sign. He then proceeded to attach the "shock electrodes" to the subject's right hand. Another 2-minute period of base-line recording followed. Next, the threat instructions were given:

> You will receive a strong electric shock. I repeat: You will receive a strong electric shock. It will be harmless, but unpleasant. You will not know exactly when it is going to come, but you will have some partial information about the timing. There will be three warnings: A, B, and C. The shock can appear any time after Warning C. Warning A will be given by the red signal going on and off once [at this point the experimenter demonstrates the procedure by switching a red light in front of the subject on and off once]. Warning B will be given by the red light blinking twice [demonstration]. At the onset of the last warning, C, the light will be switched on and stay on until the shock is given [demonstration]. Are there any questions? [The experimenter stops the tape and, only if the subject responds with "no," proceeds with the remaining phrase.] Wait for the start.

It should be mentioned that the instructions were a recording made by the experimenter so that there was no change in the voice throughout the entire experiment. The brief warning signals were controlled by a preset timer, with the red light on for 1 second. The last, continuous warning was controlled by the experimenter manually.

Now followed 3 minutes of the first session of anticipation according to the particular group to which subject was allocated. Group E received only Warning A for 3 minutes, whereas Group L received all the three warnings, A, B, and C, each lasting 1 minute.

After 3 minutes of anticipation, the threat was canceled: "This time the alarm was called off. I repeat: This time the alarm was called off. There will be no shock. You can now relax."

After two minutes of relaxation, the second threat instructions were given: "We are now starting a new session. You will receive . . . [continuing as in the previous threat instructions]."

Then came the full 6-minute period of the second anticipation of the shock, according to groups. It was terminated by the second and final cancellation: "The danger has passed, and there will be no more danger. I shall now remove the shock electrodes, and you can completely relax."

An additional 5 minutes of relaxation followed before the subject was disconnected from the polygraph. Following the removal of the electrodes, the questionnaire was administered. The subject was then taken back to the first room, paid for his participation and debriefed about the purpose of the experiment. The total duration of the experiment was about 60 minutes.

RESULTS

The Psychophysiological Indexes

All heart-rate scores were transformed into beats per minute, and all GSR readings were transformed into conductance scores. Twelve discrete readings of GSR were sampled for each minute. Previous research using a similar method indicated that the arithmetic mean based on such sampling satisfactorily represents the entire period tested.

Our first analysis tested the effects of the threat instruction, the cancellation of the threat, and the second threat, on the various indexes of fear. Table 5.2 presents the mean fear reactions of both groups for the entire experimental sequence. Before attempting to test the statistical significance of the relevant ups and downs in the intensity of the autonomic reactions, a few preliminary points deserve mentioning.

To begin, it appears that in spite of the random allocation of subjects to the two experimental groups, their mean initial heart rates differ. This difference, although not statistically significant, makes it imperative that all intergroup analyses be made with scores relative to the respective base levels. It should be

TABLE 5.2
Mean Autonomic Reactions of Both Groups for the Entire
Experimental Sequence

	Heart Rate		Skin Conductance	
	Group L	Group E	Group L	Group E
Initial Pulse	77.7	82.0		
Base Level	76.5	84.5	6.72	7.49
Stress Instructions	79.2	86.5	8.23	9.58
Base Level	75.6	82.4	9.54	9.85
First Threat	86.7	94.9	12.79	16.77
Minute 1	83.1	88.7	11.56	15.71
2	82.5	86.1	12.46	13.58
3	83.2	86.7	13.81	13.97
Cancellation	76.2	81.0	12.39	12.86
Second Threat	82.7	90.8	15.70	14.07
Minute 1	79.2	86.1	16.39	14.49
2	80.4	85.0	18.72	15.46
3	78.1	85.4	16.98	17.74
4	77.8	85.5	19.51	20.19
5	78.2	86.5	17.78	17.87
6	79.3	87.3	17.67	20.44
Relaxation 1	79.3	83.7	18.24	17.14
2	78.6	83.1	17.05	16.43
3	79.4	85.6	18.24	16.32
4	78.9	84.7	18.43	17.03
5	78.0	84.6	18.28	17.25

noted that the present procedure does not allow for any meaningful base-line recording in view of the stressful nature of the experiment. Furthermore, as the subject learns more and more about what is in store, his apprehension may continually change. There is thus no true base line available, nor could one be easily obtained considering the artificial situation of being attached to a polygraph. The notion of base line in its quantitative, parametric sense is questionable both on the theoretical and the practical levels.

In the present experiment there are several base-line scores. The first is the initial pulse taken even before entering the psychophysiological laboratory. Next there are two periods of 2 minutes each preceding and following the initial stress instructions. The cancellation of the threat is also a manipulation that provides scores on a return to a base level. The final cancellation and relaxation period provide still another measure on the base line issue. Needless to say, these various scores do not necessarily correspond with each other.

Observing the entire experimental sequence in the skin-conductance channel reveals a major difficulty, namely, that there seems to be a continuous rise in this response channel. More specifically, while the effects of the various stress-inducing parts of the experiment can be seen, there seems to be little evidence for the effect of cancellation and relaxation. The skin-conductance channel appears to take much longer than heart rate to return to any base line from a previously increased level of responding. Even more important is the absolute recovery time necessary, which seems to be much longer than the few minutes allowed in this experiment.

A study of relaxation from threat (see Breznitz, 1965) can shed some light on this issue. Seventeen subjects were threatened with a strong electric shock, and immediately after the threat was given, it was cancelled. The experimenter removed the shock electrodes and told the subjects that the purpose of the experiment was to study relaxation. The heart rate and skin-conductance channels were then monitored for 12 minutes. Figure 5.1 presents the results.

The results indicate that whereas 2 minutes were sufficient to allow the recovery of the heart rate, at least 8 minutes were needed for the recovery of skin conductance. The data from the present experiment seem to replicate this basic

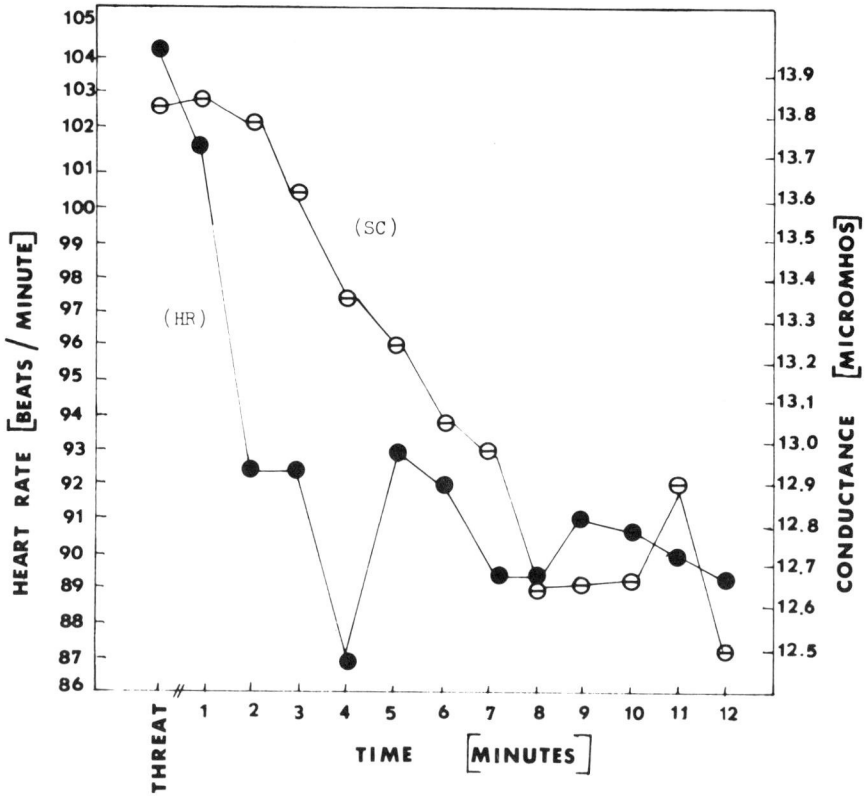

FIG. 5.1 Recovery from threat: heart rate and skin conductance.

TABLE 5.3
The Effect of Instructions on Heart Rate

	Variable	Mean	Diff.	Std. Error	Corr.	t	df	p
Group E	Initial Pulse	82.05	−12.85	3.44	.55	−3.74	19	.001
	First Threat	94.90						
	Warning A_1	87.70	6.70	1.49	.91	4.50	19	.000
	Cancellation 1	81.00						
	Cancellation 1	81.00	9.80	1.74	.83	5.64	19	.000
	Second Threat	90.80						
Group L	Initial Pulse	77.75	−8.90	1.94	.69	−4.60	19	.000
	First Threat	86.65						
	Warning C_1	83.15	6.95	1.78	.66	3.89	19	.001
	Cancellation 1	76.20						
	Cancellation 1	76.20	6.45	1.24	.88	5.19	19	.000
	Second Threat	82.65						

asynchrony in relaxation speed between the two autonomic channels. For our purposes, the effectiveness of skin conductance as a measure of fear reaction is thus partly reduced because of the need for repeated measures. For practical reasons, the intertrial intervals cannot, unfortunately, be sufficiently long for the full recovery of the skin-conductance channel. In this connection it is worth mentioning yet another psychophysiological measure, namely, that of nonspecific electrodermal responses. Katkin (1965, 1966) was the first to demonstrate the potential value of this index, and this was subsequently reinforced by Szpiler and Epstein (1976). Considering the "law of initial value" as stated by Lacey and Lacey (1962), and in view of the difficulty with the conductance channel as described earlier, this nonspecific index appeared to be problematic as well. The major emphasis must, therefore, shift to the heart-rate channel.

Effectiveness of the Experimental Instructions

T tests between means for dependent samples were used separately in each experimental group. The results appear in Table 5.3. The heart-rate channel is obviously sensitive to the experimental procedure; threat instructions increase it,

The Effect of Warnings on Fear

The discrete warnings paradigm makes it possible to test the impact of each warning on fear. The specific design used in this study employed three warnings: A, B, and C. On the first trial only Group L experienced all three, whereas on the second trial both groups did. The impact of transition from one warning level to another can be tested in both the heart-rate channel as well as the subjective reports on tension experienced during the various stages of anticipation. Subjects rated their tension on a 7-point scale, with 7 indicating the highest tension level. Tables 5.4 and 5.5 present the data for the heart-rate and the tension scores, respectively. When a warning lasts for more than 1 minute, the heart rate for the first minute is used.

The contrast between the two tables could hardly be more obvious. The subjective tension measures are highly sensitive to warnings. With each transition to a more advanced warning stage, the reported tension is significantly

TABLE 5.4
The Effect of Warnings on Heart Rate

	Variable	Mean	Diff.	Std. Error	Corr.	t	df	p
Group E	Warning A_2	86.10	−0.35	1.01	.94	−0.35	19	.732
	Warning B_2	86.45						
	Warning B_2	86.45	−0.85	1.25	.94	−0.68	19	.506
	Warning C_2	87.30						
Group L	Warning A_1	83.10	0.60	0.82	.94	0.73	19	.476
	Warning B_1	82.50						
	Warning B_1	82.50	−0.65	1.12	.88	−0.58	19	.569
	Warning C_1	83.15						
	Warning A_2	79.20	−1.20	0.68	.96	−1.76	19	.095
	Warning B_2	80.40						
	Warning B_2	80.40	2.30	0.80	.94	2.88	19	.010
	Warning C_2	78.10						

TABLE 5.5
The Effect of Warnings on Subjective Tension

	Variable	Mean	Diff.	Std. Error	Corr.	t	df	p
Group E	Tension A_2	3.55	−0.65	0.15	.89	−4.33	19	.000
	Tension B_2	4.20						
	Tension B_2	4.20	−1.00	0.14	.89	−6.89	19	.000
	Tension C_2	5.20						
Group L	Tension A_1	3.70	−0.35	0.17	.84	−2.10	19	.049
	Tension B_1	4.05						
	Tension B_1	4.05	−0.95	0.20	.80	−4.79	19	.000
	Tension C_1	5.00						
	Tension A_2	3.40	−0.25	0.16	.82	−1.56	19	.135
	Tension B_2	3.65						
	Tension B_2	3.65	−0.65	0.24	.72	−2.67	19	.015
	Tension C_2	4.30						

increased. No such effect can be found in the heart-rate scores. The only statistically significant change is the *decline* in fear reaction following the transition from Warning B to Warning C on the second trial in Group L. The implications of this finding to the main hypothesis of this study are discussed shortly.

Are the subjective experiences of differential tension more sensitive to the psychological effects of warnings than the heart rate, which is monitored "online"? Although such a possibility cannot be ruled out offhand, another explanation is possible. If our subjects have an implicit theory about the presumed effects of imminence of the danger on their fear reaction, they might be influenced by their assumptions when filling out the postexperimental questionnaire. Needless to say, both high sensitivity and the previously mentioned mechanism can operate jointly. However, their relative contribution cannot be ascertained at the present level of our knowledge.

Testing False Alarm Effect

The FAE can be tested by comparing each segment of the anticipation sequence with its counterpart following the experience of threat cancellation. Thus, all those scores obtained on both trials are relevant for the testing of the FAE. Tables 5.6 and 5.7 present the results for the heart-rate and tension scores, respectively.

The data indicate a clear and reliable FAE in both heart-rate scores and tension scores. This effect reaches statistical significance in all but two instances. The t tests in our tables are all two tailed, whereas the FAE hypothesis clearly states the anticipated direction of the change. Interestingly, the statistical significance of the FAE appears to be strongest in Group L during Warning C. This is the case in both response channels, and it fits an earlier finding in the same direction mentioned earlier.

The postexperimental questionnaire includes two direct questions about the credibility of the danger. The first question relates to the first threat; the second question relates to the second threat. In those questions the subjects are asked to state how sure they were that the shock would be given. The alternatives were: 100% sure (scored as $+2$), quite sure ($+1$), about 50% chance (0), less than 50% chance (-1), sure that the shock would *not* be given (-2). Table 5.8 presents the data for both groups, testing for the FAE.

Once more, it appears from comparison of significance levels that the credibility loss is greater in Group L than in Group E. But, after all, that is the main

TABLE 5.6
The FAE in the Heart Rate Channel

	Variable	*Mean*	*Diff.*	*Std. Error*	*Corr.*	*t*	*df*	*p*
Group E	First Threat	94.90	4.10	1.71	.92	2.39	19	.027
	Second Threat	90.80						
	Warning A_1	88.65	2.55	1.86	.89	1.37	19	.185
	Warning A_2	86.10						
Group L	First Threat	86.65	4.00	1.73	.77	2.31	19	.032
	Second Threat	82.65						
	Warning A_1	83.10	3.90	1.48	.80	2.63	19	.016
	Warning A_2	79.20						
	Warning B_1	82.50	2.10	1.19	.87	1.77	19	.093
	Warning B_2	80.40						
	Warning C_1	83.15	5.05	1.22	.85	4.13	19	.001
	Warning C_2	78.10						

TABLE 5.7
The FAE in Tension Scores

	Variable	Mean	Diff.	Std. Error	Corr.	t	df	p
Group E	Tension A_1	4.47	.89	.31	.39	2.85	18	.011
	Tension A_2	3.58						
Group L	Tension A_1	3.70	.30	.21	.68	1.45	19	.163
	Tension A_2	3.40						
	Tension B_1	4.05	.40	.22	.71	1.80	19	.088
	Tension B_2	3.65						
	Tension C_1	5.00	.70	.18	.86	3.91	19	.001
	Tension C_2	4.30						

hypothesis of this research, namely, that late cancellation leads inevitably to a stronger FAE than does early cancellation. We can now proceed to make a direct test of this issue.

Pacing of Warnings and the False Alarm Effect

If the release of warnings is followed by a false alarm experience, the warnings should be less likely to evoke a fear reaction in the future. By contrast, transition to warning stages, which were never experienced before, should increase fear reaction. In the present study, subjects in Group E were not exposed to the more advanced stages of warning during the first trial; they were first experienced following the false alarm. Group L subjects were issued all three warnings prior to the cancellation. Thus, on the second trial, the more advanced warnings, particularly the last warning (C), should evoke higher fear reaction in Group E than in Group L.

TABLE 5.8
Credibility of the Two Threats

	Variable	Mean	Diff.	Std. Error	Corr.	t	df	p
Group E	Credibility 1	.15	.40	.31	.21	1.29	19	.214
	Credibility 2	−.25						
Group L	Credibility 1	.47	.58	.23	.52	2.48	18	.023
	Credibility 2	−.11						

5. PACING OF WARNINGS AND THE FAE

In order to control for initial differences in heart rate, a new C2NET score was computed for each subject by subtracting from his C2 score his initial pulse. Table 5.9 presents the analysis of variance on C2NET heart-rate scores according to groups. Unlike in Table 5.4 which tested for the impact of warnings, comparison between groups made it necessary to use the last minute as the data base, as it was only during minute 6 that Group E experienced Warning C.

The results clearly support the hypothesis. By withholding the last warning during the first trial, it was to some degree protected from the FAE following the cancellation of that threat. This general effect could also be seen to some extent in Tables 5.4 and 5.8. The significant decline in heart rate from Warning B2 to Warning C2 in Group L is particularly striking, in view of the imminence of danger signified by the transition to the last warning.

The fact that the subjective credibility loss reported by our subjects is significantly lower only in Group L (see Table 5.8) implies once more some sensitivity on their part to internal events occurring during the various phases of the experiment. As they could not know about the existence of different treatments for different experimental conditions, it does not seem plausible that in this instance they just reacted on the basis of some implicit theory of FAEs. Because this finding is based on intergroup comparisons rather than on comparisons of different segments of the experiment within each subject, the "implicit theory" notion is practically ruled out. This adds extra credibility to the differential FAE in the subjective credibility scores.

Our hypothesis received yet more interesting support from the data on time estimation. As mentioned before, earlier research indicated that in conditions similar to the present experiment, intensity of fear reaction was found to correlate with underestimation of the duration of anticipation. If such is the case, the comparison of the duration of the two trials may prove to be of some relevance to

TABLE 5.9
Heart-Rate Scores During Warning C_2

Group	Sum	Mean	SD	Sum of Sq.	N
Group E	105	5.25	12.31	2878	(20)
Group L	7	0.35	7.44	1052	(20)
Within-Group Total	112	2.80	10.17	3930	(40)

Analysis of Variance					
Source	Sum of Sq.	df	MS	F	Sig.
Between Groups	430	1	430.0	4.16	.05
Within Group	3930	38	103.4		

TABLE 5.10
Which Threat Was Longer?

Group	Sum	Mean	SD	Sum of Sq.	N
Group E	−1.0	−.08	1.04	19.52	(13)
Group L	−12.0	−.86	0.53	3.71	(14)
Within-Group Total	−13.0	−.48	0.82	16.63	(27)

Analysis of Variance					
Source	Sum of Sq.	df	ms	F	Sig.
Between Groups	4.103	1	4.103	6.166	.02
Within Group	16.637	25	0.665		

the testing of the differential effects of warnings on fear reaction in the two groups.

Translating the hypothesis to the time estimation issue, the following logic applies: Subjects in Group L could be expected to be more frightened during the first threat than those in Group E. This is due to their exposure to Warnings B and C, which signify that the shock is imminent. If the FAE is greater in Group L than in Group E, exactly the opposite should be found during the second threat, and subjects in Group E should now experience more intense fear reactions. Assuming that fear is negatively related to time estimation, we should predict that Group E perceived the second trial as shorter and the first trial as longer, relative to Group L. The very first question in the postexperimental questionnaire requires the direct comparison of the two durations. Subjects who responded by stating that the first session was shorter than the second received a score of −1, those who perceived them as equal in duration received a score of 0, and those who perceived the second session as shorter received a score of +1 (see Table 5.10).

The hypothesis was once again supported by the data. It should be noted that the time estimation test is quite dramatic in view of the simple fact that in terms of objective duration, the second session took 6 minutes, whereas the first took

TABLE 5.11
Mean Estimated Durations of the Threats

	First Threat	Second Threat
Group E	300.0	271.7
Group L	224.1	302.1
Real Time	180.0	360.0

only 3 minutes. The a priori chances of a subject actually perceiving the second session as shorter are thus quite minimal. And yet, subjects in Group E often did so. As a matter of fact, their mean estimated duration of the second session is actually shorter than that of the first. Table 5.11 presents the data on the basis of Question 2 of the postexperimental questionnaire. All times are given in seconds.

The results are even more surprising in the context of theories of time estimation (e.g., Ornstein, 1969). Considering the prevalent notions in this area, we would expect that time would seem longer when the subject is given greater amount of information. Consequently, a trial with three warnings (Group L, first session) would be perceived as longer than a trial with just a single warning (Group E, first session). The strong effect in the opposite direction is based on the rationale that self-produced information is as important as external information. Subjects with more intense fear reactions are thinking primarily about the danger, whereas those less afraid may be more distracted by letting their mind

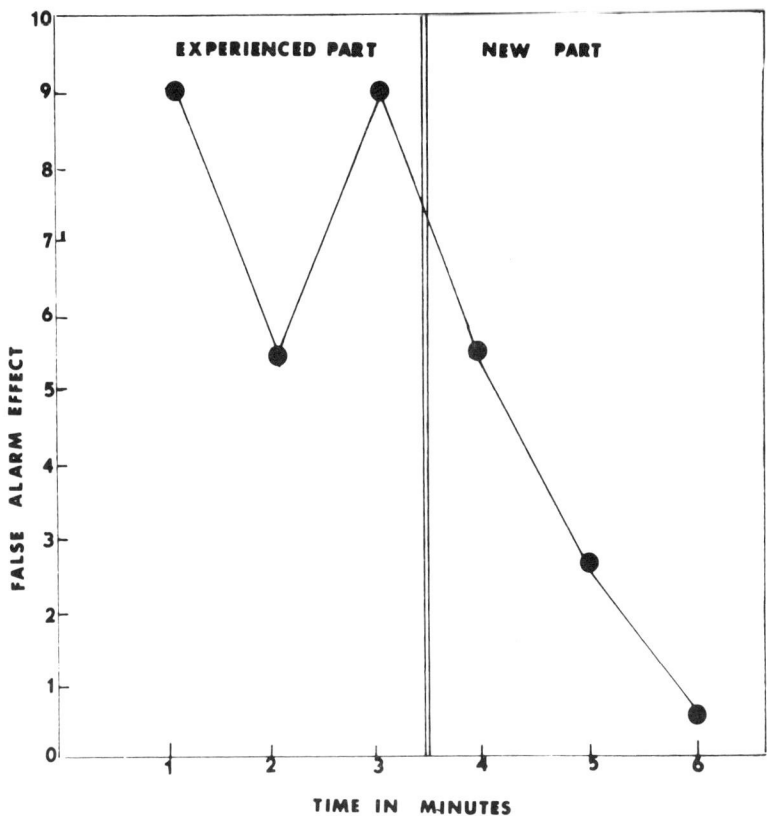

FIG. 5.2 The effect of late cancellation on the FAE (heart rate).

wander from one topic to another, thus providing a greater amount of self-produced information (Anner, 1972; Breznitz, 1972).

By calling off the first threat after 3 minutes, the present design forfeits the possibility of measuring the FAE of the last 3 minutes of anticipation. In order to have access to some preliminary evidence in this matter, the responses to the second threat were compared to two control groups taken from an earlier study employing the same paradigm (Breznitz, 1972). The reader may recall that the subjects in these groups were given a single trial only, which corresponded with the duration and pacing of warnings of our two experimental groups during the second threat. These comparisons give a clue about the FAE that could have been obtained if Groups E and L were given a full 6 minutes of anticipation on the first trial.

By subtracting the reaction of the experimental groups (second threat) from the reaction of the appropriate control groups (first threat), we obtain a rough estimate of the FAE. This procedure is based on different subjects for the two trials and thus can only provide a basis for generating some preliminary suggestions, not for parametric comparisons.

The heart-rate data are presented in Figs. 5.2, 5.3, and 5.4. Figures 5.2 and 5.3 illustrate that the FAE is greater during the first minute of each warning. As time goes on and as there is new information coming from the warning system, both the fear reaction and the FAE are reduced. Figure 5.4 brings evidence to bear on our central hypothesis. The FAE is systematically greater in Group L than in Group E. A closer look at these figures raises two interesting problems:

1. Although smaller than in Group L, why is there any FAE at all in Warnings B and C of Group E? These warnings were never experienced before, and their credibility might have been protected by canceling the threat prior to their appearance.
2. Why is there a higher FAE to Warning A in Group L than in Group E? After all, both experienced A during the first threat before its cancellation.

The answer to both of these questions may well turn out to be essentially the same, that is, a process of generalization. More specifically, subjects generalize from the experienced part to the unexperienced parts of the warning system. The credibility loss following a false alarm reflects to some extent on the warning system as a whole. Thus, even though certain warnings were not directly subjected to the FAE, they were indirectly influenced by those that were. By the same token, the greater FAE experienced by subjects in Group L generalized to the part they shared with Group E (i.e., Warning A). From their point of view they were given three items of information, all of which turned out to be false alarms, compared with one item of Group E.

This analysis has some sobering implications. It may be possible to reduce the FAE by appropriate pacing of warnings and an early cancellation, but the cred-

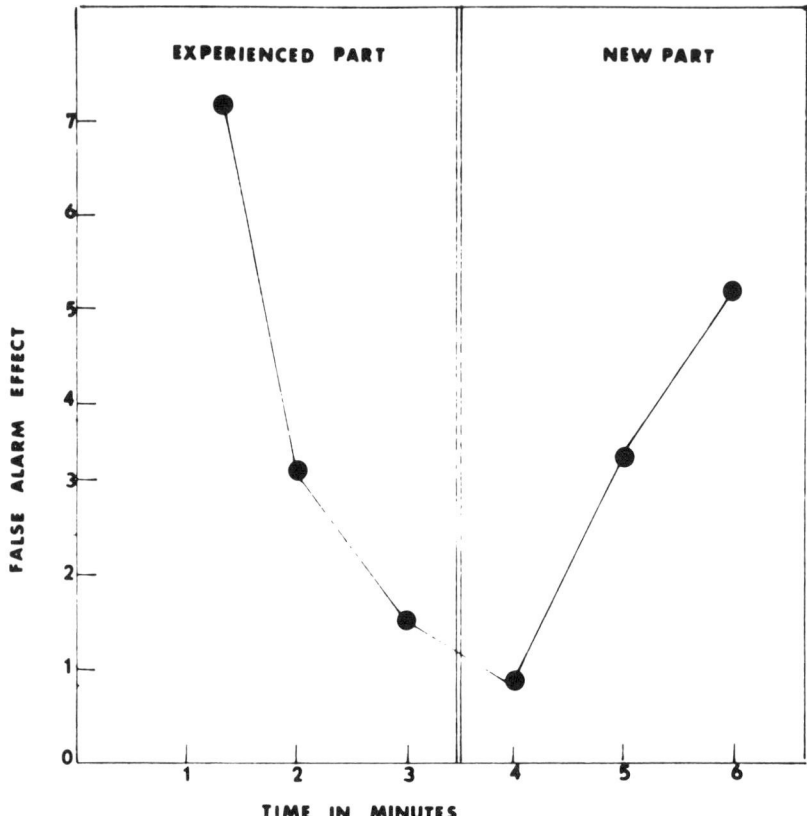

FIG. 5.3 The effect of early cancellation on the FAE (heart rate).

ibility loss extends well beyond the person's immediate experience. Such nonspecific FAE substantially reduces the effectiveness of steps taken to protect a warning system from credibility loss. As our story unfolds, the status of this nonspecific FAE gradually becomes more apparent.

Optimal Pacing of Warnings

Earlier in our discussion, the point was made that the main function of a warning system is to provide opportunity for protective action in the face of impending danger. Information concerning the psychological distance of the danger should consider effectiveness of protective behavior as its main guiding principle. Upgrading the threat by transition from a low-level warning to a higher level warning cannot, therefore, depend only on temporal cues of imminence. In other words, the fact that the danger is definitely coming closer is not a sufficient reason for issuing the next warning, unless that warning implies some new action. In the absence of a requirement for specific behaviors contingent upon the new warning, the long-term cost of releasing it can become prohibitive. The present study provides clear evidence that cancellation of the threat in its more advanced stages of warnings augments the FAE. This results in substantial credibility loss to the warning system. Thus, any unnecessary upgrading of the warnings (i.e., unrelated to contingent activity) is not only ineffective, but actually harmful.

We shall know more about the particular behavior contingencies and their impact on safety as our investigation proceeds to include protective behavior in addition to fear reaction. At this point, however, the case can already be made for the efficacy of keeping the warning system at its lower possible level. Such is the case particularly when the chances are that the danger will not materialize.

Here now is a practical problem: Individuals or agencies responsible for the release of warnings are often more sensitive to the requirements of the present than to long-range requirements. It is only "natural" to assume that they will be

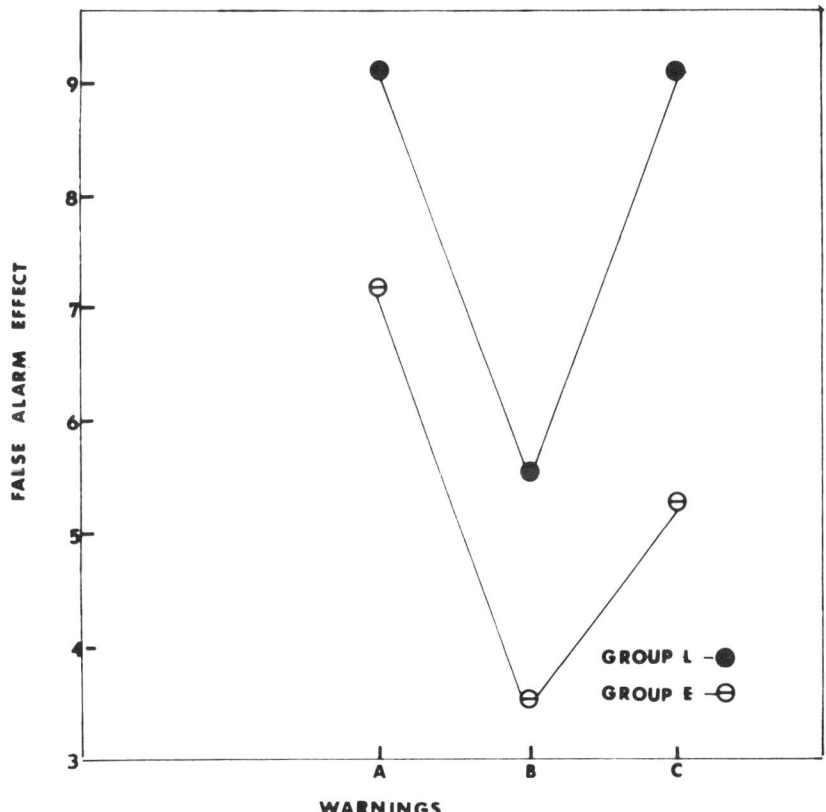

FIG. 5.4 FAE according to timing of cancellation (heart rate).

more concerned with making sure that this time the receiver(s) will be well prepared and thus reduce any responsibility on their part for lack of preparedness. There is a distinct tendency on the part of information managers to actually upgrade the threat in order "to play it safe." Such upgrading and transition, say from Warning A to Warning B or from Warning B to Warning C, can actually take place on a local level, even without the knowledge of a more central authority. It is not an uncommon practice by local commanders or officials to try and do better than the stated Warning A requires by issuing the Warning B on their own initiative. At a lower level such a warning can be further upgraded to C by another official. These initiatives, even though taken with the best of intentions, can cause irreparable damage to the warning system if the danger is called off. This illustrates a built-in dilemma between short-term preparedness, which advocates the upgrading of the threat and dramatization of its intensity and proximity, and long-term preparedness, which calls for practices exactly the opposite in nature.

The logic of the argument calls for a more differentiated warning system as one way of dealing with this problem. Inasmuch as the next chapter provides an additional illustration of the same basic dilemma, we ought to postpone a more thorough analysis of these questions until later in the discussion.

6 Probability of Threat and the False Alarm Effect

Our next attempt to discover variables that may protect a warning system from a particularly intense false alarm effect via the information-management subsystem deals with an especially potent variable, the probability of the threat. The rationale for the anticipated potency of the probability issue rests on the analysis of the concepts of credibility and probability. Credibility reflects the belief that particular information is trustworthy and should be taken seriously. The announced probability of a threat indicates the chances that the threatening information will be followed by an actual danger. Thus, from the point of view of the receiver, objective probability reflects the amount of credibility that the warning system attaches to the danger signals at its disposal. Needless to say, the receiver's subjective probability is entirely indistinguishable from his or her perception of a warning system's credibility. The two are intimately intertwined; consequently, by manipulating probability, we are at the core of the credibility issue.

A slightly different formulation of this point may be helpful. If a warning system issues information indicating that the probability of a given threat to materialize is P, this can be viewed as implying that there is a given probability, $Q = (1 - P)$, that the threat will be a false alarm. Subsequently, if such is indeed the case, the warning system was "wrong" by the factor of P, but at the same time was "right" by the factor of Q. The higher the P value, the lower the corresponding Q value, and of course, the greater the anticipated credibility loss. The central hypothesis of the present experiment is that the higher the announced probability of the threat, the greater the FAE following its cancellation.

A word of caution is needed at this point. There is no reason to assume simple linear functions or simple algebraic summation of the effects involved in the final psychological outcome. Thus, if the stated probability of a danger is lower than

50% and consequently the stated probability of a false alarm is higher than 50%, it does not follow that the warning system actually gains credibility by issuing the threat and then calling it off. We submit that even the cancellation of a low-probability threat results in credibility loss, but one smaller than if the probability was high. This may happen because the subjective probabilities may be entirely different than the objective ones in terms of actual parametric values, and their correspondence to the objective ones may be only in terms of an ordinal scale rather than a ratio scale. Other psychological factors may be operative which will make the fact that the warning was unnecessary more salient than the fact that it was a low-probability warning. It is our contention that in the absence of very specific extrinsic information, a false alarm can never increase the credibility of a warning system. The only question is: How great will the credibility loss be? One possible example of such specific extrinsic information is the case where the initial warning was issued by an entirely different source stating a high probability of danger, upon which another warning system issued information to the effect that the probability is much lower than the one stated by the original source. A false alarm episode will in this case vindicate the second warning system and perhaps even increase its credibility. But in this case the second warning system did not act as a warning system at all; it only reacted to a different warning system. This other warning system, which issued the original threat, should be seen as the main actor in this event. Needless to say, its own credibility will be substantially reduced by the FAE.

In light of the foregoing, perhaps we should qualify our definition of a warning system by requiring that it be the initiator of the threat. When more than one warning system relates to a particular kind of danger, the first one to report it (not necessarily to detect it, but to release the information) becomes the active warning system. It has the most to lose by a subsequent cancellation of the threat. This illustrates in yet a different framework the strong relationship between early warnings and the FAE, and the warning system that first issues a warning will have the greatest FAE if the danger does not materialize. The same warning system will of course increase its credibility if the danger does materialize.

To complicate the issue further, whether an early warning system produces a FAE or not depends significantly on the probability that the danger materializes. Thus, if the objective probability of the danger is high, the chances that a FAE will follow are smaller than in the case of a low-probability event. Once such a FAE occurs, however, its intensity will be much greater, for the reasons mentioned earlier. From the point of view of the warning system itself, there is a built-in negative relationship between the probability of causing a FAE and its intensity.

Early detection of danger is usually correlated with low probabilities in view of the weak remote signals on which the threat is based. Distance in time is another factor that increases the chances of new developments and thus change in the situation. Consequently, early warnings are typically low-probability warnings having high chances of turning out to be false alarms. However, once a false alarm occurs, the tactical considerations that governed the information-management subsystem become irrelevant, and the degree of FAE according to our hypothesis will depend on the initially stated probability of the threat.

EFFECT OF PROBABILITY OF THREAT ON FEAR

The potential role of fear reaction in the intensity of subsequent FAE is an open question. Although the possibility remains that a stronger fear reaction to the first threat may lead to a greater FAE after its cancellation, there is as yet no direct evidence on this issue. It is quite conceivable that the differential FAE of early versus late cancellation, as tested in Chapter 4, is at least partially determined by the stronger initial fear of Group L. The particular contribution of fear to the FAE becomes of special interest in the context of probability of threat. If our hypothesis is supported by experimental data and the FAE is found greater in subjects threatened with high-probability danger than in subjects given a low-probability threat, it could be argued that intensity of fear reaction is the mediating mechanism.

Thus, if fear reaction could be assumed to be stronger when the probability of the impending danger is higher, the subsequent FAE may be due to the fear level rather than to a directly recognizable influence of probability as such. In other words, the possibility will remain that only because of higher fear reaction was the FAE found to be differentially affected by probability. Although the theoretical status of such an argument must await the demonstration of its relevance, the present experiment can help clarify the issue of the effect of probability on fear.

Studies in this area have yielded conflicting results thus far. Monat, Averill, and Lazarus (1972) present the conflicting theoretical arguments:

> What is the effect of event uncertainty on the *degree* (amount of stress experienced?) It might be expected, on the one hand, that degree of stress should be proportional to the probability of harm. If there is little likelihood of harm, one may simply forget about it and relax; but under conditions where the likelihood of harm is high, a premium might be placed on active psychological efforts to prepare oneself for the harm. On the other hand, event uncertainty itself may increase anxiety and thus add to the disturbance (e.g., Berlyne, 1960). This leads to the prediction of a curvilinear relationship between arousal and expectancy with maximum event uncertainty (50% predictability) leading to greater levels of anticipatory arousal than smaller levels of uncertainty, even when shock is more probable [p. 238].

The available research on this question (e.g., Epstein & Roupenian, 1970; Jennings, Averill, Opton, & Lazarus, 1970; Niemela, 1969; as well as the previously cited Monat et al., 1972, study) has not produced a clear picture.

Why is it that such obviously different treatments as a threat with a probability of 100% and one with a probability of just 5% do not produce reliably different psychophysiological responses? Does this imply that the response systems that have been studied are insensitive to the psychological implications of differential probabilities of threat? Such a statement, if true, would have far-reaching implications to problems of warning systems. Are we justified in claiming that it is not important whether warning systems are able to predict the *chances* of a danger correctly, as long as they accurately predict its potential *imminence*? It is our belief that reliable effects of probability on fear have not yet been discovered because of two methodological reasons:

1. The intensities of the anticipated danger have been too low. This has made the impact of "uncertainty" as such more important than would be the case in more intense danger.
2. The experimental paradigm used has been one of totally predictable timing of the danger. Whether by a clock or by similar exact counting methods, subjects in these experiments have had full knowledge about the proximity of the danger.

When discussing the advantages of the discrete warnings paradigm (Chapter 4), the danger that knowledge of imminence will dominate the experimental situation to the exclusion of all other parameters of threat was mentioned. Monat et al. (1972) also refer to this possibility: ". . . under conditions in which the person knows exactly when the aversive event is to occur, and regardless of how certain or uncertain he is about whether it will occur, his thoughts turn increasingly toward vigilant examination of the anticipated event as it grows imminent; and this increased vigilance is accompanied by an increase in arousal [p. 250]."

It is conceivable that such monopolizing of a person's attention due to continuous cues of imminence wash out any variance normally under the control of probability. Because the present experiment utilizes the discrete warnings paradigm and attempts to maximize the stressful impact of the threatening instructions, we argue that a clear positive relationship between probability and fear reaction should be demonstrable.

EXPERIMENTAL DESIGN

The main consideration in designing this experiment was the utilization of information available from previous relevant studies, particularly the study reported in Chapter 5. The following design was used: Subjects were threatened with a strong electric shock to be given at any time following the onset of the last warning. They were told that there would be three warnings: A, B, and C. The first trial lasted 3 minutes, with each warning lasting exactly 1 minute. In all respects this treatment was identical with that of Group L in the previous experiment. The data from that group of subjects could thus be utilized in this experiment as well.

Altogether there were three different groups. Group L was instructed that there was certainty that the threat would materialize; hence, in the context of this experiment it would be relabeled as Group 100. But there were two additional conditions. In Group 50 the subjects were instructed that there was a 50% chance that the shock would be given, and Group 5 was told that the probability of shock was 5%.

On the first trial, after 1 minute into Warning C, the threat was canceled, and following a brief relaxation a new trial began using the same warning system but with 100% chances for all groups. Group 50 and Group 5 were given a third trial in which the stated probability for Group 50 became 5%, and for Group 5 it became 50%. Table 6.1 presents the experimental design.

The two main independent variables in this study were differential probability and false alarm. The dependent variables were exactly the same as in the study reported in Chapter 5, namely, heart rate, subjective ratings of tension, subjective beliefs in the credibility of the threats, and time estimation of the various phases of the experiment. Skin conductance was also measured in order to maintain comparability with previous experiments. However, the data from this psychophysiological channel were not analyzed in view of the aforementioned limitations in a repeated-measures design.

As in the previous experiment, all subjects were male volunteers from the student population of George Washington University, Washington, D.C. In addition to the 20 subjects in Group 100, 36 subjects were randomly assigned to Groups 50 and 5, 18 in each, bringing the total number of subjects to 56.

The entire procedure and instructions were the same as in the experiment described in Chapter 5, with the only difference being the stating of respective probabilities and the attempt to produce two false alarms in Group 50 and in Group 5 by the introduction of a second cancellation and a third subsequent threat.

TABLE 6.1
The Experimental Design

	Threat 1	*Threat 2*	*Threat 3*
Group 100	100%	100%	
Group 50	50%	100%	5%
Group 5	5%	100%	50%

RESULTS

Effectiveness of Instructions

Prior to the testing of our specific hypothesis, the impact of the experimental indication of threats and their cancellation must be ascertained. This is particularly important in view of the fact that by contrast to previous groups, the two new groups were issued threats with lower probabilities. Are such threats sufficiently potent to influence the fear reaction of our subjects significantly?

Table 6.2 presents the data for the heart-rate channel according to groups and instructions.

The heart-rate results indicate that the critical segments of the procedure were once more effective in controlling the intensity of the reaction. Thus, both threats systematically increase fear reaction, and the cancellation instructions decrease it. This allows us to proceed to more refined analyses.

As in the previous study, the transition from one warning to another was not reflected in the heart rate, but could be clearly demonstrated in the subjective reporting of tension. Table 6.3 presents the data. It appears that subjects perceive

TABLE 6.2
The Effects of Instructions on Heart Rate

	Variable	Mean	Diff.	Std. Error	Corr.	t	df	f
Group 5	Initial Pulse	75.33	−8.11	2.22	.73	−3.66	17	.002
	Threat 1	83.44						
	Warning C_1	72.72	2.94	1.02	.93	2.88	17	.011
	Cancellation 1	69.78						
	Cancellation 1	69.78	−10.50	1.03	.96	−10.23	17	.000
	Threat 2	80.28						
Group 50	Initial Pulse	74.61	−10.17	2.08	.86	−4.90	17	.000
	Threat 1	84.78						
	Warning C_1	77.39	4.94	1.44	.92	3.43	17	.003
	Cancellation 1	72.44						
	Cancellation 1	72.44	−12.17	1.62	.91	−7.53	17	.000
	Threat 2	84.61						

TABLE 6.3
The Effect of Warnings on Subjective Tension

	Variable	Mean	Diff.	Std. Error	Corr.	t	p
Group 5	Tension A_1	3.28	−0.33	.16	.85	−2.06	.055
	Tension B_1	3.61					
	Tension B_1	3.61	−0.83	.20	.76	−4.12	.001
	Tension C_1	4.44					
Group 50	Tension A_1	3.44	−0.67	.18	.87	−3.69	.002
	Tension B_1	4.11					
	Tension B_1	4.11	−1.17	.23	.78	−5.02	.000
	Tension C_1	5.28					

the transition from lower level warnings to those indicating greater imminence as increasing their tension. This highly reliable finding must, however, be viewed in the context of their ability, post facto, to reconstruct their assumptions about their behaviors. Be that as it may, this response channel is exceptional;y sensitive to the cognitive appraisal of the situation. As such, it should prove very useful with the increasing cognitive complexity of our experiments.

Probability of Threat and Fear Reaction

We are now ready to test the hypothesis that probability of threat is positively related to fear reaction. In the heart-rate channel, the analyses of variance were performed on net scores (i.e., raw scores minus initial pulse scores). Although the data in all warning segments were in the predicted direction (i.e., Group 100 > Group 50 > Group 5), they reached statistical significance only during the last warning (C). Table 6.4 presents the analysis of variance.

The heart-rate channel gives clear support to the hypothesis only during the last warning. Why is that so? Is the proximity of the danger an amplifier of the differential signals of the threat instructions? Or, perhaps, is it the elapsed time since the announcement of the threat rather than proximity of impact that makes the difference? It is quite conceivable that a certain amount of cognitive appraisal of the threat is needed before the stated probability can demonstrate its effect. Such cognitive appraisal needs time, and hence the longer the time at its disposal, the greater its effect.

It is of course possible that mechanisms of defense are the important mediating factor. This would be in line with the reasoning of Monat et al. (1972). We

TABLE 6.4
Probability of Threat and Fear Reaction (Warning C)

	Sum	Mean	Std. Dev.	Sum of Sq.	N
Group 5	−47	−2.61	10.03	1710	(18)
Group 50	50	2.78	7.77	1027	(18)
Group 100	108	5.40	10.18	1969	(20)
Within-Group Total	111	1.98	9.42	4706	(56)

Analysis of Variance

Source	Sum of Sq.	df	ms	F	Sig.
Between Groups	625	2	312.5	3.52	.037
Within Group	4706	53	88.8		

submit that in the absence of powerful cues of imminence, low-probability threats encourage avoidant-like thoughts more than do high-probability threats. The defensive process also requires time to show its effect, a condition able to explicate our results.

The effect of probability of threat could be demonstrated in the subjective reporting of tension as well. In this case, the predicted order of tension (i.e., Group 100 > Group 50 > Group 5) was statistically significant for all three warnings. These evaluations were given after the experiment proper, and thus subjects had sufficient time to be influenced by their appraisals and defenses prior to answering the questions.

Here too, net scores were calculated by subtracting from the raw tension scores the amount of tension subjects reported experiencing when they first heard the general stress instruction. Table 6.5 presents the summary of these analyses. It includes the results of the direct question on credibility of the first threat, which also show clear support for the hypothesis.

We were thus able to demonstrate that under conditions of sufficiently intense manipulations and utilizing the discrete warnings paradigm, probability of threat is positively related to intensity of fear reaction. This finding is of obvious relevance to a variety of warning systems as well as to the basic body of knowledge in the area of psychological stress. The specific values of 100%, 50%, and 5% probability were chosen following Monat et al.'s study to allow direct comparisons between the two. Although in the time-known condition of their study no effect of those dramatically different probabilities was found, the present paradigm was able to support the underlying rationale for our prediction. The role of time, particularly empty time, in providing the opportunity for these effects to occur remains a fascinating question in need of further systematic investigation.

Probability of Threat and the False Alarm Effect

We are now closing in on the heart of the matter. Do the results of this experiment support the notion that a high-probability threat, if canceled, leads to a strong FAE? The difference between responses to the first threat and the second threat was defined as the FAE. It could be measured in all of the segments that were systematically reproduced on both trials. Analyses of variance were performed for heart-rate scores, tension scores, and credibility scores, respectively. A summary of the statistics appears in Table 6.6.

The results lend significant support to our hypothesis. The FAE during the last stages of anticipation is greatest in Group 100, followed by Group 50, and finally Group 5. This is replicated in both the heart rate and the subjective tension response channels. The credibility loss due to the cancellation of the first threat as reported by the subjects is also significantly greatest in Group 100, followed by Group 50, and lastly Group 5. Data on comparisons of estimated durations of the two trials followed the same order, but they did not reach statistical significance.

The finding that probability of threat determined to some degree the intensity of FAE especially during Warning C should by now in view of the foregoing analysis be almost obvious. Because we have found that it is during the last stages of the first threat that the impact of differential probabilities becomes particularly evident, we should expect that the same will apply concerning the additional psychological consequence on subsequent FAE. One can view the same factor, which leads to differential fear reaction to different probabilities of threat, as causing the FAE if the threat does not materialize.

TABLE 6.5
Probability of Threat and Subjective Tension: Between Groups

Variable		Mean	Sum of Sq.	df	ms	F	Sig.
Warning A_1	Group 5 Group 50 Group 100	−1.28 −1.17 −0.15	14.89	2	7.45	5.02	0.01
Warning B_1	Group 5 Group 50 Group 100	−0.94 −0.50 0.20	12.71	2	6.36	4.51	0.02
Warning C_1	Group 5 Group 50 Group 100	−0.11 0.67 1.15	15.23	2	7.61	4.19	0.02
Credibility 1	Group 5 Group 50 Group 100	−0.72 −0.56 0.47	15.64	2	7.82	5.59	0.01

6. PROBABILITY OF THREAT AND THE FAE

TABLE 6.6
Probability of Threat and the FAE: Between Groups

Variable		Mean	Sum of Sq.	df	ms	F	Sig.
Warning A Heart Rate	Group 5 Group 50 Group 100	−0.17 0.89 3.90	171.0	2	85.5	2.99	0.05
Warning B Heart Rate	Group 5 Group 50 Group 100	0.17 2.61 2.10	60.3	2	30.1	1.29	0.28
Warning C Heart Rate	Group 5 Group 50 Group 100	−1.17 1.83 5.05	367.0	2	183.5	8.43	0.00
Warning A Tension	Group 5 Group 50 Group 100	−0.39 −0.17 0.30	4.74	2	2.37	2.37	0.10
Warning B Tension	Group 5 Group 50 Group 100	−0.22 −0.11 0.40	4.24	2	2.12	2.02	0.14
Warning C Tension	Group 5 Group 50 Group 100	−0.61 0.33 0.70	17.08	2	8.54	7.74	0.00
Credibility	Group 5 Group 50 Group 100	−1.44 −0.83 0.58	40.06	2	20.03	13.78	0.00

A close parametric analysis of the FAE reveals that the mean heart rate for Group 5 actually *increased* on the second trial. The same is true in relation to subjective tension and credibility, with Group 50 joining in the "negative FAE." But can FAE be negative? The argument has already been made that this should not happen, even with a very low-probability threat. Why, then, is a negative FAE implied by the data?

The evidence that may totally refute the negative FAE notion does not exist, unfortunately, at the present time. However, highly plausible alternative explanations can be presented. In the design of this experiment, all three groups were issued exactly the same instructions on the second trial. Only such a design could insure that whatever differences were discovered between the groups would be due to their different histories during the first trial. It was for this reason that all three groups were issued a 100% probability threat on the second trial.

But this raises a new problem. Group 5 and Group 50 were threatened with a higher probability threat on the second trial than on the first. Our study indicates that higher probability should lead to a stronger fear reaction. This effect in turn runs contrary to the tendency to reduce fear reaction due to a FAE. The actual intensity of fear is thus a combination of these two opposing tendencies. When the effect of higher probability is stronger than the FAE, this should lead to an increase in the fear reaction. Such an increase is, therefore, another indication of support for our first hypothesis and does not constitute a demonstration of a negative FAE. As a matter of fact, if there had been no FAE at all, the increase in fear reaction in Group 5, for instance, would have in principle matched the difference between Group 5 and Group 100 on the first trial. Even a crude comparison reveals that the increase in fear reaction is well below the one anticipated on the basis of assuming no FAE. In the absence of full factorial design having nine separate groups, these parametric issues cannot, however, be resolved.

Yet another approach to our results can put the emphasis on the contrast between the two consecutive threats. The contrast is greatest in Group 5, then in Group 50, and smallest in Group 100, which is undergoing the exact repetition of the first trial. Because fear reactions can be at least partially under the control of the cognitive implications of such contrasts, this may contribute to a rise in autonomic as well as subjective indicators of fear. The same applies to the credibility of the second threat, which by contrast to the first may appear much higher for Group 5 and Group 50. Once again, the apparent negative FAE can be explained by such a contrast effect taking place in spite of a FAE, which in Groups 5 and 50 cannot be measured directly without independent estimates of various factors involved in determining this complex effect.

The contrast effect and the FAE are intimately interdependent in yet another fundamental sense, namely, the amount of learning from past experience. The analysis of the FAE was based on the notion of learning from experience. Such learning is facilitated by similarities between the past and the present. Consequently, the more dissimilar the events, (i.e., the greater the contrast between them), the smaller the generalization from one to the other and the smaller the FAE.

It seems that whatever our analytic starting point, the ultimate predictions and outcomes are the same: The higher the probability of a canceled threat, the greater the credibility loss it produces. Future research in this area will hopefully be able to untangle these mutually interrelated psychological variables, but in terms of the actual results of different practices, this may prove unnecessary. From the point of view of a warning system, a canceled high-probability threat is damaging to its credibility for two reasons:

1. By producing a higher FAE.
2. By reducing the chances that a subsequent threat will, by contrast to the previous threat, be more credible. The higher the probability of a threat, the more difficult it is to initiate a much higher one in the future. The

warning system is in fact to some extent determining both its present and future effectiveness at the same time.

The notion of a contrast effect as possible important cognitive variable emphasizes the role of recent history. The very same threat may be perceived differently if it follows upon different recent experiences. Thus, as implied in Chapter 3, the analysis of sequences may be necessary for any attempt to arrive at a more refined prediction.

This discussion is not entirely divorced of relevance to schedules of reinforcement. Although a more detailed analysis of the status of the FAE phenomenon must await a later stage of our inquiry, the analogy between the effect of probability on FAE and the partial reinforcement effect deserves mention. Responses maintained on partial reinforcement schedules are more resistant to extinction than are 100% reinforced responses (e.g., Skinner, 1953). Like intermittent reinforcements, low-probability threats, if canceled, contribute less to the extinction of a warning system's credibility. It is perhaps not entirely a coincidence that a very central theoretical attempt to explain the partial reinforcement effect relies heavily upon the contrast between the acquisition stage and the extinction stage. There is more about this later.

Is the False Alarm Effect Fully Determined by Reactions to the Canceled Threat?

From a theoretical point of view, the mediating mechanisms involved in the production of the FAE can at this stage of our knowledge at best be seen as speculations. Among the numerous possible approaches to this problem an entire family of explanatory principles relates to the following issue: Is it possible to anticipate the magnitude of the FAE from the reactions to the initial threat? In other words, does the subsequent threat contribute to the FAE, or does it only serve as a tool for measuring the FAE, which was determined by the previously canceled threat? Furthermore, to what extent is the intensity of the original reaction to that initial threat the sole determinant of the FAE? More specifically, is the decline in fear reaction a function of the intensity of the fear reaction to the first threat and, by the same token, the decline in tension and reported credibility a function of initial tension and credibility, respectively?

This issue is particularly relevant to the analysis of the present experiment in view of the fact that the main independent variable (i.e., the probability of the first threat) was found to affect the intensity of fear reaction during the first trial significantly. Thus, within the context of this study, the question should be phrased as follows: Is the differential FAE in the three groups determined by their differential reactions to the first threat? Because both the FAE and the reaction to the first threat were stronger in Group 100 than in Groups 50 and 5, it seems that there is a positive relationship between reactions to the first threat and the FAE.

Direct measures of the correlations between the two, though always very high, are misleading because they are at least partially mathematically determined. The correlation between a measure of fear reaction to the first threat (e.g., the heart rate during Threat 1 and the difference between Threat 1 and Threat 2) will always be positive due to the common element of Threat 1. The same difficulty applies to any other index if correlated with a difference score.

In order to overcome the mathematical limitations, the partial correlation statistic was used. The correlations between probability of the first threat and the FAE were computed after partialing out the initial reaction. This provides a direct measure of the effect of probability on FAE, which is not mediated by reactions to the first threat. Thus, if these partial correlations are not significantly high, this indicates that the effect of probability on the intensity of the FAE is accounted for mostly by its effect on reactions to the first threat. If such is the case, we are justified in viewing initial commitment and fear as the principal mediators of the FAE.

The correlations and partial correlations were computed twice in order to test their sensitivity to the specific values of the probability variable. In one instance, this variable was defined ordinally by allocating to Group 5 the value of 1, to Group 50 the value of 2, and to Group 100 the value of 3. The correlations obtained were then compared with those found when defining probability by assigning each group its actual probability value. In this case, Group 5 received a score of 5, Group 50 a score of 50, and Group 100 a score of 100. The comparisons indicated that the correlation matrixes obtained by the two methods were almost identical, with occasional minor differences following the third decimal point. Consequently, we use the second definition, that is, the one allocating to each subject the value of the stated probability on the first trial. Table 6.7 presents the correlation matrix between all the variables tested in this context, and Table 6.8 presents the relevant partial correlations.

TABLE 6.7
Intercorrelations Between Probability of Threat$_1$, Indexes of Initial Stress, and FAEs

	p	Net HR-C_1	HR C_1-C_2	Cred. 1	Cred. 1-2	Ten. C_1	Ten. C_1-C_2
Probability	1.00	.33	.50	.39	.58	.13	.47
Net Heart Rate C_1	.33	1.00	.51	.03	.15	-.06	.12
Heart Rate C_1-C_2	.50	.51	1.00	.14	.40	.08	.40
Credibility 1	.39	.03	.14	1.00	.66	.27	.24
Credibility 1-2	.58	.15	.40	.66	1.00	.14	.42
Tension C_1	.13	-.06	.08	.27	.14	1.00	.27
Tension C_1-C_2	.47	.12	.40	.24	.42	.27	1.00

6. PROBABILITY OF THREAT AND THE FAE

TABLE 6.8
Partial Correlations Between Probability of Threat and Indexes of
FAE, Partialing Out Initial Reactions

	Corr.	N	Sig.
Heart Rate C_1–C_2	.40	56	.00
Credibility 1–2	.46	56	.00
Tension C_1–C_2	.45	56	.00

Table 6.8 shows that all of the partial correlations are significantly higher than 0. This implies that probability of threat affects the subsequent FAE via more than one mediating mechanism. In addition to its effect through the impact on initial fear scores, tension scores, and credibility scores, it influences the FAE in all these channels by other avenues as well. In order to estimate these direct and indirect causal effects, a path analysis was performed for each of the response channels by means of stepwise regressions. Following the arguments of Kim and Kohout (1975), the unstandardized path coefficients were chosen as appropriate for our purposes. Figure 6.1 presents the results.

Because the temporal sequence of the variables is given a priori, the foregoing models of causal relationships are the only ones possible. The reconstruction of the expected correlations on the basis of these models yields an almost perfect fit to the observed correlations, which appear in Table 6.7. The partial correlations as well as the path coefficients indicate that there is a major direct effect of probability of threat on the FAE. Considering the nature of the threat instructions, it is highly probable that some cognitive processes related to initial probability either start to operate only after the cancellation of the threat or represent effects that could not find their expression in the reaction to the first threat. There is also the possibility that both these alternatives are operative to some extent.

The above data further refute the possibility that the effect of probability on the FAE was entirely due to its effect on fear reaction. A closer look at Table 6.7 provides an additional clue to this riddle. Note that the intercorrelations between the various reactions to the first threat are much smaller than the intercorrelations between the different measures of the FAE. This suggests that although the heart-rate, credibility, and tension scores initially measure different aspects of the threat reaction, their mutual interrelations grow with the cancellation of the threat. In other words, the FAE has a significant nonspecific effect in addition to its specific effects. Because the correlations of probability with indexes of FAE are also higher than with the initial reaction, it stands to reason that probability plays a meaningful role in determining the magnitude of such nonspecific FAE. In line with our earlier analysis of the concept, it is conceivable that the general credibility loss of the warning system corresponds to the nonspecific FAE.

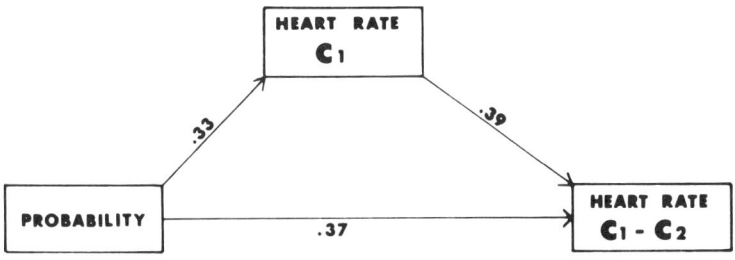
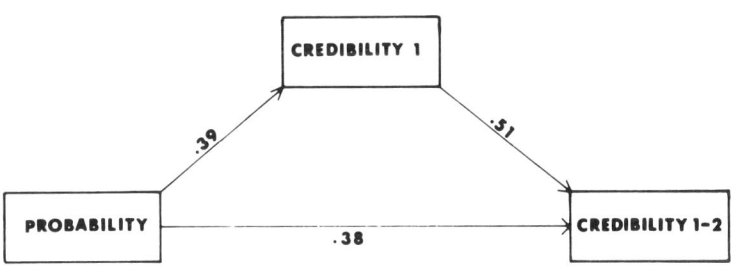
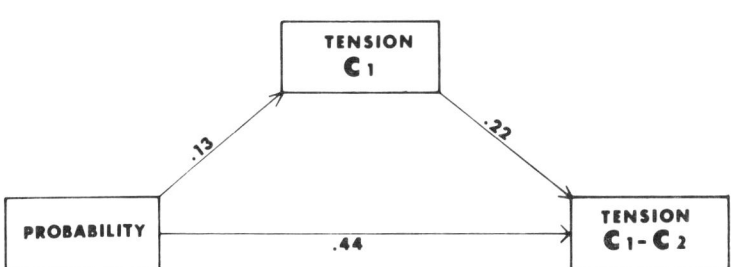

FIG. 6.1 Path analysis on the effect of probability on the FAE in heart rate, subject credibility, and tension.

Implications of the Findings

From the point of view of a warning system, it appears that informing a receiver of the probability of the threat is not without risk. The higher the stated probability of a threat, the greater is the FAE following its cancellation. The credibility loss is partly due to unnecessary fear reaction and partly due to other factors. Any attempt to protect a warning system from the FAE should, therefore, stress the value of keeping the stated probability of a threat as low as possible. This refers to the advantages of presenting a threat in as low a key as possible. The limiting factors to such a policy are numerous, particularly if free media compete for the role of information distribution. Even within given objective constraints, however, there are certain degrees of freedom to present a particular threat in a more or less dramatic way. Our results clearly support the latter practice.

As with the issue of pacing of warnings, so too in this case we face the dilemma of short-term versus long-term effectiveness. A warning situation can be upgraded and dramatized by issuing a higher level warning or by stating a higher probability that it will materialize. These two avenues, though partially independent, often covary. As the danger comes closer, its probability increases, and vice versa. Thus, a warning system will often upgrade the warning stage following a meaningful increase in probability.

Considerations of immediate effectiveness often prescribe dramatization of the danger in order to insure that protective measures will be carried out by the receiver. Such a practice poses a serious long-term danger to any warning system due to the increased credibility loss following the cancellation of highly dramatized threats.

7
Protective Behavior and the False Alarm Effect

BEHAVIORAL MEASURES OF THE FALSE ALARM EFFECT

Our research so far has demonstrated both the prevalence and the importance of the false alarm effect following a single cancellation of a threat. This was found in the affective domain by the psychophysiological index of heart rate as well as in the cognitive domain by a variety of subjective reports. Furthermore, we discovered two variables that affect the magnitude of the FAE, namely, the warning stage during which cancellation occurs and the initial probability of the threat. In addition, the data indicate that credibility loss is mediated by a variety of mechanisms, such as the intensity of fear reaction to the first threat, contrast effects between the two consecutive threats, and additional cognitive mediators that take place during various stages of the entire experience.

In all of this, however, the behavioral measures of the FAE are clearly missing. Besides the affective and cognitive indicators, the availability of behavioral cues would complete the picture to some extent. It is particularly important to include in our research behavioral measures of the FAE that are functionally related to the effectiveness of warning systems. One obvious choice is *protective behavior*. The central role of protective behavior in any analysis of warning systems has already been elaborated and needs no additional rationale. It is, after all, the primary cause for having a warning system in the first place. The systematic investigation of the FAE made it imperative to start with a closer approximation to basic threat, but now that some of the critical procedures have been found effective and some of the main effects have been discovered, there is little justification in further excluding this pivotal element from the research paradigm.

Needless to say, any attempt to consider the potential practical application of this work would be quite useless without direct knowledge about protective behaviors and their relationship to the FAE. The only kinds of coping available for subjects in the previous experiments were those aimed at palliating the fear and anxiety experienced during the anticipation of the impending danger. Various forms of avoidant-like thought can help some individuals distract their mind and perhaps by virtue of such distraction reduce to some extent the negative emotions instigated by the threat instructions (e.g., Lazarus, 1966; Monat, Averill, & Lazarus, 1972). Such intrapsychic coping devices do not, however, change the essential passivity and objective helplessness of the situation.

Protective behavior is an entirely different mode of coping, because it provides objective control over certain features of the threat. It is therefore a form of active coping, which is instrumental in reducing the danger. As such, it can also reduce the fear of the danger.

Considering the importance of human protective behavior, the paucity of information about it is quite surprising. This is in sharp contrast to the relatively extensive exploration of active coping in infrahuman subjects. The obvious relevance of escape and avoidance conditioning to a variety of theoretical as well as clinical issues generated substantial efforts in this direction, but almost exclusively with animals. Although important in its own right, this body of knowledge cannot easily translate to the human situation in view of the central role of cognitive appraisal in determining the effects of psychological stress induction. The analysis of clinical data describing a variety of stress syndromes is relevant and rich in information but cannot replace the need for a systematic experimental program in this area (Horowitz, 1976). Students of stress are left with a situation in which certain kinds of functional relationships are assumed to operate on the basis of best available knowledge, but these relationships have never been clearly demonstrated.

Consider the case of a military unit that has just experienced a false alarm concerning danger from the enemy. Our experiments indicate that the fear reaction the soldiers experience following a subsequent similar threat will be reduced. What can we expect to happen to some specific instrumental coping behavior that was instigated by the threat? Would the FAE affect that activity at all? Common sense prescribes that whatever reduces the fear should also reduce active coping, but this has never been properly tested, and the safety of that unit may conceivably depend on it. The few post hoc studies of protective behavior in natural disasters do not offer a clear answer to this question either (Baker & Chapman, 1962).

We submit that false alarms reduce a person's willingness to engage in protective behavior in the future. The main purpose of the experiment reported in this chapter is to put this hypothesis to a direct empirical test. The inclusion of the additional measure of FAE in the protective behavior channel provides the opportunity to learn something in addition to the main effect of threat cancellation on protective behavior. Thus, the present experiment can shed some light on the complex interrelationships between fear reaction and protective behavior.

Psychological theory is undecided about the exact causal relationships, and there are at least three different models concerning the presumed interaction between a fear arousing stimulus and the various response systems, the affective and the behavioral. Is the avoidance (or escape) response mediated by fear (Mowrer, 1950), does it produce the fear (James, 1890), or are these two systems parallel and independent (Leventhal, 1970)? It is this missing link that forbids the simple extrapolation from existing knowledge about fear reaction to protective behavior. The aim of this chapter is to provide at least a partial answer to this set of problems using human subjects. Last but not least, we wish to provide a satisfactory research tool that will make further systematic research of this area more feasible.

METHODOLOGICAL CONSIDERATIONS

As we take a further step in the direction of making the basic research paradigm employed here more complex, the requirements of a satisfactory measure of protective behavior should be spelled out. This additional dependent variable ought to be operationalized to have the following properties:

1. It should be easily quantified. This obvious advantage for any index is a virtual necessity in the present context due to the fact that we need to measure the FAE by comparing the protective behavior before and after a false alarm.

2. It should be reliable. We search for an ojectively recordable response that is unequivocal in its meaning. Furthermore, the stressful nature of the experiment should not interfere with the ability to emit these behaviors.

3. It should be sensitive, that is, differentiated, allowing more than just a yes/no score.

4. It should be free operant. Our emphasis on motivational factors, which may decrease the willingness to engage in protective behavior, prescribes that it be free. If possible, it should also be continuous to facilitate comparison with the continuous variable of heart rate, which measures fear reaction.

5. It should be reversible. Protective behavior in real life has this quality in a variety of situations, and considerations of practical application prescribe that our experiment attempts to simulate this characteristic as well. People may at one point during a threatening episode take certain precautions against the impending danger, then later decide that they were not necessary, and undo them. Another major reason for this requirement is that because fear reaction can either rise or

decline continuously, protective behavior should be at least be given the opportunity to follow suit.

6. It should protect against intensity of the danger. This last requirement is perhaps theoretically the most crucial one. If the protective behavior in this study could reduce the probability of the danger, there would be no way for our subjects to find out whether the threat did not materialize because it was a false alarm or because of their actions. By allowing control over imminence of the danger, we would likewise have changed it from a naive to a cynical danger. This would have been a major departure from the research paradigm used successfully so far. Thus, the protective behavior should reduce the anticipated intensity of pain on impact, without having any effect on either the probability or timing of the impact as such. Needless to say, the intensity should not be allowed to be reduced all the way, as this would again affect the probability.

In addition to all these methodological requirements considering the inclusion of protecctive behavior, the transition from a two-trial to a three-trial procedure seemed desirable. This makes it possible to study the effects of two consecutive false alarms on the various indexes. Such a possibility was pretested in Group 5 and Group 50 of the previous experiment and was found feasible both in terms of the longer durations involved and in terms of the status of the postexperimental questionnaire.

LABORATORY SETTING AND INSTRUCTIONS

All the procedures reported in relation to the previous experiments remained intact. The only addition was the introduction of the device measuring protective behavior. In the subject's room, directly facing the subject, was an event counter set at the number 50. Two foot switches were attached to the counter in such a way that by pressing his right foot the subject could reduce the number appearing on the counter and by pressing his left foot he could increase the number, though never above the initial level of 50. Every action by the subject was monitored directly by the polygraph indicating the direction of the action (up or down) as well as its exact timing and frequency. A second event counter, which operated in parallel with the one facing the subject, was in the experimental room giving the experimenters immediate visual information about the subject's status of protective behavior.

The experimental procedures and instructions remained unaltered until just before the threat instructions. Immediately after attaching the dummy shock electrodes, the experimenter presented the subject with a "pain scale" and put it in front of him near the event counter. Figure 7.1 shows the pain scale. He then shut off the main light in the subject's room, leaving him in semidarkness with just a weak light illuminating both the counter and the pain scale. Next followed

SHOCK INTENSITY

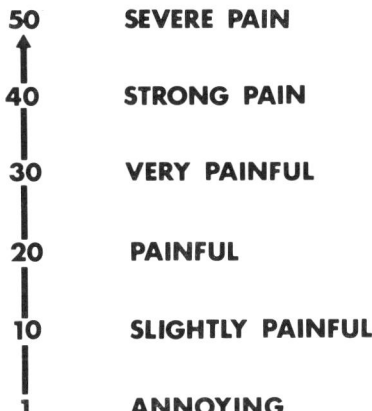

FIG. 7.1 The pain scale.

the usual threat instructions about the impending electric shock and the three discrete warnings: A, B, and C. After demonstrating to the subject the onset of these warnings, the specific instructions concerning protective behavior were given:

> Unless you take action, you will receive a shock of 50 points on the scale, which is the highest safe intensity. As the chart indicates, severe pain is associated with this shock intensity. The actions you may take and the cost of taking them will now be explained. You may reduce the shock intensity any number of points down to a level of 1 intensity point. You may reduce it any time and as many times as you wish during the course of this experiment. The shock intensity is reduced by pressing the pedal with your right foot. Each press reduces the shock intensity by 1 point. Thus, if for instance, you want to reduce the shock intensity by 9 points, press down your right foot nine times.

Next, subjects were told that in addition to their fee for participating in the experiment they would be given an additional sum of money. However, each point of shock intensity reduced by them will cost them a fixed sum to be subtracted from this additional allocation. They were instructed about the possibility of subsequently readjusting the shock intensity upwards by pressing with their left foot. Each such increase of shock intensity would gain them any money lost on previous decreases. Next, subjects practiced once with their right foot and once with their left. It was made clear that any action they take must be carried out before the onset of the shock.

Following these instructions, the first warning (A) was issued. It lasted exactly 1 minute at the end of which Warning B was given. It too lasted for 1 minute, followed by the last warning (C). One minute later, the first threat was canceled, as usual. Two minutes of relaxation followed, terminated by the second threat. The event counter was readjusted to the initial level of 50 before the onset of the second threat. The procedure was repeated exactly as on the first trial, giving each warning 1 minute. The second cancellation, the third threat, and the three warnings all followed the same pattern, terminating with the third and final cancellation. The postexperimental questionnaire, which included specific additional questions, was administered after 5 minutes of relaxation.

The particular arrangement chosen to measure protective behavior satisfies all of the aforementioned major requirements. Thus, it is easily quantified, reliable, sensitive, free operant, continuous, reversible, and related to intensity of the anticipated danger. It also involves an element of some cost to the subject, for reasons to be elaborated later.

There were 30 subjects, all male students at the University of Maryland, Baltimore County, that participated in this experiment. As in the previous experiments, the subjects were all in good health and agreed to the screening of their medical records.

RESULTS

The Effect of False Alarms on Protective Behavior

Like any response, the protective behavior in this experiment can be measured by the following three indexes:

1. Probability of protective behavior. Though for any given subject this is an all-or-none affair, the probability of protective behavior can be estimated on the group level from the proportion of subjects who engage in it. Such an estimate can then serve as a basis for comparing different groups undergoing different treatments. On the single-subject level, it is conceivable that the decision whether or not to engage in protective action is at least to some extent psychologically unrelated to the next decision (i.e., if yes, how much?).

2. Amplitude of protective behavior. Within the context of the present experiment, the amplitude for each trial varies between zero and 49.

3. Latency of protective behavior. How soon after the onset of the first warning did the first response occur?

In addition to these indexes, others were devised at a later stage of the analysis to provide more detailed information about the underlying psychological processes.

There were two false alarms, the effects of which could be tested. The third and final cancellation, though obviously yet another false alarm, could not be effectively utilized in the absence of data from a hypothetical fourth threat. The effects of false alarms were analyzed for each index of protective behavior separately. Figures 7.2, 7.3, and 7.4 illustrate the FAE for probability, amplitude, and latency of protective behavior, respectively.

Figure 7.2 indicates that the great majority of subjects did take advantage of the option to reduce the intensity of the anticipated shock, even though such action cost them money. Following each experience of false alarm, the probability of coping decreases significantly, $t_{12} = 2.41$, $df = 29$, $p < .05$; $t_{23} = 2.20$, $df = 29$, $p < .05$.

It is of some interest to note that in no case did a subject start using the protective action option after refraining from doing so during an earlier trial. In

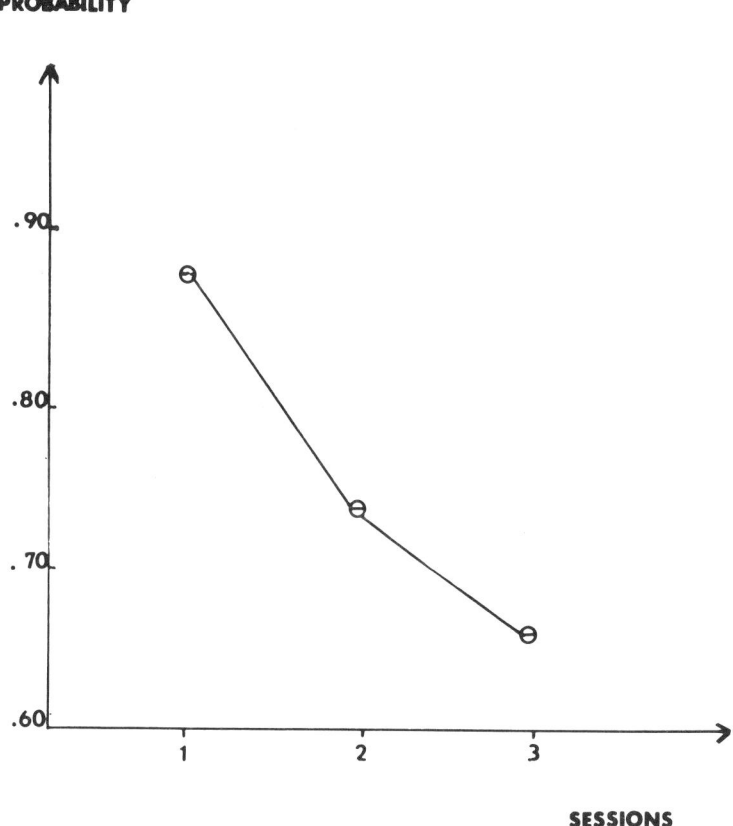

FIG. 7.2 Probability of protective behavior according to sessions.

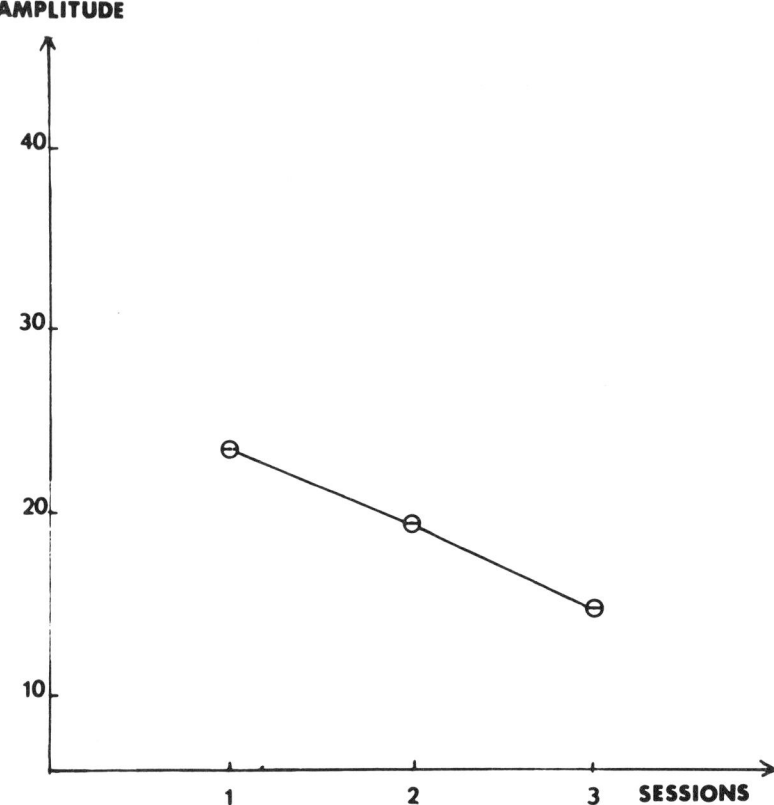

FIG. 7.3 Amplitude of protective behavior according to sessions.

other words, once a person takes a chance with the highest shock intensity, he continues to do so on all subsequent trials. This is not surprising in view of the fact that such behavior was post facto vindicated by the cancellation of the threat. Probability of protective behavior fulfills, therefore, the requirements of a perfect Guttman Scale (Guttman, 1944).

In the absence of data related to a fourth threat it is difficult to anticipate the value of probability on subsequent trials, but it stands to reason that additional false alarms can further reduce it. Whether the asymptotic level is at zero point (i.e., that not a single subject will eventually reduce the intensity of the shock) remains an interesting open question. The alternative remains that all those who can be influenced by the FAE will soon cease responding, whereas others will continue to protect themselves, but perhaps at a lower rate.

This brings us to the analysis of amplitude of protective behavior. Figure 7.3 indicates that there is a systematic FAE in the amplitude index as well. This

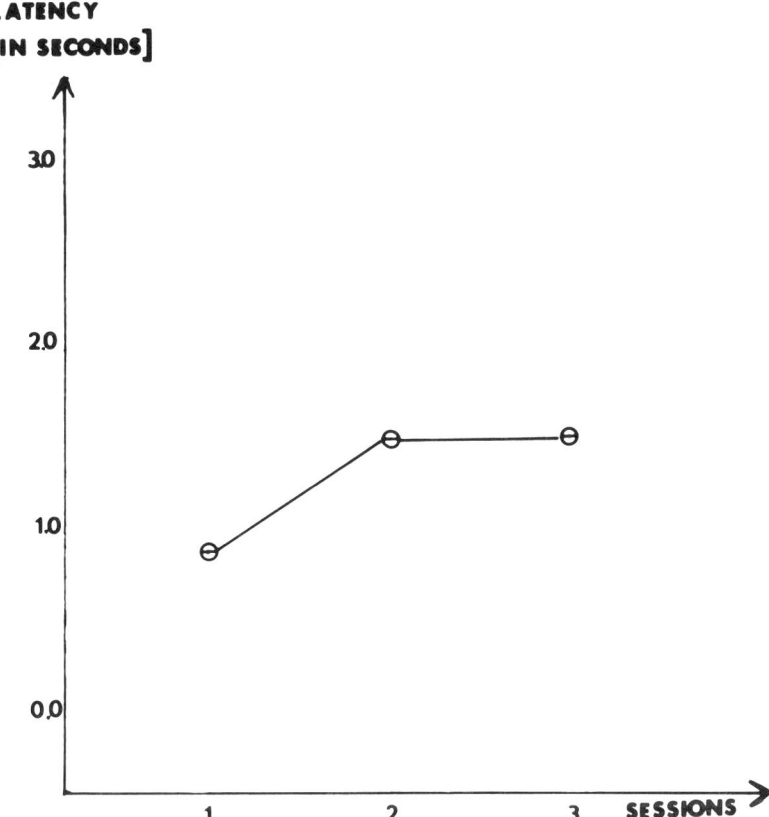

FIG. 7.4 Latency of protective behavior according to sessions.

implies that the transition from responding to not responding can be gradual and passes through certain stages. In view of the fact that probability of protective behavior has been shown to decrease by false alarms, the amplitude issue should be tested separately after excluding those who did not respond at all. In other words, in order for the amplitude data not to be contaminated by the probability data, all subjects who did not respond during a particular trial were excluded from the analysis. The results for amplitude with and without such control appear in Table 7.1, which indicates that the FAE is significant in all cases both between the first and second trial (one tailed) and between the second and third trial. In order to test the interindividual reliability of the FAE, a special sign test was performed comparing the level of protective behavior in each subject across all the sessions. Table 7.2 presents the results, which demonstrate that the previously found FAE is a highly prevalent characteristic, not due only to a few individuals. At the same time it shows that not everybody reduces the amplitude

TABLE 7.1
Amplitude of Protective Behavior

	Variable	Mean	Diff.	Std. Error	Corr.	t	df	p
All Subjects	Prot. B. 1	23.3	4.0	1.80	.84	2.22	29	.034
	Prot. B. 2	19.3						
	Prot. B. 2	19.3	4.5	1.75	.84	2.55	29	.016
	Prot. B. 3	14.8						
Only Subjects Who Acted	Prot. B. 1	27.7	3.6	2.03	.82	1.74	23	.094
	Prot. B. 2	24.1						
	Prot. B. 2	25.3	3.1	1.39	.92	2.20	19	.040
	Prot. B. 3	22.2						

of protective behavior after one or two false alarms. There are two subjects who actually acted in a way contrary to the FAE.

Figure 7.4 shows a distinct FAE in the latency of the protective behavior between Session 1 and Session 2 ($p < .05$). No such FAE occurred between Sessions 2 and 3. This may be at least partly due to the fact that as the experiment proceeds subjects often decide during the by now familiar threat instructions what action they will take, and there is no reason to expect increasingly longer latencies.

To sum up, the results clearly support the hypothesis that protective behavior is reduced by false alarms experiences.

The Course of Protective Behavior During the Entire Anticipation Sequence

The data concerning this question are clear and simple. The subjects in this experiment made up their minds rather early during the ancitipation sequence, carried out their decisions, and almost never changed their minds at a later point

TABLE 7.2
FAE in Protective Behavior

	Session 1 Versus 2			Session 2 Versus 3		
	$1 > 2$	$1 = 2$	$1 < 2$	$2 > 3$	$2 = 3$	$2 > 3$
N	15	13	2	13	15	2
p		$p < .001$			$p < .01$	

in time. Thus, out of 26 subjects who engaged in protective action during the first session, 22 acted during Warning A, 2 during Warning B, and 2 during Warning C. The reader should recall that the instructions do not force any such early execution of protective behavior. The only provision is that the action be carried out before the onset of the shock itself. Even if we assume that subjects were afraid to miss the chance by postponing their action to Warning C, the duration of which they could not anticipate, this does not explain why not during B. Furthermore, the same pattern of clear preference for immediate action was found even during the last two sessions, even though the subjects already experienced the relatively long warning periods. The response itself could be easily executed, and even the longest action of reducing 49 points could be carried out in just a few seconds.

To strengthen this point further, we ought to pay attention to the fact that not only did the vast majority of subjects act during the first warning, but they did so almost as soon as that warning was issued. The mean latency of the first response was .9 seconds on the first session and 1.5 seconds on the next two sessions. This is almost the minimal reaction time necessary for immediate response. It appears that at least some subjects decided ahead of time whether to reduce the intensity of the shock or not during the long and partially redundant threat instructions.

Another interesting feature of protective behavior is its frequent single-eventlike experience. Even though subjects could monitor the intensity of the impending shock continuously, most of them did not take advantage of this option and appeared to be committed to their initial responses. Only three out of the thirty subjects activated the left foot pedal and raised the intensity after reducing it. Two of these three reduced it back again at a later stage. Thus, within the context of the present experiment, protective behavior is often a single event rather than a series of ongoing decisions and adjustments. The implications of this characteristic are discussed later.

The Effect of False Alarms on Fear Reaction

Why should it be necessary to retest a phenomenon that has been reliably established by all the data from our previous experiments? There are three main reasons:

1. The availability of protective behavior could in principle change the psychological impact of the various experimental instructions, as well as the significance of the false alarm itself. It is therefore essential to find out whether the various indexes of fear exhibit a clear FAE in these new conditions.

2. The inclusiveness of a third session allows the testing of two consecutive FAEs. Their effects on fear reaction can add to our knowledge about some parametric constraints of the processes involved. Needless to say, a single FAE

is more open to a variety of interpretations than a more systematic curve based on more trials.

3. On the basis of some parametric tests, we have changed the scoring system of the heart-rate channel. Instead of representing each segment by the actual count of all heart beats taking place during that segment, it was thought that more interesting information could be gathered using the highest heart rate as well as the lowest heart rate during each segment. Though the correlations between the highest readings, the lowest readings, and the total number of heartbeats are all very high (the median correlation being .92), there are some advantages to the two discrete scores. First, they are less likely to regress during the relatively long period of each warning. Thus, in a full minute of anticipation the impact of the various warnings is bound to be reduced by the subsequent relaxation that invariably occurs. The highest reading does not have this problem, and it represents the informational component of the threat better. The first 5 seconds of a warning were always discounted in order to eliminate the intrusion of the orienting reflex. Second, we obtain two separate indexes concerning the same period. They provide additional information of great relevance to the analysis of fear reaction. Third, it allows us to measure the exact timing of such highest or lowest read-

TABLE 7.3
Highest Heart-Rate Readings (HR-H) According to Sessions

Variable	Mean	Diff.	Std. Error	Corr.	t	df	p
Warning A_1	110.2						
		5.5	1.76	.89	3.11	28	.004
Warning A_2	104.7						
Warning A_2	104.7						
		6.2	1.75	.84	3.54	28	.001
Warning A_3	98.5						
Warning B_1	108.0						
		7.4	1.78	.91	4.14	28	.000
Warning B_2	100.6						
Warning B_2	100.6						
		3.6	1.53	.89	2.39	28	.024
Warning B_3	97.0						
Warning C_1	109.4						
		8.4	1.55	.93	5.44	28	.000
Warning C_2	101.0						
Warning C_2	101.0						
		4.6	1.43	.91	3.18	28	.004
Warning C_3	96.4						

ings. Any attempt to investigate the intricate relationships between protective behavior and fear must be based on such temporal considerations.

Tables 7.3 and 7.4 present the results for the highest heart rate readings (HR-H) and the lowest heart rate readings (HR-L) for all the experimental segments, respectively. The results are unequivocal. The FAE is clearly evident throughout the entire experimental sequence, including the new part introduced by the second cancellation and the third session. Furthermore, it is highly systematic and significant in both the HR-H and the HR-L scores. This implies that the HR-L scores do not represent a return to a static base line and constitute another index of fear reaction.

We may therefore safely conclude that the FAE in the heart-rate channel is by now established as a robust phenomenon, which occurs reliably in a variety of experimental settings. The fact that the option of protective behavior did not diminish, cancel, or significantly alter the FAE is of special theoretical interest.

The postexperimental questionnaire used in this study included questions concerning the additional third session. Figure 7.5 presents the mean tension scores for all sessions and all warnings. The pattern of responding to the ques-

TABLE 7.4
Lowest Heart-Rate Readings (HR-L) According to Sessions

Variable	Mean	Diff.	Std. Error	Corr.	t	df	p
Warning A_1	84.4						
		10.2	1.92	.93	5.31	28	.000
Warning A_2	74.2						
Warning A_2	74.2						
		3.9	1.35	.93	2.88	28	.008
Warning A_3	70.3						
Warning B_1	83.1						
		9.6	2.35	.89	4.06	28	.000
Warning B_2	73.5						
Warning B_2	73.5						
		4.2	1.92	.87	2.18	28	.038
Warning B_3	69.3						
Warning C_1	83.4						
		8.4	1.60	.96	5.27	28	.000
Warning C_2	75.0						
Warning C_2	75.0						
		3.0	1.28	.94	2.36	28	.025
Warning C_3	72.0						

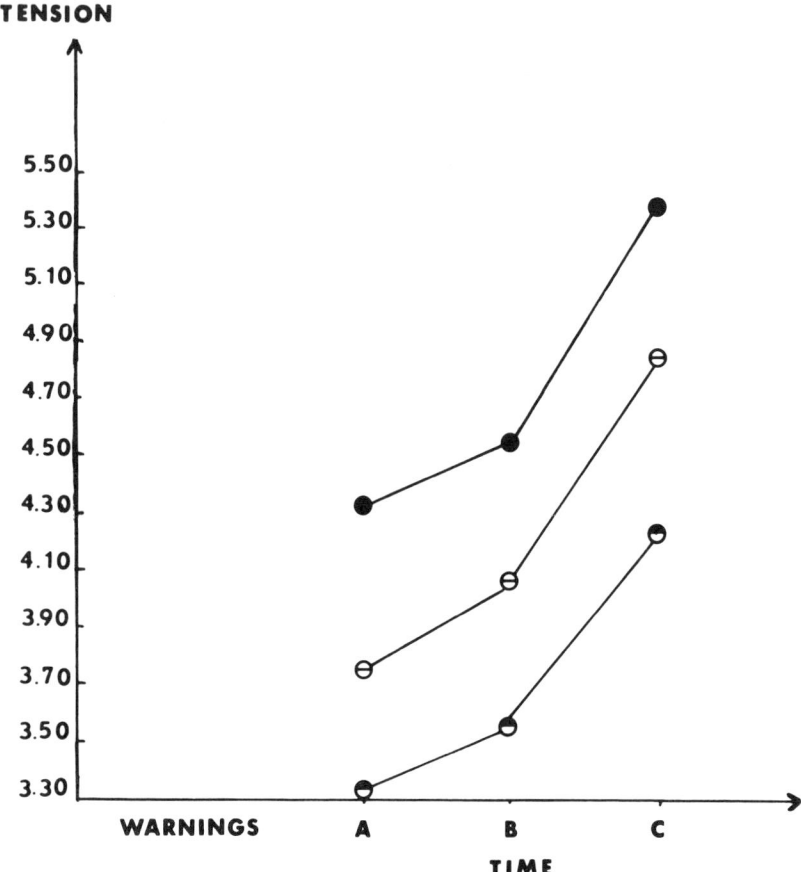

FIG. 7.5 Mean tension scores according to sessions.

tions concerning subjective tension is typical: Subjects report increasing tension with each warning, and they report a systematic FAE following each cancellation of the threat. The increases from A to B and from B to C, as well as all FAEs, are statistically significant at least at the $p < .01$ level.

The introduction of protective behavior did not change the responses in this channel as well. The results in this experiment are very much the same as those in the previously reported experiments, with the additional systematic FAE between the second and third sessions. The parallel curves in Fig. 7.5 indicate that the two main factors of warnings and FAEs are entirely independent of each other.

Finally, Table 7.5 presents the results concerning the reported credibility of the various threats. The table shows a clear FAE in the perceived credibility channel following each cancellation. It follows that on all measure of fear reaction that were available to us in previous experiments the pattern of responding did not change because of the availability of protective behavior. This permits the comparison between the earlier studies and this study, as well as all subsequent studies, which include the protective behavior option. In terms of the cumulative implications of our research program, these findings are particulary comforting.

Self-Reported Distraction

Starting with this experiment, a few additional questions were included in the postexperimental questionnaire. One of them followed Monat et al. (1972) attempt to measure avoidant-like thoughts, with some modifications. Whereas they asked their subjects to respond after each trial, we decided to postpone it until the very end of the experiment. As with other measures of subjective reports, we believe that the earlier testing may influence subsequent psychological processes during the following trials. The other change was that instead of asking our subjects to report about their thoughts during the various stages of the same trial, a single trial was taken as one reference unit. At the same time, subjects were asked to give a quantitative estimate of the percentage of time they spent thinking of things unrelated to the threat. Thus, we have three indexes of subjective distraction, one for each session. Table 7.6 shows the results.

Self-reported distraction exhibits significant FAEs. With each new trial, the percentage of time spent thinking of topics unrelated to stress increases. This is clearly in line with the rest of our results, because it is safe to assume that distraction should be related to lower stress levels than continuous vigilance. The causal relationship between fear reaction and distraction is, however, a complex

TABLE 7.5
Credibility of the Threats

Variable	Mean	Diff.	Std. Error	Corr.	t	df	p
Cred. 1	1.07	.87	.16	.54	5.28	29	.000
Cred. 2	0.20						
Cred. 2	0.20	.76	.16	.71	4.75	26	.000
Cred. 3	−0.56						

TABLE 7.6
Percentage of Time Distracted Over Sessions

Variable	Mean	Diff.	Std. Error	Corr.	t	df	p
Distraction 1	30.5						
		−10.0	3.14	.80	−3.19	22	.004
Distraction 2	40.5						
Distraction 2	40.5						
		−12.8	3.80	.68	−3.37	21	.003
Distraction 3	53.3						

one. Monat et al. (1972) argue that avoidant-like thoughts (i.e., distraction) are a way of coping, which to some extent determines the intensity of the fear reaction. Following their approach in the present context, the argument could be made that the cognitive appraisal following threat cancellation leads to an increase in thoughts unrelated to the threat, and this in turn reduces the fear reaction. Stated in this way, distraction would be seen as one of the cognitive mediators of both fear and the FAE.

Self-Initiated Versus Reactive Distraction

Although cognitive factors and processes are obviously very important as mediators of stress, their causal impact can be easily overstated. This is particularly the case because stress can lead to certain cognitions rather than depend on them. Distraction is a good case in point. A person's cognitive preoccupation with an impending danger might increase his fear, but at the same time his fear might increase his preoccupation with it. Which is the cause and which is the effect? According to Monat et al. (1972), the cognitive process should be seen primarily as the cause and the fear reaction as the effect.

The analysis of this dilemma may profit from a distinction between self-initiated and reactive distraction. Whereas the latter is the response to an external distractor (i.e., a stimulus or a task requirement that commits the person's attention in a new direction), the first takes place in the absence of external distraction. Both may be empirically related to lower fear reaction, but for entirely different reasons. Whereas reactive distraction causes reduction of fear, we submit that self-initiated distraction is the product of lower fear. In other words, only subjects who are under less stress can distract their minds passively. A still better way to describe this would be to claim that people do not control their own thoughts, and therefore distraction is never active. In one case it is a reaction to an external stimulus (i.e., reactive distraction), and in the other it is an outcome of an internal state (i.e., the lower fear). As such, it is a symptom rather than a cause and should be used as a diagnostic rather than as a predictive tool.

The ability of an external distractor to reduce fear in our paradigm is established in experiments reported in later chapters of this volume. However, the second half of the argument—namely, that self-initiated distraction is the outcome rather than the cause of fear—can be tested now.

The Pearson correlation coefficients between distraction and heart rate were computed for each warning segment over the three trials. The highest heart-rate score for each segment was used. Table 7.7 presents the correlations. As expected, all correlations are negative, indicating that the higher the reported percentage of time thinking of things unrelated to threat, the lower the fear reaction, or if our interpretation is correct, the higher the fear reaction, the lower the self-initiated distraction. So far, the data support both interpretations. Is there a way to distinguish between them?

A closer inspection of Table 7.7 reveals that the heart-rate scores of the first session are best correlated with Distraction 3, which took place two trials later. The same is true for heart-rate scores of the second session and, to a lesser degree, of the third one. The only way this could have happened was if the degree of fear preceded the amount of distraction and not the other way around.

That Distraction 3 scores produce overall higher correlations is undoubtedly related to the proximity of the third trial to the postexperimental questionnaire itself. But once again, we find that Distraction 3 scores are best related to the heart-rate scores obtained during the first trial. In addition, these correlations, which are quite impressive and statistically significant, are highest with Threat 1 and Warning A, which take place before any distraction could occur. The correlations with Warnings B and C are slightly lower. If distraction caused reduction in heart rate, the opposite pattern should have been found.

TABLE 7.7
Pearson Correlations Between Distraction and Heart Rate

	Distraction 1	*Distraction 2*	*Distraction 3*
Threat 1	−.33	−.30	−.51
Warning A_1	−.34	−.27	−.51
Warning B_1	−.27	−.23	−.38
Warning C_1	−.34	−.28	−.47
Threat 2	−.19	−.19	−.41
Warning A_2	−.24	−.18	−.47
Warning B_2	−.26	−.21	−.44
Warning C_2	−.31	−.28	−.50
Threat 3	−.40	−.28	−.41
Warning A_3	−.22	−.12	−.32
Warning B_3	−.18	−.14	−.35
Warning C_3	−.33	−.24	−.46

The notion of self-initiated distraction and its dependence on fear and anxiety are obviously too important to be evaluated by such limited post hoc analyses. A person's ability to divert his thoughts purposely from a disturbing or frightening theme to more neutral areas is often the focus of cognitive behavior therapy as well as other attempts to increase adjustment (e.g., Meichenbaum, 1975, 1977). I am rather sceptical about a person's ability to control his own thoughts without resorting to external help in the form of objective distraction. This is what the process of worrying is all about (Breznitz, 1971). Although we may choose to increase the chances of external stimuli distracting our minds for us, in their absence we are to a great extent at the mercy of our thoughts.

Fear and Protective Behavior

We have seen that cancellations of the threats lead to FAEs in both the indexes of fear and the indexes of protective behavior. In this sense, they have been shown to covary over trials. The next questions deserving our attention are: How are these two behaviors related within a single trial? Can the intensity of one be predicted by knowing the other? Is protective behavior under the control of fear reaction? If so, at what stages of the anticipation sequence? These and many other related questions are dealt with throughout the rest of this volume, and with each additional study, our ability to at least partially answer some of them grows. The initial analysis that sets the tone for much of what follows is based on specific indexes of fear reaction with particular temporal relevance to protective behavior.

These indexes were defined for the heart-rate channel utilizing the availability of sensitive continuous readings. All indexes were measured for the entire three sessions if and when a subject engaged in protective behavior. Table 7.8 de-

TABLE 7.8
List of Protective Behavior-Related
Psychophysiological Indexes

Highest HR reading during 5 seconds before start of avoidance ($-5H$)
Lowest HR reading during 5 seconds before start of avoidance ($-5L$)
The exact HR reading 3 seconds before start of avoidance (-3)
The exact HR reading at start (Start)
The exact HR reading at midpoint of avoidance (Midpoint)
The exact HR reading at end of avoidance (End)
The exact HR reading 3 seconds after end ($+3$)
Highest HR reading during 5 seconds after end of avoidance ($+5H$)
Lowest HR reading during 5 seconds after end of avoidance ($+5L$)
When (in seconds) was highest HR reading before start? (When $-5H$)
When (in seconds) was lowest HR reading before start? (When $-5L$)
When (in seconds) was highest HR reading after end? (When $+5H$)
When (in seconds) was lowest HR reading after end? (When $+5L$)

TABLE 7.9
The Effect of False Alarms on Protective
Behavior-Related Psychophysiological Indexes

Index	Session 1	Session 2	Session 3
(−5H)	107.70	96.60	93.00
(−5L)	98.80	84.20	80.10
(−3)	104.90	93.20	85.90
(Start)	101.80	89.80	89.20
(Midpoint)	104.80	83.80	80.70
(End)	103.10	90.80	91.70
(+3)	107.50	94.70	87.60
(+5H)	108.80	99.60	96.20
(+5L)	102.40	89.70	84.60
(When −5H)	2.84	3.46	2.60
(When −5L)	2.86	1.91	3.13
(When +5H)	2.73	3.27	3.28
(When +5L)	3.01	2.66	2.49

scribes the indexes. All these indexes were correlated with the amplitude of protective behavior, and no significant correlations were found. At the same time, however, these indexes also exhibited a FAE. Table 7.9 presents the mean responses to each of the indexes over the three sessions.

We have already mentioned that most of the subjects who engaged in protective behavior did so very early after the beginning of Warning A, with mean latency of response being well before 2 seconds. This makes it almost impossible to evaluate the indexes of heart rate relating to the period prior to the start of protective behavior, because it coincides with the onset of Warning A and in some instances even precedes it. The results of Table 7.9 were therefore not subjected to statistical analysis and should serve only as crude indicators of the general trends in our data. Here are some interesting features:

1. All the heart-rate scores without exception show a systematic pattern of FAEs, and they decrease over sessions.

2. The heart rates just before the beginning of action are lower than immediately following it. This can be seen by comparing the readings on Start with those at End, as well as the readings at −3 seconds with +3 seconds, and the highest and lowest readings within 5 seconds before and after protective behavior. This systematic increase in heart rate following protective behavior is especially interesting in view of the aforementioned latency, which inflates the heart-rate scores preceding protective behavior. The "true values" would probably reveal an even stronger increase following protective behavior. This suggests that protective behavior may in itself constitute a stressor, perhaps due to the need to be highly attentive while pressing the foot pedal. Such an interpretation is supported

by the fact that on the second and third trials there is a substantial relaxation at Midpoint through the action, a segment where the attentional effort is probably lower than at Start and at End, respectively.

The implication of increase in heart rate immediately following the termination of protective behavior for any analysis of the relationship between fear and protective behavior in terms of learning and conditioning is quite obvious. It makes untenable the argument that protective behavior, like escape or avoidance learning, is reinforced by fear reduction. Because the conditioning paradigm puts great emphasis on the immediate temporal contingencies, it must be rejected in its simple form.

Subjective reports of tension do not, however, confirm these findings. We have included in the postexperimental questionnaire direct questions about tension before and after protective behavior in each session. Table 7.10 presents the results for the subjects who engaged in protective behavior in the various sessions.

All the FAEs as well as the before/after effects are statistically significant at least at the .01 level. The scores are higher than those of the corresponding tension for Warning A of each session (see Fig. 7.5), even though the behavior occurred during that period. This indicates that subjects perceived the particular time segment during which they engaged in protective behavior as more stressful. This is in line with the heart-rate results mentioned earlier. However, the report that protective behavior reduced tension is not supported by the heart-rate data. What could be the reasons for this discrepancy? Two nonexclusive possibilities come to mind:

1. It is conceivable that the tension scores and the heart-rate scores do not relate to the same period. Whereas the heart-rate scores dealt with the seconds immediately following protective behavior, the tension scores may reflect a slower process relating to longer durations.
2. Subjects' reported tension may be an expression of their theory of protective behavior rather than the actual tension experienced. When directly asked to compare their tension before and after such behavior, they assumed that they must have felt tenser before.

The opposite result is counterintuitive and poses the question of why to engage in protective behavior in the first place. We have already seen a similar discrepancy

TABLE 7.10
Mean Reported Tension Before and After Protective Behavior According to Sessions

	Session 1	Session 2	Session 3
Before	5.33	4.90	4.42
After	4.24	3.74	3.68

between the heart-rate and tension scores in relation to the impact of warnings, which could be due to the same basic reason.

In order to further explicate the possible relationship between fear and protective behavior, the correlation between amplitude of protective behavior and the heart-rate scores representing the various segments of the anticipation sequence were computed. Each segment was represented by both the highest and the lowest heart-rate readings. None of those correlations was significant, and most of them were close to 0. This indicates that subjects who were more afraid of the various threats and warnings did not necessarily utilize the active coping option at their disposal to a greater extent. Obviously, if fear and protective behavior are related, it must be in a much more complex way than originally anticipated. The following analysis provides a theoretical framework in that direction.

If fear motivates people to engage in protective behavior, we must assume that the two will be positively correlated. Once people decided to protect themselves, this should reduce their fear of the impending danger, because they anticipate a lower intensity pain. In this case, the early decision to reduce the pain will lead to a negative correlation between the two, because the greater the amount of pain that will be reduced, the smaller should the fear reaction be. The type of relationship thus depends on the timing of the decision concerning whether and how much protective behavior to emit. If all or most of our subjects decided early (i.e., before the onset of the first warnings), we should have found significant negative correlations between fear and protective behavior. If all or most of our subjects did not decide ahead of time, but rather let their actual fear reaction determine whether and how much to protect themselves, we should have found significant positive correlations. Neither of the two happened, but it might be that both types occurred about equally, in which case the outcome would be zero correlations.

It is impossible to test the plausibility of this analysis without independent information about the timing of our subjects' decisions. As the findings and their possible interpretations were not anticipated at the onset of the experiment, any attempt to categorize our subjects along this dimension is by necessity ad hoc in nature.

In order to diagnose whether a subject made his decision in advance or not, the following indexes were used:

1. A protective behavior sequence can be a set of consecutive responses carried out in one block, or alternatively, subjects may reduce the intensity of the shock by a few points, pause, reduce some more, pause, reduce some more, and so on. Operationally, a single block was defined as a sequence of responses in which no two adjacent responses are more than 2 seconds apart. We assume that subjects who decided in advance how much they are going to reduce the shock intensity used one block only.

2. Short latencies of the first response indicate early decision, whereas long latencies indicate late decisions.

3. Early decision was assumed to be more schematic than a late one in the sense that one would not ordinarily decide to reduce the intensity by say 17 points. This assumption was made on the basis of the pain scale (see Fig. 7.1) and the broad categories is used. Thus, if a subject pressed his foot by a round number (e.g., 5, 10, 15, 20, etc.), he was assumed to carry out an earlier decision, whereas numbers that were not round were taken as an indication of on-line factors rather than early decision.

If the foregoing reasoning is correct, the various indexes of early decision should correlate with each other. Highly significant correlations between the three indicators were found for Trials 2 and 3, but not for Trial 1. The first trial is different from the other two in some important relevant features. Thus, subjects had no idea about the duration of each warning and the imminence of the danger. More important, they were exposed to the instructions for the first time and did not have much time to plan their course of action. This is not the case in Sessions 2 and 3.

With the exception of the first session, the data support our analysis. For the same reason, and in view of the general argument about decision time as the mediating factor between fear and protective behavior, we would assume that certain correlations between heart rate and protective behavior should become increasingly negative over sessions, because more subjects can decide ahead of time. It is interesting that the highest heart rate during threat instructions, which did not correlate with protective behavior during Sessions 1 and 2, $r = .00$ and $r = .02$, respectively, was significantly and negatively related to protective behavior during Session 3, $r = -.32, p < .05$. This result again supports the proposed model. It suggests that during the third threat instructions, subjects have already made up their minds about their subsequent protective behavior.

Finally, the correlations between amplitude of protective behavior and fear were indeed negative in the early-decision subgroup and positive in the late-decision subgroup, but the small number of subjects in each category did not permit a meaningful test of statistical significance. Particularly on the second and third trials, as fewer subjects maintained their protective behavior, this became a major constraint. A more systematic analysis of the model can be attempted after the inclusion of additional comparable experimental groups.

MUCH ADO ABOUT NOTHING

Protective behavior is always costly, even though the cost itself may vary depending on the intensity of the anticipated danger, ranging all the way from such mild outcomes as taking a pause from ongoing activities or spending some money on an insurance policy through such major costs as evacuating homes, overloading communication systems, the destruction of information, relinquishing property, and the like. In psychological terms, the cost of protective behavior is a major force against the taking of action, particularly if the parameters of the threat are not well defined. Thus, a person's reluctance to leave his or her home in the face of an approaching flood, for instance, will take advantage of any existing ambiguity concerning the probability, intensity, or imminence of the danger. People will often convince themselves and others that there is no real need to take drastic measures, or at least not yet. Consequently, the greater the cost of protective behavior, the greater the danger that a person will take unnecessary risks. The following illustration taken from our research is quite illuminating in this respect.

The initial pretests of the protective behavior used in the last experiment were at first conducted while the subject and the experimenter shared the same room. The reason for this was that the laboratories were not yet prepared, and we did not want to postpone the pretesting until they were ready. But after testing a few subjects, it seemed that the setup was wrong, the instructions were wrong, or both were wrong, because not a single subject engaged in protective behavior. They were attached to the polygraph and their psychophysiological measures indicated a very high intensity of fear, and yet, no protective behavior. Fortunately, before abandoning what eventually turned out to be a very successful research tool one of our subjects was able to verbalize the problem for us. He stated that as long as he was closely watched by the experimenter, he felt reluctant to demonstrate his fear by reducing the shock intensity. The physical presence of another person increased the social cost of self-protection beyond a level accepted by our subjects. We tested this by informing the following subjects that the mean level of intensity reduction by other subjects was 27. Having heard that, all subjects started to reduce the anticipated shock intensity, but by less than 27 points. In this way, they could protect themselves without at the same time appearing to cowardly. When the laboratories were finally ready and there was no longer a need for the experimenter to stay in the same room with the subject, the extra instruction concerning presumed mean level of intensity reduction became unnecessary. This is particularly interesting in view of the fact that subjects were well aware that they were closely watched by the experimenter, even though he was in another room. Thus, physical proximity, as such, appears to be a major factor.

In certain situations self-protection implies fear, a factor which may further reduce a person's willingness to protect himself, particularly in the presence of others. Those subjects who did not protect themselves at all were not necessarily less afraid of the shock; rather, they may have been more afraid than others to show their fear.

We used only young males as our subjects, and the foregoing seems an especially fitting description of their dilemma. Needless to say, such a possibility adds another element to the already complex issue of the relationship between fear and protective behavior.

An Interesting Paradox. The very existence of the active coping option may decrease the tendency to use it. By giving a person a certain amount of control over a threat, the subjective intensity as well as the quality of the threat may be dramatically reduced. Seligman (1975) claims that a "safety switch," which eliminates the sense of helplessness, often remains unused; its availability reduces the need for it. The paradox relates to the fact that the probability of self-protection is maximal when it is unavailable. In their analysis of people's willingness to tolerate risks, Slovic, Fishoff, and Lichtenstein (1980) make the point that sense of control increases the level of acceptable risks (see also Starr, 1969). This suggests that measuring the actual usage of the protective option may not be a fair estimate of its importance. To give it justice, protective behavior ought to be evaluated by its total impact on the psychological well-being of the receiver by comparison to its absence.

False alarms are vindications of risk taking, even unnecessary risk taking. Judged from hindsight, the cancellation of the threat justifies the risk. After all, the protection turned out objectively unnecessary. Considering its cost, refraining from self-protection is reinforced by a false alarm experience. It is not surprising, therefore, that those subjects who were willing to take the risk of the highest shock intensity and refrained from protective behavior were reinforced by the cancellation of the threat and proceeded to take that risk on all subsequent trials.

On the other hand, those who protected themselves at some cost turned out to be objectively wrong. The false alarm experience defined their active coping as unnecessary and wasteful. This might very well be the most important and most dangerous outcome of false alarms. The "wisdom" of hindsight leads to a strong FAE in the self-protection response channel, particularly if the cost of protective behavior is high. It becomes psychologically a case of "much ado about nothing," with all its implications for the future.

In terms of attribution of responsibility, people may be reluctant to blame their own judgment for wasteful self-protection and would rather shift the entire blame to the warning system itself. Thus, we may assume that the credibility loss suffered by a warning system should be to some extent positively related to the amplitude of protective behavior before the cancellation of the threat. In other words, the fact that a person perceives his or her own protective behavior as incurring a major waste of time and other resources makes the warning system so much more wrong.

TYPOLOGY OF THREAT REACTIONS

The intricate relationships between fear and active coping may turn out to be more comprehensible with the help of a schematic typology of threat reactions. The types described should not be viewed as the outcome of empirical research,

TABLE 7.11
The Four Response Types

	High Protection	Low Protection
High Fear	A	B
Low Fear	C	D

but rather as "ideal types" that serve primarily an analytic function. Their relevance to real data, though obviously important and encouraging, is secondary to their primary purpose, which is theoretical. Table 7.11 presents the four ideal response types. Needless to say, by resorting to extreme dichotomies we exclude the majority of reactions falling somewhere along these essentially continuous variables. At the same time, however, the simplicity gained by dichotomization has obvious analytic advantages.

Let us start by restating our account of the zero correlation between the two variables as observed in the present study. A positive correlation could be found only if Types A and D were the most frequent. This in turn implies that the causal chain is from fear to protective behavior. Early decision leads to a predominance of Types B and C, implying the reverse causal chain and a consequent negative correlation. The zero correlations obtained indicate the occurrence of all four response types in about the same frequency.

Considering the FAE next, we may assume that a highly credible warning system will on the first occasions lead primarily to Type A behavior. Following a series of false alarms, Type D behavior will gradually predominate, serving as an absorbing state for all other response patterns.

Questions. What is the particular route of transition from A to D? Does it pass through B or through C? Or perhaps it changes gradually on both dimensions? These questions are very important considering the differences between Type B and Type C. Thus, whereas Type C behavior is perhaps the most effective within any warning system, Type B is the least effective, and the unnecessary risk taking has some obvious neurotic aspects. It may be argued that the explicit goal of an effective warning system is to produce Type C behavior (i.e., high protection without high fear). Such behavior implies that the protective behavior is not determined by the intensity of the fear reaction, but rather by some other determinants. A great amount of training is often thought to be the best way to produce Type C behavior, particularly when protective behavior is instrumental to personal or organizational safety.

Another Question. Because FAEs lead from Type A to Type D behavior, is it possible to increase the chances that the transition will pass through Type C rather than Type B? This can be achieved only if the impact of a FAE influences the two response channels differentially. A prerequisite for such a response is the desynchronization of the FAE. More specifically, the fear reaction should be more strongly affected than protective behavior.

We submit that any attempt to desynchronize the FAE should rest on manipulations that are a priori more relevant to one of the dimensions than to the other. The research reported in the following chapters attempts to achieve that goal.

8 It's Now or Never: Protective Behavior Under Time Pressure

Any attempt to desynchronize the false alarm effects in the fear reaction and in protective behavior must retain the basic features of the experimental paradigm that has been used so far. In order not to throw the baby out with the bath water, the new manipulation attempted in the next experiment capitalized on the discovery that most of the subjects who engaged in protective behavior did so immediately after the onset of Warning A. This regularity ought to be judged in the context of instructions that allow complete freedom in the choice of the timing of protective behavior, as long as it takes place before the onset of the shock. In other words, subjects could act from the onset of Warning A, throughout A, throughout B, and well into Warning C, having 3 full minutes at their disposal. In view of our claim that the exact timing of the decision concerning protective behavior may well be the key to the understanding of the relationships between it and the fear reaction, it was particularly tempting to manipulate the decision time by instructions.

The least innocuous manipulation consists of instructing the subjects to behave as they prefer anyway. Thus, a new group of subjects were tested. These subjects were explicitly told that if they wish to reduce the anticipated intensity of the shock, they must do so during Warning A. Because Warning A is issued immediately following the threat instructions, they had very little time to make up their minds. The same was true of the subjects in the previous experiment, who voluntarily took such a course of action. Therefore, the main difference between this new group (Group A) and the one in which subjects were free to choose their timing (to be called Group Free) is in the psychological implications of *must* versus *wish*. Another difference lies in the fact that with the onset of Warning B, Group A could no longer change mind, whereas Group Free could.

The fact that almost nobody in Group Free took advantage of this option does not necessarily constitute proof against its importance. As in the case of transition from helplessness to partial control, the psychological impact of the option may reduce the need for its usage.

In order to provide more information on the effect of decision time on protective behavior, two additional groups of subjects were tested. Group B was instructed that any attempt to reduce the intensity of the shock must take place during Warning B, and Group C was told it could act only during the last warning (C). With this exception, all the procedures and instructions for Groups A, B, and C were the same as for Group Free. The exact phrasing of the temporal constraints of coping did not abolish its continuity or reversibility; it only shrinked the total duration during which this was possible. To illustrate, subjects in Group A were instructed:

> You may reduce the shock intensity any number of points down to a level of 1 intensity point. You may reduce it any time during Warning A and as many times as you wish, as long as it is before the onset of Warning B. [And later] Remember, any action you take must be finished before the onset of Warning B. Once Warning B starts, there is nothing you can do to affect the intensity of the shock.

The instructions for Group B and Group C followed the same pattern. Forty-five subjects were randomly assigned to the three groups, fifteen in each.

RESULTS

Probability of Protective Behavior

It is only fair to mention that in addition to learning something about the role of decision time in situations of impending danger, we also hoped to desynchronize the fear and active coping channels. This hope was based on the rationale that by time-locking the protective behavior we might exercise some influence over it without at the same time producing a similar impact on the fear reaction. But we were clearly unprepared for the dramatic results that we obtained. Having by now pursued long and tedious pretesting of the procedures and having analyzed the previous experiment, we did not anticipate major shifts in the probability of active coping. Fortunately, however, we were wrong! In Group A on the first session, all subjects without exception engaged in protective behavior, in Group B 60% did the same, and in Group C only 33% did so. Figure 8.1 illustrates the results for all three groups.

Analyses of variance indicate that the differences between groups are significant for Session 1, $F = 10.2$ $df = 2/42$, $p = .000$, and for Session 2, $F = 7.35$, $df = 2/42$, $p = .002$. In Session 3 the three groups were exactly identical. The FAE was significant only in Group A.

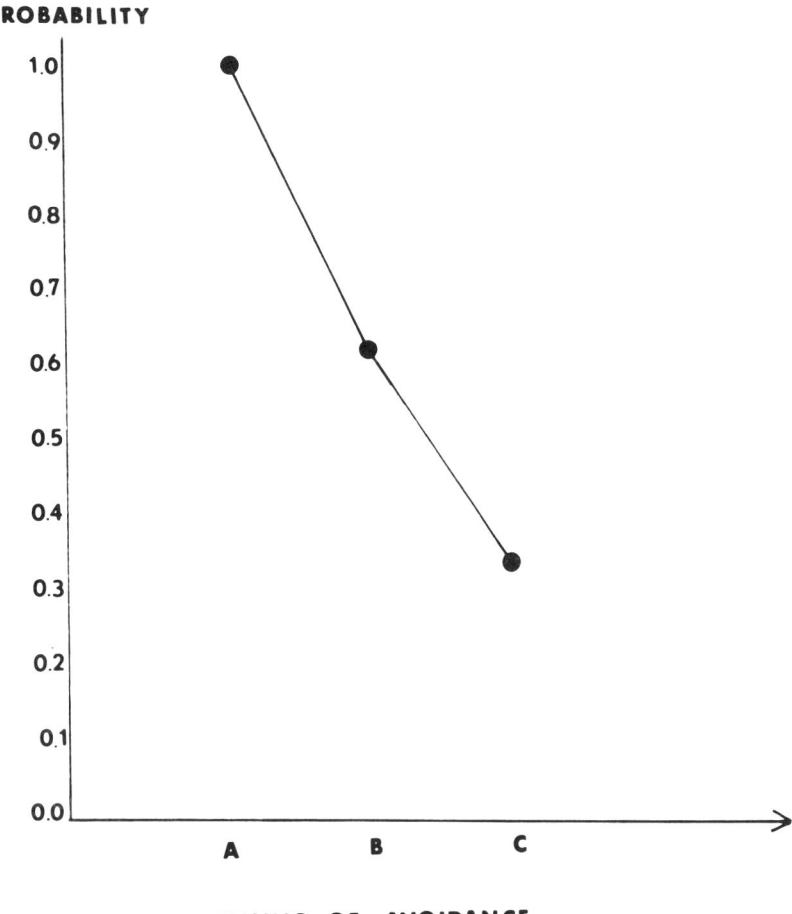

FIG. 8.1 Probability of protective behavior according to groups.

Subjects in Group Free voluntarily placed themselves primarily in Group A in terms of the timing of protective behavior, and it is of some interest to note that their probability score of .87 fits that position quite well. At the same time, however, the psychological difference between free timing and forced timing is sufficiently powerful to motivate virtually all subjects in Group A to protect themselves.

What are the reasons for such strong dependence of probability of coping upon its timing? Why does delay in carrying out the protective behavior reduce the tendency to do so? Four partially independent explanations come to mind:

1. In situations of time pressure, Group A subjects are particularly at the mercy of the most available alternative. There is not sufficient time for extensive

deliberation of other alternatives, and the most available one is immediately chosen. Thus, time pressure is seen as an amplifier of the availability heuristic (Tversky & Kahneman, 1974), not unlike Hull's notion of "drive." Assuming that immediately after the threat instructions, which dwelled extensively on the high intensity of the shock as well as the means to reduce it, consideration of one's safety is the most available alternative, and under time pressure it will invariably be chosen.

2. It is conceivable that under conditions of stress, individuals prefer the more conservative alternatives. In addition to the stress produced by the threat of impending shock, the time pressure in Group A might have augmented the stress even more. Data based on all our previous experiments indicate that fear reaction is highest during Warning A, even in the absence of the additional strain produced by time pressure. Thus, if stress increases conservatism, this could explain our findings. I am now actively engaged in research indicating the plausibility of this argument.

3. Can the function of protective behavior be seen solely as the reduction of the intensity of the future danger? We submit that protective behavior serves yet another function: that of reducing fear and anxiety. This is in line with a variety of formulations of the two-factor theory of avoidance learning. Such fear reduction can be seen as a major cause of protective behavior, in the same way that buying an insurance policy attempts to maximize one's peace of mind irrespective of whether it will ever be necessary. This argument is most potent in the context of investigating the FAE, because it modifies the dependence of protective behavior on the credibility of the threat. A person may be well aware that the chances of a particular danger are very small and yet invest in reducing his or her fear reaction, however unwarranted. Furthermore, if a threat turns out to be a false alarm, the protective behavior could still be perceived as instrumental in reducing the fear prior to the cancellation of the threat. Thus, a hindsight analysis may view the fear as unnecessary but the protective behavior as a good response to fear. Assuming the foregoing to be a true determinant of protective behavior, we can now understand why most subjects in Group Free act immediately. If fear is a factor, it is most effective to reduce it as early as possible. By contrast, subjects in Group C who had to wait for the onset of the last warning before being allowed to protect themselves had very little to gain in terms of fear reduction, because they have been through most of it already!

4. Finally, it is quite possible that the particular instructions of Group A were effective in motivating all subjects to engage in protective behavior, because they simulated the conditions conducive to panic behavior. As was discussed earlier, panic behavior is typically induced in situations where there is a great imminent danger, which can be escaped, but in which the escape route is perceived as quickly closing. Thus, subjects in Group A were threatened with a powerful shock, they were instructed that they may escape the high-intensity pain by reducing it, but unless they do so immediately, it would be too late. During the

first session in particular, subjects had no way to estimate the duration of Warning A, and the only way they could insure their safety was by acting immediately. This analogy to the panic situation may provide a clue to the dramatic finding that there was not a single person in Group A willing to take the risk of the highest shock intensity.

Whatever is the most appropriate explanation of our unexpected results, a great deal of additional systematic research is needed before their theoretical status can be clarified. Their practical implications need not necessarily await such theoretical elaboration, and they are explicated later.

Amplitude of Protective Behavior

Analysis of the data reveal additional findings worthy of our attention. Let us start by considering the effect of timing upon the amplitude of protective behavior. In order to obtain scores uncontaminated by probability, the mean amplitude of protective behavior was calculated taking only those subjects who engaged in this behavior. Table 8.1 presents the results.

Analysis of variance established that neither the between groups nor the FAE were statistically significant. However, it is interesting to note that unlike the probability of protective behavior, its amplitude, though not statistically significant, was highest in Group C of all groups. This indicates that probability and amplitude may very well reflect different underlying processes. The decision whether to take action cannot be seen as equivalent to the decision of if yes, how much action should one take. The distinction between these two must be kept in mind if for no other reason than that there are protective measures that are all-or-none affairs. A decision to take them gives rise to new problems which must be decided upon, but which were totally irrelevant prior to the initial decision.

Consider the example of evacuation in the face of an approaching tropical storm. There is no half evacuation or double evacuation. When people decide

TABLE 8.1
Amplitude of Protective Behavior by Groups and Sessions

Sessions	Group A	Group B	Group C
First Session N_1	29.8 (15)	25.7 (9)	35.8 (5)
Second Session N_2	26.9 (14)	20.1 (8)	35.4 (5)
Third Session N_3	24.2 (11)	17.6 (7)	34.6 (5)

that they are going to evacuate their homes, they will be confronted by the need to make some new decisions, such as what to carry with them and so forth. However, these decisions are conceptually, as well as psychologically, sequential and at least to some extent independent. In our case this difference ought to be made explicit because the continuous nature of the protective behavior measured may be mistakenly overrated. The difference between zero protection and some protection cannot be viewed as psychologically equivalent to the difference between some protection and some more protection. In Group Free, which was discussed in the previous chapter, both probability and amplitude showed a clear FAE following the cancellation of the threat, but such is not the case in the present study. Furthermore, probability is highly sensitive to timing of protective behavior, whereas amplitude is not.

Subjects in Group C exhibit a paradoxical pattern of behavior. They tend to refrain from self-protection, but the few that protect themselves maintain their behavior in face of two consecutive false alarms. This can be seen both in the probability measure illustrated in Fig. 8.1 and in the amplitude measure in Table 8.1.

Why is there virtually no FAE in Group C? A distinct possibility is *preselection*. The forces against protective behavior in Group C are so powerful that all those who could have been influenced by considerations of credibility yield to them during the first session and refrain from self-protection. Stated differently, it is conceivable that there is a ceiling effect beyond which subjects are not sensitive to determinants intrinsic to the warning system. They act for reasons extrinsic to the credibility issue and continue to do so in spite of two false alarms. Another possibility is that subjects in Group C, who are acting against great odds to the contrary, argue that if it is so difficult to decide for protection, it should at least be worth the trouble and effectively reduce the anticipated pain.

In the same vein, it can be argued that the prolonged deliberation preceding the action of Group C increases the commitment to its members' decision. Thus, the theory of cognitive dissonance (Festinger, 1957) would predict higher persistence in Group C subjects and consequently greater resistance to the FAE.

All of these speculations share a common thread: They relate the smaller FAE to the forces that reduced the probability of protective behavior in the first place. This common element reduces the chances of discovering a magic formula that will combine the advantages of Group A (i.e., high probability of protective behavior) with those of Group C (i.e., small FAE). If one or more of the foregoing suggestions are true, there is a built-in incompatibility between the two.

The paradox cannot be explained by referring to the longer duration preceding the action on the second and third trials, because the FAE is more evident in Group B than in Group A. If the FAE could be reduced as a function of extra time to think about the implications of the preceding false alarm, Group A should have exhibited the highest FAE.

To complicate the issue further, it appears that whereas Group C did not show any FAE in the protective behavior channel, it demonstrated a clear FAE in fear reaction as measured by heart rate. However, such a discrepancy is the best proof of our success in desynchronizing the two response channels. This leads us directly to the next analysis.

The Effect of Decision Timing on the Relationship Between Fear and Protective Behavior

One of the main reasons for the present study was to manipulate the timing of a person's decision concerning protective behavior. We propose a theoretical formulation to the effect that early decision leads to negative correlations between fear and protective behavior, whereas late decision would produce positive correlations. Contrary to our earlier efforts to categorize our subjects by having to rely on post hoc measures, the design of this experiment allows a more direct testing of our predictions. Although the unanticipated low number of subjects in Groups B and C who protected themselves makes it impractical to calculate correlations between fear and protective behavior in those groups, there is no such constraint concerning Group A. On the contrary, not only did all the subjects in Group A engage in protective behavior, thus making it possible to include them in our analysis, but for logical reasons Group A is best suited for testing. It is most closely related to Group Free, with the important difference that by the time we deal with Warnings B and C, the decision must have not only been made but actually carried out irrevocably. If our analysis is correct, the correlations between fear and protective behavior for those late warnings must be negative.

The results were obtained by calculating the Pearson correlation between amplitude of protective behavior and heart-rate scores for each warning. The heart-rate scores consisted of the net highest heart rate, that is, the highest heart rate minus the highest heart rate preceding the stress instructions. Such a net score eliminated some obvious effects due to individual differences in base levels. The correlations appear in Table 8.2.

The results are as predicted by our theory. There is already some tendency for a negative correlation during Warning A, but it is not statistically significant.

TABLE 8.2
Pearson Correlations Between Heart Rate and
Protective Behavior in Group A

	Warning A	*Warning B*	*Warning C*
Correlation	−.24	−.46	−.44
N	15	15	15
Probability	.19	.04	.05

This is not surprising considering the fact that for certain subjects the highest heart rate reading during Warning A could have very well preceded the termination of the protective behavior. Only from Warning B can we be absolutely sure that all protective behavior was already carried out. The rest follows: Those subjects that reduced the intensity of the anticipated shock more than others had less to fear during the rest of the anticipation sequence! The smaller the amount of protective behavior, the more frightening the impending danger.

Timing of the Coping Option as a Source of Stress

The present experiment offers two possibilities to test whether the stress during the time when the coping option is open differs from stress during the rest of the anticipation sequence. Both heart-rate and tension scores for each of the warning segments are available and may provide an initial answer to this question. There is, however, a complication due to the fact that the already established main effects make it difficult to detect any secondary pattern superimposed upon them. In order to increase our chances of discovering a lawful relationship between the timing of the coping option and indexes of fear reaction, the means for the entire population were subtracted from each corresponding score. This was in addition to the usual adjustments for base levels implied by the net scores. Table 8.3 presents the data.

The results suggest that subjects are particularly stressed during the warning in which the coping option is open. Thus the mean adjusted heart rate of Group A is highest during Warning A, of Group B during Warning B, and of Group C during Warning C. The chances of this order are 1:27 ($p = .037$). Exactly the same pattern can be seen in the adjusted tension scores.

The psychological processes providing the basis for this finding ought to be further explored by experiments deliberately designed for that purpose; however, our post hoc analysis can carry us one additional small step in that direction. The following question is of special interest: Is the increase in stress during the period when the coping option is available more manifest in subjects who used that option or in those who did not use it?

TABLE 8.3
Adjusted Fear Reaction Scores According to Groups and Warnings

		Group A	Group B	Group C
	Warning A_1	+3.00	−1.80	−1.20
Heart Rate	Warning B_1	−1.00	+3.30	−2.30
	Warning C_1	−0.90	+0.30	+0.60
	Warning A_1	0.75	−0.92	0.09
Tension	Warning B_1	0.46	−0.57	0.06
	Warning C_1	0.53	−1.08	0.57

TABLE 8.4
The Effect of Protective Behavior on Indexes of Fear, Group B

	Variable		Mean	t	p
Net Heart Rate	Warning A_1	Coping	14.78	1.49	.16
		No Coping	6.33		
	Warning B_1	Coping	19.56	2.30	.04
		No Coping	5.67		
	Warning C_1	Coping	10.22	0.15	.88
		No Coping	9.33		
Net Tension	Warning A_1	Coping	−0.62	1.24	.24
		No Coping	−2.00		
	Warning B_1	Coping	0.25	1.31	.22
		No Coping	−1.33		
	Warning C_1	Coping	0.12	0.83	.43
		No Coping	−1.00		

As Group C has too few subjects who protected themselves and Group A has none who did not, this question can be reasonably tested only in Group B. Table 8.4 presents t tests for differences in both the heart-rate scores and tension scores between Group B subjects who acted during Warning B and those who did not.

The results suggest that the additional stress experienced during Warning B was probably related to actual coping. Thus, the heart rate of subjexts who cope is significantly higher during Warning B that than of subjects who do not. A similar tendency can be seen in the tension channel as well, but it did not reach statistical significance. At this point it stands to reason that the activity as such may be viewed as the critical variable rather than the freedom to act during that particular time. Such an interpretation is in line with results reported in the previous chapter to the effect that protective behavior actually increased the heart rate immediately after its termination. Another way to view these results is to focus on attentiveness and vigilance as the chief factors contributing to the action-related increase in stress. Even though the actual activity of pressing the foot pedal while observing the event counter in order to insure the desired number of responses is a simple task, which subjects practiced once during the instructions period, it cannot be properly carried out without the full commitment of one's attention. This indeed may well be the cause of the extra stress that we detected.

Additional insights into the effects of limiting the coping option to a single warning period can be obtained by comparing the results of Group Free with the results of Group A only. As the reader should recall, subjects in both groups acted during Warning A, but whereas in Group Free they did so on their own volition, Group A subjects had no choice in the matter. We already know that the two groups differ significantly in probability of protective behavior. Whereas 87% of Group Free protect themselves, 100% of Group A do so in the first session. Considering our immediately preceding analysis, it should come as no surprise that during the first session Group A subjects reported higher tension than those of Group Free. This was highly significant during Warning A, as indeed it should be, if activity increased tension.

Though there were no additional differences between these two groups during the first session, an interesting and totally unexpected finding emerged in Sessions 2 and 3. Subjects in Group A had significantly higher distraction scores than those in Group Free. This may suggest that by limiting the coping option to a particular segment of the entire duration of anticipation, the rest of that duration becomes somewhat less stressful. Not only is there no possibility to act, but there is also no reason to dwell on the subject, because such cognitions will be of no practical value. Such a "timeout" caused by delineating the temporal availability of the coping option may have the advantage of reducing vigilance and increasing avoidant-like thoughts. There need be no difference in the total amount of stress between the free operant condition and the temporally limited one. The difference lies in the way stress is distributed over the various segments of anticipation. Thus, our results suggest that the stress may be increased during the critical period when action is possible, particularly if carried out, while at the same time it will decrease by comparison when that option is closed. If future research supports this analysis, the effects of timing of protective behavior could be seen as demonstrating the positive aspects of control as well as some of the positive aspects of helplessness (e.g., Brady, 1958).

SUMMARY

Our first attempt to desynchronize the two main response channels of fear and protective behavior turned out to be successful. Not only were we able to obtain new support for the idea that decision time determines the relationship between these two, but our choice of manipulation turned out to be particularly lucky. It yielded a bounty of serendipitous findings that shed new light on the complex issues we are trying to understand. Chief among them is the discovery that the timing of the active coping option may determine the probability of its usage. Besides some of the theoretical implications of this result, its potential practical importance should not be overlooked.

Thus, whenever confronted by a danger in which it is absolutely essential to engage in protective behavior, postponing the threat until such time that action is imminent may increase the motivation for self-protection. Incidentally, such postponement is in line with our previous findings concerning the pacing of warnings as well as their announced probability. Time pressure, however, may be a mixed blessing, particuarly if the desired action is complex and requires a certain amount of improvisation. The added stress of time pressure may further increase the performance deficit anticipated under conditions of psychological stress.

9 Attempts to Restore Credibility by Explaining the Causes of False Alarms

When the all-clear signal is given, people take stock. Having spent some time under the shadow of an impending danger, the lifting of that shadow becomes a meaningful and interesting moment. The cognitive appraisal of this new information starts an immediate process of recovery from stress, as indicated by the gradual decline in arousal. Understanding that the danger is over is probably a sufficient cause for reducing the fear reaction.

At the same time, however, or shortly afterwards, a more elaborate reckoning must take place. This relates to the interpretation of the entire episode, not just its termination. It is then that the initial warning is perceived as a false alarm. Thoughts that such may be the case might already have existed during the anticipation proper, but they were unfounded and represented attempts to defend against the threatening future. When the threat is officially canceled, interpreting it as a false alarm becomes a logical conclusion rather than a matter of convenience.

Suddenly a whole set of questions must be answered: Is it really over? Maybe it wasn't coming in the first place? Was all this fuss for nothing? Couldn't they have known better? Sooner? If they were wrong about the danger, how can I trust them? Are they wrong, perhaps, about the cancellation as well? The initial attempts to provide answers to these and other similar questions are probably within receivers' existing beliefs and schemata. Their notions about the nature of the world and the nature and quality of the warning system provide the context in which the new information is assimilated. If too dissonant and unexpected, the new information cannot be effectively assimilated within the limitations imposed by existing cognitive structures, and these structures themselves must undergo some modification. In line with Piagetian formulation concerning assimilation and accommodation (Flavell, 1977; Lipsitt & Reese, 1979; Piaget, 1970), the greater the surprise value of a threat cancellation, the greater the need for accommodation. The false alarm effect is the end result of the accommodating process, and its magnitude reflects the magnitude of cognitive restructuring (i.e., learning from experience).

Our research has already documented that the initial probability of the threat and the pacing of warnings affect the accommodation process. The greater the "surprise value" or "information value" of the cancellation proper, the greater the need to change existing belief systems, and consequently, the greater the FAE.

These changes can focus on the nature of the danger or on the nature of the warning system. Earlier discussion of this issue emphasized the central role of intrinsic versus extrinsic information in determining the focus of change. During the period when receivers attempt to answer the questions raised by the cancellation of the threat, they are particularly in need of additional information. Thus, it is of great importance to note whether this need for information will be satisfied by the warning system itself (i.e., by providing intrinsic information) or by other, extrinsic sources. Needless to say, the credibility of this new information is also questioned by receivers who have just experienced the consequences of what they perceive as unwarranted credibility.

If a warning system attempts to provide information concerning its recent failure to predict the course of development of a particular danger correctly, it may furnish some explanation of the entire episode. We submit—although cannot prove it at this point—that if the warning system is the first to analyze its failure, it stands to gain more psychologically than if the analysis of its failure is presented by external sources. The psychological gain in this case consists of cutting the losses rather than actual gain. The possibility exists, however, that by providing a plausible and convincing explanation for its recent failure a warning system may salvage part of the inevitable credibility loss. If indeed this is a valid possibility, what are the central parameters of such information? How exactly can the deleterious effects of a warning system's failure (real or apparent) be minimized through explanations and actions that aim to at least partially restore credibility?

Before trying to address this issue, which constitutes the central theme of this chapter, let us have a closer look at the situation of the subjects in our experiments. In all the experiments so far the cancellation of the threat was announced by the experimenter without any additional information. It was simply issued as a totally unexplained new fact. The exact words used were: "This time the alarm has been called off. I repeat, this time the alarm has been called off. There will be no shock. . . . You may now relax."

Even though there is no explicit information to that effect, the subjects clearly understand that the experimenters knew all along that the danger would be canceled. Because there was no indication that the cancellation was contingent on something that the subjects did, it must have been planned well in advance. The postexperimental questionnaire contains an explicit question about subjects' views on the reason for calling off the alarm. More specifically, they are asked whether they think that the cancellation is related to anything they themselves did. Only 15% of all subjects tested believe that they might have had something to do with the cancellation, without, however, having any clear idea what it might have been. The cancellation of the threat, just as its onset, was thus predetermined purely by the experimenters following a certain plan of action.

From the receivers' point of view, the experimenters could not be perceived just as the warning agents, but rather they themselves were the danger! Following the false alarm experience, the subjects had to reinterpret what they thought about the purpose of the experiment. The possibility that the shock would not be administered even on the second trial now became subjectively more probable, leading to the various indexes of FAE. The absence of explicit information encouraged our subjects to speculate about the nature of the experiment, increasing the subjective probability of those hypotheses that stressed the harmlessness of the entire experience.

Any attempt to introduce debriefing procedures into the existing experimental paradigm could not, therefore, be made before first creating a warning system as an entity separate from the omnipotent experimenter. Within the confinement of the laboratory and as long as the subjects agree to continue their participation, the experimenter is indeed the lawmaker, and it is his whims and arbitrariness that a proper warning system should detect and bring to their attention. Our next experiment solved this problem by having a second subject, who was an accomplice, play the role of the warning system proper.

Before explicating the details of the design and its rationale, we should, however, take a closer look at the kinds of causes for false alarms that might be most useful to simulate. The various reasons for false alarms fall into two broad categories:

1. A false alarm may represent the basic limitations of a particular warning system in predicting complex events in advance. Thus, the state of the world may actually change during the various stages of anticipation and justify calling off the threat. A warning system's failure may be the direct outcome of inadequate knowledge, which serves as the basis for its operation. Short of scientific progress, such constraints impose the upper limits on the warning system's performance.

2. On the other hand, a warning system may function below its optimal level because of some shortcomings in its mode of operation. These shortcomings can be a system error due to inadequate instrumentation, a human error, or a procedural error. By contrast to the first type of causes, these causes of a warning system's failure can in principle be corrected.

From the receiver's viewpoint, it may be totally unimportant what the source of a false alarm was. It remains to be empirically tested whether individuals who are given information explicating the reasons why both the threat and its subsequent cancellation were "justified" at the time they were issued will indeed respond with a FAE or not.

A warning system based on imperfect knowledge might fail more than once for the same reason. Consequently, a false alarm experience provides the individual with data about the competence of a system, and in the absence of evidence to the contrary, one may infer that failing once, it might fail again.

On the other hand, it is possible to provide the subject with information implying that the source of failure was temporary. Thus, if following a cancellation of a threat one is made to understand that the false alarm was due to a system failure, which was diagnosed and is being repaired, the credibility loss may not necessarily carry over fully to the next experience with a similar threat, and the FAE can be reduced.

METHODS

In order to facilitate comparisons with our earlier work, the experimental paradigm in this study retained the basic features of the preceding experiments. Thus, subjects were threatened with a painful electric shock, using three discrete warnings to indicate the proximity of the shock. Protective behavior was available through which the shock intensity could be reduced at some monetary cost. Following the last warning the threat was called off.

Two new groups of subjects were tested: Group Info in which the false alarm was explained as a consequence of new information, and Group Error in which it was presented as a result of a correctable human error. Group Free from the previous experiment served as the control group (Group C), because the subjects in that group did not receive any explanation whatsoever.

The effects of these debriefing manipulations were tested by confronting the subjects with a new similar threat. This was repeated twice. The dependent variables were the same as in the previous studies.

Forty undergraduate students at the University of Haifa served as subjects in this experiment. They were randomly allocated to Group Info or Group Error, twenty to each group. Subjects were invited to come to the laboratory in pairs. One of the pair was an accomplice well trained in the role he would have to play. Upon arrival at the laboratory, subjects were told that the experiment deals with alerts before dangers. One of them would play the role of the "warning agent" (Subject A), and the other would be the receiver of the first subject's "decisions" (Subject B). A prearranged unfair lottery insured that the accomplice would always be the warning agent. Both subjects were seated in the subjects'

118   9. ATTEMPTS TO RESTORE CREDIBILITY

room, but in separate cubicles barring eye contact. The accomplice was issued earphones through which—so both subjects were told—he would receive information about the potential dangers. On the basis of this information, he would then decide whether and when to alert Subject B by asking the experimenters to deliver the various warnings. All this was stated publicly for the naive subject to hear. Next followed the usual steps of attaching Subject B to the polygraph, reading the general stress instructions, and base-line recordings.

At the end of the 2 minutes of base-line recordings, Subject A said aloud: "Threat instructions please." The exact timing of this request was secured by one of the two experimenters telling the accomplice through the earphones exactly when to make that request. Immediately following this prearranged request, the pretaped threat instructions were given through the intercom, as in all our previous experiments. These included the description and brief practice of the protective behavior option.

Immediately following the threat instructions, Subject A asked for Warning A to be issued, and the red light was switched on and off once, accordingly. After 1 minute, Subject A asked for Warning B to be issued, and 1 minute later for the last warning (C). All times were controlled by the experimenter who communicated with the accomplice via the earphones. At the end of 1 minute from the onset of Warning C, Subject A asked the experimenter to cancel the threat. The experimenter then read the usual cancellation instructions.

We thus created a situation in which Subject A is perceived by the naive Subject B as being the warning agent. Though the various signals and instructions are entirely controlled by the experimenters and Subject A is only carrying out requests by the experimenters, from Subject B's point of view it is exactly the other way around, and the experimenters are carrying out the explicit requests of Subject A.

Explaining the Cause of the False Alarm

Information about the cause of the false alarm was given to the naive subject indirectly. He could overhear Subject A explaining to the experimenter the reason for his behavior. It was thought to be a more credible way to use this indirect method rather than attempting to explain the failure of the warning system directly to the affected person.

Thirty seconds following the cancellation instructions, the experimenter told Subject A to remove his earphones and explain why he acted the way he did. This request, as well as all subsequent communication between the experimenter and Subject A, was carried over the intercom with the deliberate purpose of having Subject B hear all that was being said.

In Group Info, Subject A said after removing the earphones: "Judging by the information I had, I was almost sure that the shock will be given, and I did not want him to be surprised. Then, when item Number 17 arrived, it became clear that the situation had changed and the danger was over."

Subject A was then told to attach his earphones again, and 2 minutes after the first threat was canceled, a new, second threat was issued immediately after the accomplice asked for it. The same procedure was followed until the second cancellation. The debriefing followed a similar pattern using different words. The same sequence was repeated again, making a total of three threats and three cancellations.

In Group Error, Subject A said after removing the earphones: "Judging by the information I had, I was almost sure that the shock will be given, and I did not want him to be surprised. Then, when item Number 17 arrived, it became clear that the situation had changed and the danger was over."

At this point the experimenter said: "We feel that you did not understand the instructions. Your decisions do not correspond to the information that you are receiving. Are the instructions clear now? Try to concentrate on the information and decide according to it. We shall start a new experiment."

Following the second cancellation, the decision maker is again chastised: "This time again your actions did not correspond to your information. I believe that you did not understand the experiment, and we can not proceed like this." Then, in order not to arouse his suspicion, the naive subject "overhears" the following conversation between the two experimenters.

Experimenter A states: "He does not understand his task. I suggest to call him out."

Experimenter B says, "Okay," then directly to the accomplice: "Please come to our room." He enters the control room, and there he is again being told that he did not understand his task. Finally, Experimenter A says: "I am going to look for a replacement. If I don't find one soon, we will terminate the experiment."

He then enters the subject's room and tells him what he has already overheard through the intercom. The main lights are switched on, and the heart-rate channel is disconnected.

Three minutes later a second "accomplice" enters, the lights are switched off, and the heart-rate channel is again connected. The "new subject" is then instructed via the intercom:

> This experiment deals with stress. Your task is to be a warning agent. You will receive information through the earphones, and on the basis of that information, you will decide whether and when to alert your partner about an impending danger. The kinds of warnings and kinds of information to be given will become clear to you as you start listening. Put on the earphones please, and announce whether you hear us properly. We are starting a new experiment.

One minute later, the third and final threat was issued.

Thus, in Group Error the naive subjects are made to believe that the false alarm occurred due to a human error caused by Subject A. Following the first cancellation, Subject A is warned to perform better on the next trial, and following the second false alarm, he is actually replaced by a new subject. Thus, any error caused by him has now been potentially corrected, and the warning system potentially rehabilitated.

In Group C no postcancellation information was given, and subseqeunt threats followed a silent 3-minute post cancellation interval.

RESULTS

Before presenting the data, it should be emphasized that not a single subject in Groups Info and Error indicated suspicion of the experimental procedures. We were particularly worried about Group Error, which involved two experimenters and two collaborators playing complex roles. It appears, however, that the subjects were naive throughout the entire experimental sequence.

TABLE 9.1
Means, Standard Deviations, and Two-Way
Analysis of Variance of HR Readings According
to Groups and Sessions

Session Group		*1*	*2*	*3*	*Mean*
C	M	109.03	101.00	96.89	102.27
	SD	17.93	14.65	12.98	
I	M	112.48	104.18	99.29	105.31
	SD	15.13	14.59	13.43	
E	M	106.81	100.39	98.90	102.03
	SD	16.29	15.05	14.61	
Mean		109.44	101.86	98.36	

Source	df	MS	F	p
Groups	2	3576.15	<1(ns)	
SwG	67	10177.03		
Sessions	2	34636.95	95.56	<.001
Groups × Sessions	4	719.27	1.98(ns)	
Sessions × SwG	134	362.47		

TABLE 9.2
Means, Standard Deviations, and Two-Way Analysis of Variance of
Active Coping Responses According to Groups and Sessions

Group		1	2	3	Mean
C	M	23.30	18.63	14.83	18.92
	SD	17.83	16.68	16.87	
I	M	24.05	20.45	15.35	19.95
	SD	17.06	16.76	16.60	
E	M	18.37	18.58	18.47	18.47
	SD	15.10	14.81	15.14	
Mean		21.91	19.22	16.22	

Source	df	MS	F	p
Groups	2	37.96	<1(ns)	
SwG	66	708.25		
Sessions	2	536.32	9.99	<.001
Groups × Sessions	4	141.35	2.63	<.05
Sessions × SwG	132	53.66		

Fear Reaction

Typically following a false alarm, heart rate as well as other indexes of fear reaction to a subsequent similar threat are reduced. Table 9.1 presents a two-way analysis of variance of the highest heart-rate readings according to groups and sessions. The results indicate that in terms of fear reaction as measured by heart rate, postcancellation explanation of reasons for a warning system's failure does not reduce the FAE. A clear reduction in heart rate follows each of the two cancellations in all three groups.

Protective Behavior

Table 9.2 presents a two-way analysis of variance of the amplitude of protective behavior according to groups and sessions. The data again indicate the FAE, implying that following a cancellation of a threat the intensity of active coping during a similar subsequent threat is reduced. However, the significant interaction between groups x sessions warranted a closer look. The results of tests on simple main effects (Winer, 1971) show that in Group Error there are no significant differences between sessions (Group C: $F = 10.05$, $df = 2/132$, $p < .001$; Group Info: $F = 7.12$, $df = 2/132$, $p < .0.5$; Group Error: $F < 1$).

Table 9.2 clearly illustrates that there is actually no FAE in protective behavior in Group Error. This is in marked contrast to both Groups Info and C, as well as all other previous findings, using a similar research paradigm. Not only for the first time in a series of experiments could a manipulation be found that protects the warning system from credibility loss in the protective behavior channel, but potentially even more interesting is the split between this channel and the psychophysiological one. Thus, the fear reaction is reduced, even though a correctable explanation for the false alarm was furnished, but the active coping is not.

It appears that the manipulation in Group Error was successful in desynchronizing the two main response channels and actually produces the desired Type C behavior discussed in Chapter 7. This behavior pattern of lowering the fear, but at the same time maintaining the previous level of self-protection, is optimal in most situations of danger, and often a great amount of deliberate training is directed toward obtaining and maintaining this pattern.

The successful desynchronization was achieved by providing an explanation that is presumably appraised by the receiver as indicative of actions that may to some extent neutralize the cognitive implications of the false alarm experience. On the theoretical level, these findings suggest that fear reaction in this situation is not under the complete control of mediating cognitive factors because they were unable to control the heart rate (Schachter & Singer, 1962), nor is protective behavior governed by the emotional reaction. Thus, the same cognitive appraisal of a threat as having a particular credibility or change of credibility can have a differential impact on the two response systems.

Such an analysis is quite compatible with Lazarus' (1966, 1977) classification of coping, which in its openness allows discrepancies between the emotional and the cognitive modes. A similar phenomenon appears to be central to the process of worrying (Breznitz, 1971).

A speculation may be offered that the autonomic reaction is much more stimulus bound than active coping, and consequently more affected by the stimulus aspects that remained invariant over the three sessions. The constant laboratory setting and the repetitious instructions may lead to some FAE independently of the actual content of the messages. On the other hand, active coping is the outcome of complex decisions about the probabilities of gain and loss and their implications; therefore, it is presumably more affected by cognitive factors.

In this context it is worth noting that analysis of subjective tension scores as well as credibility scores showed a clear FAE in all groups, including Group Error. The fact that these indexes demonstrated a pattern closer to the heart-rate scores than to protective behavior scores may reflect subjects' post hoc knowledge of the actual outcome of all three threats.

An interesting exception was self-reported distraction. Though a clear FAE could be seen in both Groups C and Info, no such effect took place in Group

Error. This may very well be due to the fact that postcancellation debriefing provides a variety of new information that has to be processed by the subjects. Their ability to think of topics unrelated to the threat is thus markedly reduced in Group Error.

The results of this study demonstrate that in principle it is possible to salvage part of the credibility of a warning system following a false alarm experience. At the same time, however, they suggest that a certain specific condition must be fulfilled for a postcancellation explanation to be effective. Thus, even though Group Info obtained explanations relating to the changes in the "state of the world," its FAE was just as intense as that of Group C, which received no explanation whatsoever. Although the possibility must always be granted that this reflects only a specific failure of the particular operational definition of the manipulation as used in this study, the much broader conclusion should also be considered. By that I imply the principle that explaining false alarms by pointing out the uncertain nature of the danger and by pointing out the objective limitations of a warning system simply does not work. The warning system may be doing its best under the circumstance, but in the absence of viable change in those circumstances, there is no reason to doubt the lesson learned by a false alarm experience. The failure of such a warning system to predict the course of development of the threat correctly becomes objective evidence of its limitations. The loss of credibility is based upon this evidence.

A warning system that is perceived as not operating at its optimal level has the paradoxical advantage that it can be improved. If as in Group Error, receivers are made aware of the source of a warning system's failure, which is then perceived as corrected, the FAE can be reduced. Furthermore, the reduction of FAE will be effective predominantly in the protective behavioral channel, thus leading to the optimal Type C behavior pattern.

In terms of our earlier discussion, information concerning the detection of the cause of a false alarm may serve an important function in a person's attempt to assimilate the false alarm experience. The warning system itself provides the much needed cognitive framework for attempting to understand what took place. By pointing to a concrete system error, the task of an intelligent subject who tries to make sense of the entire episode is significantly simplified. If the explanation itself is sufficiently credible and if subsequent to it viable steps are taken to correct the system error, the credibility can to some extent be restored.

Can it be restored or, perhaps protected from being lost in the first place? In the absence of evidence from research designed to test this question directly, there is no way of knowing which is the case. And what a fascinating research problem it is, touching on the very process of the FAE. Is the FAE a quick process? Does it take place immediately following the cancellation of the threat? And in more practical terms: Is it important to intervene quickly? If a debriefing procedure such as the one effectively used in Group Error is contemplated, will it reduce the FAE, or will it rebuild part of the credibility from a necessarily lower level? If the former is the case, then the intervention should be as quick as possible, not allowing the accommodation due to the false alarm experience to consolidate. On the other hand, if the latter is the case, time may turn out to be unimportant.

Whether protected or restored, a warning system's credibility will never remain at its original, precancellation level. These attempts to interfere with the usual FAE must be considered only partially successful at best, because the detection and correction of a system error is at the same time indicative of the credibility of the warning system as a whole. These procedures and practices may delay the ultimate loss of credibility, but if one error follows another or one change of instruments follows another, the entire system will soon be questioned.

The mechanism underlying the success of this type of postcancellation explanation may very well turn out to be one akin to *discrimination learning*. By stressing the corrections and changes introduced to the warning system, it is perceived as different from what it was when it failed. This in turn makes any learning from the false alarm experience less justified.

The detection, isolation, and replacement of the weak link in the warning system chain is a particularly inviting solution to credibility loss, because it protects the main elements of the system. Considering the fact that the sufficient condition for this kind of protection against the FAE is that the receiver will perceive it as an improvement, there might be a strong temptation to visibly detect, isolate, and replace weak links that are not real, in a truly Machiavellian fashion. History is full of examples in which scapegoats are detected, isolated, and replaced as a way to account for a warning system's failure.

Last but not least, postcancellation information can attempt to save the credibility of a warning system by indicating that it was not a case of false alarm at all, but rather a "near miss." This is entirely different from the previous issue, because instead of explaining why a warning system failed, the focus is on explaining what actually took place. The psychological impact of a near miss is so dramatically different from that of a false alarm that it is truly outside the scope of the present volume. At the same time, however, being a "close relative" of the false alarm concept, the basic features of the near miss concept ought to be discussed.

The Psychology of the Near Miss Phenomenon

The common element shared by both a false alarm and a near miss is that insofar as the receiver of the warnings is concerned nothing objectively harmful happened. It is this similarity of objective outcomes that has been the main cause of confusion in this matter. Thus, Janis (1962), in his detailed analysis of the psychological effects of warnings, makes the surprising statement that false alarms may sometimes increase vigilance:

Unconfirmed warnings of dire disaster do not variably produce the outcome described in the popular "cry-wolf" story. This is indicated by Killian's study (1954) of reactions to a series of hurricane warnings. In September 1953 the residents of Panama City, Florida, were informed by newspaper, radio, and other media that Hurricane Florence was approaching the Gulf coast and would probably hit them with the worst storm in Florida's history. The two local radio stations broadcasted hourly an official warning advising all people near the coast to move to inland shelters. An estimated 10,000 residents followed this advice. But the hurricane suddenly changed its course. Instead of hitting Panama City with its full force, the storm center crossed the coast about 100 miles away, so that Panama City experienced a relatively mild windstorm which produced only slight damage [p. 89].

Janis proceeds to comment on the fact that in a series of intensive interviews, Killian found that few of the evacuees complained about having been "misled by the false alarm"; the vast majority said they would evacuate again under the same circumstances. Janis mentions the possibility that some kind of dissonance reduction (Festinger, 1957; Janis, 1959) could have been one of the main factors for this paradoxical effect. He is quick to note, however, that such an explanation does not hold for a sizable number of people who, in spite of the fact that they did not evacuate their homes, claimed that they would do so under similar conditions in the future.

Needless to say, had this been the entire picture of that particular episode, we would have great difficulty in explaining this "negative FAE." Fortunately, however, Janis (1962) himself provides the clue: "Evidently some additional information was obtained from the false alarm and its aftermath which induced them [the people who did not evacuate] to regret their decision and to adopt a new attitude toward the threat [p. 85]."

This additional information consisted of two important elements: (1) the exceptionally high tides and strong winds perceived by the individuals even though the storm was a full 100 miles away; and (2) reports of the enormous damage wreaked by the hurricane in areas less than 100 miles away. Both of these elements confirmed the prediction about the force of the storm and its potential consequences.

Element 2 is the key to the near miss phenomenon. In order for an individual to appraise an event as a near miss, there must be evidence that what did not happen to him happened to somebody not too far from him. Thus, the episode described by Janis was not a false alarm at all, but rather a genuine near miss. Let us now attempt a more abstract analysis of the differences between the two.

Subjective Outcomes

Whereas on the objective level the outcome in both instances might be the same, they may be entirely different on the subjective level. More specifically, the subjective evaluation of outcomes is to a great extent determined by prior expectations. Thus, if a person expects a high-probability and high-intensity danger, which fails to materialize, this typically produces an FAE. If, however, a person does not expect anything serious to happen—irrespective of the kind of warnings received—and subsequently something *almost* does happen to him, this typically is perceived as a near miss.

Question. What is almost?

Answer. The psychological proximity of the dire consequences can vary on many dimensions. Thus, geographical proximity can be very important in case of natural disasters, which invariably occur at a certain place and time. If the person spent that time at a place close by, he will perceive the event as a near miss. Another dimension is the probability of being at the point of impact. A classic example is the case of an airplane passenger who barely missed the flight, which ended in a crash. Yet another dimension of proximity is the social distance of the victim from the person. If a close friend or relative is involved, this again implies a near miss.

Such a negative outcome, particularly if unexpected, often leads to a dramatic change in people's perception of their own invulnerability. Narrow escapes, precisely because they shatter the illusion of invulnerability, sometimes lead to emotional and behavioral problems (e.g., Fraser, Leslie, & Phelps, 1943; Glover, 1942; Janis, 1951; MacCurdy, 1943; Moore, 1958a, 1958b; Wolfenstein, 1957).

Does it follow, then, that the distinction between a false alarm and a near miss cannot be made objectively? We submit that such is not the case, because in principle it is possible to evaluate the postcancellation information. Thus, if the information provides evidence of the impact of the danger elsewhere, it would increase the chances that the episode would be perceived as a near miss rather than as a false alarm. Furthermore, the psychological distance of the impact can also be objectively evaluated, even though this can be rather difficult to accomplish. Finally, evidence can be obtained about a person's expectations prior to the actual outcome. Such information is critical to the distinction between a false alarm and a near miss.

Credibility of Warnings Following a Near Miss Experience

A near miss experience is not a success from the point of view of the warning system. We have already indicated that an episode is perceived as near miss if the objective outcomes are more serious than the expected ones. Thus, a failure of a warning system to alert a person to the chances of serious consequences may be instrumental in producing a near miss, that is, with some luck, if nothing happens to the person, and yet happens close to him. Stated like an epigram, this means that: A near miss is a big surprise turned small at the last moment. Near misses can happen even without any prior warnings at all. Whatever the outcomes, being totally unexpected will be evaluated as more serious.

Theoretically, a near miss experience, just as a false alarm experience, should never increase the credibility of a warning system if it failed to predict the outcome of a threat. We submit that such indeed is the case and that following a near miss episode the credibility of a warning system usually drops, or at best, remains unchanged. Why, then, in terms of the emotional indicators of sensitization and hypervigilance, as well as the willingness to engage in self-protection, does the opposite seem to be happening?

The reason is that a near miss increases the credibility of the danger itself. Thus, threats of similar danger in the future will be taken more seriously in spite of a prior warning system's failure. The analytic framework suggested in Chapter 2 allows us to make these distinctions between processes, which although psychologically different may lead to the same behavioral consequences. It is, however, possible to measure the credibility of the danger separately from the credibility of the warning system itself. Unfortunately, a systematic attempt in this direction has not been made up to now.

Even the most exact definitions of false alarms and near misses necessarily leave a problematic "gray area" containing events that may be interpreted either way. It is particularly in such instances that postcancellation information may turn out to be a salient factor in determining the psychological outcome of an experience. Providing information about the impact of the danger "elsewhere" can increase the chances of the near miss interpretation and encourage protective behavior in the future.

10 Performance, Training, and Protective Behavior

Anticipation of a threatening event need not take place in a behavioral vacuum. Though the impending danger may very well monopolize one's attention, there are other behaviors that must go on. Life often presents situations that require instrumental coping with an impending threat, while at the same time there is a need to maintain some normal routine. Furthermore, the onset of the emergency itself may require the carrying out of certain actions not directly related to one's personal safety. From the stricly subjective point of view of the individual, we thus speak of actions and tasks that are not directly related to the threat signaled by the warning system.

The important point to consider at the outset of this analysis is that it could often happen that maintenance of a certain activity unrelated to threat may indeed interfere with a relevant activity, such as protective behavior. Needless to say, the greater the temporal constraints of the situation, the greater the amount of competition between protective behavior and other behaviors. Thus, for example, in addition to the need for self-protection, a soldier in combat is often required to perform tasks that do not concern his personal safety and actually can be in direct conflict with it. The storming of a defensive position, though in the last analysis conducive to the goals of the unit as a whole, can clearly be seen as behavior that actually endangers the individual soldier. By the same token there are certain roles, such as fire fighter, police officer, physician, and the like, which during emergencies require behaviors that are directed primarily toward the safety and well-being of the social unit as a whole rather than that of the particular individual or his or her family. These role requirements typically produce a role conflict, which has far-reaching implications to a society's response to an emergency (see the analysis by Inbar, 1969).

Our own attempts to simulate complex warning systems experimentally are now in the position to make an additional step forward. We have started with the simple case of helpless anticipation of danger, proceeded through the introduction of the active coping option, and tried to analyze the increasingly complex relationships between fear and protective behavior in a variety of situations. The study of the false alarm effect, which is of course in the center of our entire analysis, requires that certain properties of the threatening situation occur on more than one occasion in order to allow the testing of the FAE itself. In addition to investigating the effects of false alarms on psychophysiological indexes of fear, tension, credibility, and so forth and in addition to the various indexes of protective behavior itself, we are now in a position to include yet another important behavioral component, namely, *task performance*. Our step-by-step approach in which we try to maintain a basically simple experimental paradigm and complicate it one step at a time toward increasingly close approximation of real-life situations has reached a point where much of our subject's attention will have to be divided between the impending danger and another attention-demanding task.

TASK ORIENTATION VERSUS DANGER ORIENTATION

Within the context of time limitation, the particular task requirements compete with the psychological demands related to the threatened danger for the person's attention. In terms of activity, by investing more in the one, the person has to reduce his involvement with the other. Based on this very simple formulation, several consequences may follow. They are schematically presented in Fig. 10.1, which describes the postulated interactions between task performance, protective behavior, and fear.

The figure shows that because of one's limited channel capacity, performance and protective behavior interact negatively. By investing in protective behavior,

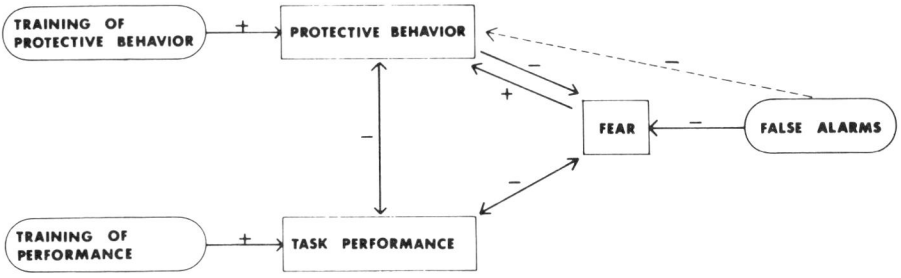

FIG. 10.1 Schematic presentation of the relationships between the variables studied.

the quality of one's performance should deteriorate. By the same token, if one concentrates on performance, protective behavior should be reduced. Looking at the third component in the situation, namely that of the fear reaction itself, we find that performance and fear should affect each other negatively, and by committing one's attention to task performance, due to distraction, the amount of fear experienced may likewise be reduced (Gal & Lazarus, 1975). The remaining interactions between protective behaviour and fear have already been detailed in this volume. We have found that although fear induces protective behavior, the protective behavior itself may reduce subsequent fear.

In order to better explicate these intricate interrelations among the various behavioral components in an anticipatory situation, it is necessary to look for ways to manipulate the various components directly. The FAE itself, as shown in Fig. 10.1, is one such manipulation. By reducing the credibility of subsequent threats, the fear reaction and to some extent the protective behavior as well were seen to be reduced. This in turn should lead to an increase in performance effectiveness. In fact, any manipulation that reduces the danger orientation is expected almost automatically to increase the task orientation. However, there are two other ways to influence the components directly. On the one hand, it is possible to train the performance on the particular task. Such training is expected to reduce the amount of attention and effort that will have to be allocated to the task. This, according to our analysis, should lead to reduced task orientation and increased danger orientation. Yet another way to test some of these factors is by training the protective behavior itself. By reducing the attentional demands of the protective behavior as such, the level of danger orientation should decrease and that of task orientation should increase. These two specific manipulations are of particular interest in view of the fact that training is often induced as a vehicle to increase effectiveness in certain situations, particularly difficult and dangerous ones.

The present chapter describes two studies that attempted to test this reasoning. In the first study task performance was introduced, and the effects of various kinds of training were investigated. In the second we discuss an experiment in which the protective behavior itself was trained. The role of training in stressful situations is particularly intriguing because it is often used as a way to protect certain behaviors from the impact of stress. The idea is often taken for granted that by training or even overtraining certain actions a state that reduces the chances of the deleterious effects of stress on performance is reached. This is relevant both to task performance unrelated to personal safety and to protective behavior as such.

An important question in many stress contexts is whether the training of behaviors that are supposed to resist deterioration under stress should be done during the stress itself or in more relaxed circumstances. The argument for the first possibility rests on the idea of stimulus generalization in learning. More specifically, it is suggested that in order to perform well under stress the behaviors must actually be carried out and trained in situations which are themselves stressful. Short of that, so goes the argument, training, though possibly helpful in maintaining the desired behavior in the training situation itself, will become ineffective when the stress alters the situation dramatically (e.g., Keinan, 1979; McGrath, 1970; Terris & Rahhal, 1969; Vossel & Laux, 1978).

On the other hand, the argument must be put forward that learning itself is quite ineffective under conditions of high stress. Consequently, training will be more effective when done under relatively relaxed conditions. Needless to say, this is a perennial problem for the military. Because much of training in the military context aims at preparing the soldier to perform well under highly stressful conditions, the question is whether to attempt to simulate the stressful component of a situation as well as possible or to train for stress in essentially nonstressful situations.

It should be mentioned that when training for stress under highly stressful circumstances, this so-called "realistic training" poses some difficulties from the point of view of our analysis of the FAE. No matter how hard one tries to simulate the conditions of real battle, the training situation cannot produce the single most important element of stress, namely, the fact that people are wounded or killed. From this point of view, then, realistic training attempts to approach the stress situation without at the same time successfully producing the active element of the stress itself. By being exposed to this kind of training one actually goes through what is presumably a dangerous situation without ever being seriously harmed. In other words, the training itself produces a FAE. The soldier may reach the wrong conclusion that certain precautions need not be taken too seriously because, after all, from his own experience, nothing truly dangerous ever took place. This effect may turn out to be particularly strong when there is an attempt to reach a high verisimilitude of stress during training. In the absence of such simulated proximity, the psychological jump from the training situation to the real stress situation is not so easily made, and consequently, the FAE is probably smaller. This paradoxical outcome is particularly hazardous when viewed from the point of view of protective behavior. Whenever such protective behavior is costly and implies complex patterns of action often requiring a great deal of time and effort, there is the possibility that based on training experiences the person will learn that these protective behaviors need not be performed meticulously and properly.

The introduction into the system of an unrelated task that a person must perform well is another strong element in exactly the same direction. If during realistic training one finds out that protective behavior often comes at some cost to task performance, this further reduces the motivation to engage in it in the future.

Performance is often seen related to stress by an inverted U-shaped function (Cofer & Appley, 1964). Thus, according to the Yerkes-Dodson Law, performance is best under an optimal level of arousal, which is higher in simple as compared to complex tasks. Several theoretical explanations have been offered for this phenomenon based on drive theory (Spielberger, 1975), signal detection theory (Welford, 1968, 1976), effort and allocation of attention (Kahneman, 1973), and attentional selectivity models (Wachtel, 1967). Our particular interest in this context is the frequently seen phenomenon of degradation of performance under highly stressful conditions. Thus, drive theory assigns performance decrements to activation of competing error tendencies by high-drive level, whereas according to signal detection theory, error tendencies result as a consequence of information overload leading to increased noise in the information-processing systems. Models of attentional selectivity deal with the effects of focusing of attention on a smaller number of cues associated with a particular task. Consequently, under mild degrees of stress, performance on tasks seen as central improves, whereas peripheral stimuli are ignored (Baddeley, 1972). Highly stressful conditions result in an increasing narrowing of the attentional field so that even relevant cues may remain unattended. Wachtel (1967) claims that under such narrowed-attention conditions, no stable orientation toward the environment can be maintained. This leads to increased scanning, reduction of one's ability to integrate informational cues, and finally to disorganized behavior.

Although empirical research has concentrated mainly on the effects of stress on performance (Broadbent, 1971; Cofer & Appley, 1964; Lazarus, Deese, & Osler, 1952), the effects of training of a task on subsequent performance under stress have not been thoroughly investigated. The main efforts in the area of training have concentrated on performance of trained personnel in the stress situation (Hammerton & Tickner, 1969; Ruff & Korchin, 1967). In addition, amount of training on a task (Bergstroem, 1970) and kind of training (Prather, 1969) were sometimes manipulated.

The main purpose of the first part of the present experiment was to investigate the effects of training under relatively relaxed versus stressful conditions on performance of various visual search tasks under stress. Because visual search tasks demand the full attention of the subject in order to perform quickly and correctly, it is difficult to specify the mechanisms by which training can facilitate performance on such tasks. Thus, experience might allow the subject to test certain scanning strategies, and familiarity as such could also be helpful.

Training can take place under relaxed conditions, prior to the stress situation, or under conditions more similar to the stressful conditions. A prevalent view based on generalization principles of learning maintains that training effectiveness is a function of the degree of similarity between the training and testing situations respectively. The applicability of this general principle to stress situations remains to be demonstrated, however.

Another related issue concerns the effects of stress and training on tasks that differ in demands imposed on search strategies and difficulty of target detection. Thus, the present research employed three kinds of visual search tasks. System-

TABLE 10.1
Experimental Design

Group	Training of Task	Training of Protective Behavior
1	Yes	No
2	Yes	No
3	Yes	No
4	Yes	Yes
5	No	Yes
C	No	No

atic search, which is characterized by routine requirements (i.e., performance should follow prescribed rules) (Task A), and nonsystematic search, which allows greater freedom for discovery of effective strategies. In addition, in the latter task, target appearance is either frequent (Task B) or rare (Task C). Thus, the differences between Tasks A and B lie in the demands imposed on the way the search is to be performed, whereas Tasks B and C differ in difficulty of target detection. It is hypothesized that the routine nature of Task A will make it less sensitive to stress effects than Tasks B and C.

Another important question concerns the way FAEs influence performance. It has been shown that FAEs reduce both fear and instrumental avoidance. If fear causes deterioration in task performance, then following a false alarm, task performance should improve.

The second part of this experiment deals with the investigation of the effect of training the protective behavior itself upon the various response channels. In view of the simplicty of the protective behavior, training in this context consists of establishing a routine checklist of all features of the apparatus related to protective behavior. The routine is trained and executed before the beginning of each session, and thus does not interfere with whatever takes place during the anticipation proper. This arrangement made it possible to test its effects on task performance, as well as on the psychophysiological responses and the protective behavior itself.

Consequently, both parts of this experiment could be carried out using the general design presented in Table 10.1. The differences between Groups 1, 2, and 3 relate to the different training conditions relevant to Part One of this experiment.

PART ONE:
TASK PERFORMANCE AND TRAINING

The laboratory setting and apparatus were the same as in the previous experiments.

Stimuli and Tasks

Two different number displays were prepared:

1. Ordered Display—360 pairs of numbers were printed on a page in an orderly fashion arranged in 15 columns. The numbers consisted of all pairs of numbers between 00 and 99, each pair appearing three or four times in random places along the 15 columns.
2. Random Display—The aforementioned pairs of numbers were used, but this time they were distributed randomly across the page (see Appendix B for examples of the two pages).

Three different tasks were constructed on the basis of these displays:

Task A—ordered search for a one-digit number in an ordered display. In this task the subject was required to search through the columns in an orderly fashion, beginning from the rightmost column and going through each column from top to bottom. The one-digit target number was written above the rightmost column marked with an X. Subjects were required to count their hits by noting the serial number of each hit (see Appendix C for detailed instructions for each task).

Task B—free search for a one-digit number in a random display. In this task subjects were asked to search for the one-digit number written at the center of the page. Again they were asked to write the sequential number of each hit. This task differs from the first in its requirements for nonsystematic search but is identical to it in the number of targets available.

Task C—free search for a pair of digits in a random display. In this task subjects were asked to find three instances of a designated pair of digits written at the center of the page and mark them with the numbers 1, 2, and 3 according to the order in which they find them. This task is more difficult than Task B because of the scarcity of targets.

Design

The experimental design consists of three groups of 21 subjects, identical in stress and false alarm conditions, but different in the amount and type of task training:

Group 1—training in a relaxed situation. Subjects in this group were instructed about the three different tasks required during the experiment and actually performed two of the tasks prior to any knowledge about the nature of the impending stress. Following threat instructions, subjects were required to perform the same two visual search tasks, once during the first warning period (A) and once during the last warning period (C) of the first session. The second session was identical to the first. In the last session subjects were asked to perform a different task four times during Warnings A and C. (The kind of tasks performed at each stage are explained later.)

Group 2—Training in a stress situation. This group was indentical to Group 1 in procedure apart from the fact that subjects did not perform the two tasks prior to the experiment but were only instructed about the nature of the tasks. Thus, the first actual performance of the tasks was done during Warning A of the first session, and this is considered to be training in a stress condition, the effects of which can be tested on subsequent performance in Warning C. In addition, this group consitutes a control group for Group 1, because first performance during Warning A can be compared with performance on the same Warning A following pretraining in relaxed conditions.

Group 3—no training. Subjects were instructed as to the nature of the tasks required but actually performed the tasks only during Warning C in the first and second sessions. Thus, Group 3 was a control group for Group 2. In the third session they performed a new task four times, during Warnings A and C, as in Groups 1 and 2. Following the termination of the experiment, all subjects performed the three tasks once more.

It was thought best that subjects would perform tasks only during Warnings A and C of each trial, because during these periods the fear reaction is particularly high. Each such period lasts for 1 minute, and each task is performed for 30 seconds. Therefore, only two tasks could be performed during each warning period. As we were interested in the performance of three different tasks, each group of subjects was divided into three subgroups, with each subgroup performing only two tasks during training and Sessions 1 and 2 and performing the third task during Session 3. The three tasks used were: Task A—ordered search for one-digit number in an ordered display; Task B—free search for one-digit in a random display; Task C—free search for a pair of digits in a random display. The division into subgroups according to tasks performed and the actual performance of tasks in each group at each stage of the experiment appear in Table 10.2.

For each group and subgroup specific booklets were arranged containing instructions and tasks to be performed. Each type of task included the same display of numbers, but differed in the target number. Because target numbers may differ in the difficulty with which they can be found, number effects were controlled for by arranging sequences according to a Latin Square design in Group 1. Groups 2 and 3 were assigned the same sequences, but these were shorter in view of the fact that subjects in these groups performed fewer tasks.

Following the manual reading of the pulse, the subject was given a booklet containing instructions for the required performance of each kind of visual search task and a number of pages arranged according to the group and subgroup to which he was allocated. Subjects were randomly allocated to groups and sub-

10. PERFORMANCE, TRAINING, PROTECTIVE BEHAVIOR

TABLE 10.2
Division into Groups and Subgroups According to Task Performance

Warnings	Training before Experiment	Session 1 A B C	Session 2 A B C	Session 3 A B C	Following the Experiment
Group 1					
Subgroup BA	BA	BA – BA	BA – BA	CC – CC	B A C
Subgroup BC	BC	BC – BC	BC – BC	AA – AA	B A C
Subgroup AC	AC	AC – AC	AC – AC	BB – BB	B A C
Group 2					
Subgroup BA	–	BA – BA	BA – BA	CC – CC	B A C
Subgroup BC	–	BC – BC	BC – BC	AA – AA	B A C
Subgroup AC	–	AC – AC	AC – AC	BB – BB	B A C
Group 3					
Subgroup BA	–	– – BA	– – BA	CC – CC	B A C
Subgroup BC	–	– – BC	– – BC	AA – AA	B A C
Subgroup AC	–	– – AC	– – AC	BB – BB	B A C

Note: A—Task A; B—Task B; C—Task C.

groups with the constraint that each nine consecutive subjects represented one full crosscut of the experimental design.

All subjects read the instructions and performed the tasks appearing on the instruction page. Subjects were instructed about the nature and requirements of the various tasks. They were promised a monetary reward for each hit and penalties for mistakes in Task A.[1] (The complete instructions appear in Appendix C.) After the subject read the instructions, the experimenter presented him with three examples, one for each task, and explained verbally the various task requirements until he was satisfied that the subject understood the differences between the tasks. Subsequently, subjects allocated to Group 1 actually performed two tasks once according to the subgroup to which they were allocated. Each task was performed for 30 seconds, timed by a stopwatch. Subjects allocated to Groups 2 and 3 did not perform any tasks at that stage.

At this point the subject was asked to give a statement to the effect that he was in good health. The subject signed this statement before proceeding with the experiment. The usual practice of attaching the subject to the polygraph followed. The stress instructions were also the usual ones.

---

[1]The subjects in this study were soldiers. Soldiers are not allowed to receive money from civilian sources, so it was arranged that for all money gained a present would be bought for the unit. This arrangement was explained to each subject.

PART ONE: TASK PERFORMANCE AND TRAINING   137

Following the threat instructions and the explanation of the avoidance procedure, subjects received instructions pertaining to the visual search task:

> During the experiment you will perform the number search task. The booklet containing the number pages is in front of you. When a "start" signal is given, turn the first page and start marking the number appearing on the page, beginning at the point marked X, in accordance with previous instructions. Perform quickly and accurately. When the "stop" signal is given, stop the search, turn the page over, and when an additional "start" signal is given, turn the white page and move to the next task. Are there any questions?

Following this, additional instructions were given in order to present the subject with the various options pertaining to performance and avoidance:

> Keep in mind—you were told that during the experiment you may reduce the shock intensity by pressing the foot switch and that you will be given a number search task. If you want to reduce shock intensity, you may stop searching or perform the search at a slower rate. If because of reducing shock intensity you stop the search or perform more slowly, you will gain less, but the shock intensity will be lower. If you perform quickly and do not reduce shock intensity, you will gain more, but then you will get a shock of the highest intensity. What you do depends solely upon your own considerations.

Immediately following the threat instructions, the first warning (A) was issued by the red signal going on and off once. Subjects in Groups 1 and 2 were told immediately following that signal to turn a white page and start the search for the target. Two tasks were performed during Warning A, each lasting 30 seconds. Subjects in Group 3 were not given any tasks during Warning A. Warning A lasted for 1 minute (plus a few seconds required for turning the pages in Groups 1 and 2), at the end of which the second warning (B) was issued. It too lasted for 1 minute, terminated by the last warning (C). At this period, all subjects were given two tasks to perform. For Groups 1 and 2 these were the same tasks as those performed during Warning A, and subjects in Group 3 performed the two tasks for the first time. One minute after the onset of C the first threat was canceled through the usual prerecorded cancellation instructions.

The three warning signals of the second session now followed, each lasting for 1 minute, and the same tasks were performed as in the first session. Then came the second cancellation. The instructions at this stage of the experiment were worded exactly the same as in the first cancellation. The relaxation period of 2 minutes was followed by the third and last threat. The instructions were the exact repetition of the second threat instructions. However, during the third session, all subjects performed the same task four times, during Warnings A and C, and this task was the one that was never performed during previous sessions. The third warning in the sequence was terminated by the third and final cancellation. Following the recovery from the stress, subjects once more performed each of the tasks.

In addition to the usual postexperimental questionnaire, there was a second questionnaire, which dealt with those features of the experiment pertaining to task performance (see Appendix D).

RESULTS

Visual Search Tasks

Several comparisons were made of measures of visual search tasks in order to test hypotheses relating to effects of training under relaxed and stressful conditions on subsequent performance and the influence of stress and FAE on performance:

1. The effect of training under relaxed conditions (i.e., before the nature of stress was revealed to the subject) was tested by comparing performance of Groups 1 and 2 during Warnings A and C in Sessions 1 and 2.
2. The effect of training under the highly stressful conditions (i.e., during Warning A, Session 1) was tested by comparing performance of Groups 2 and 3 during Warning C in Sessions 1 and 2.
3. The effect of stress on performance was tested by comparing performance of experimental groups with that of a group of subjects who performed the same tasks while not under stress. This group is named Group C.
4. The effects of false alarms on performance cannot be tested directly, because they are confounded with training effects. Performance during the third session, however, can be compared with Group C performance and with performance of the same tasks during the first session.

Analyses of variance with repeated measures on sessions and warnings were used. In the case of unequal group size, the unweighted means solution was applied (Winer, 1971). A few subjects who apparently did not understand the difference between Tasks B and C were excluded from the analysis.

Task A (Systemtic Search)

Correct Responses. Average performance for each group at each stage of the experiment in which the task was performed is presented in Fig. 10.2. Figure 10.2a presents performance before stress (B.S.) during Sessions 1 and 2 and after stress is over (A.S.). In addition, the performance of Group C on four trials is depicted. Figure 10.2b presents performance of those subjects who performed the task during Sessions 3 for the first time together with Group C performance.

A comparison of Groups 1 and 2 on performance during Sessions 1 and 2, Warnings A and C revealed a significant effect for sessions only, $F = 5.96$, $df =$

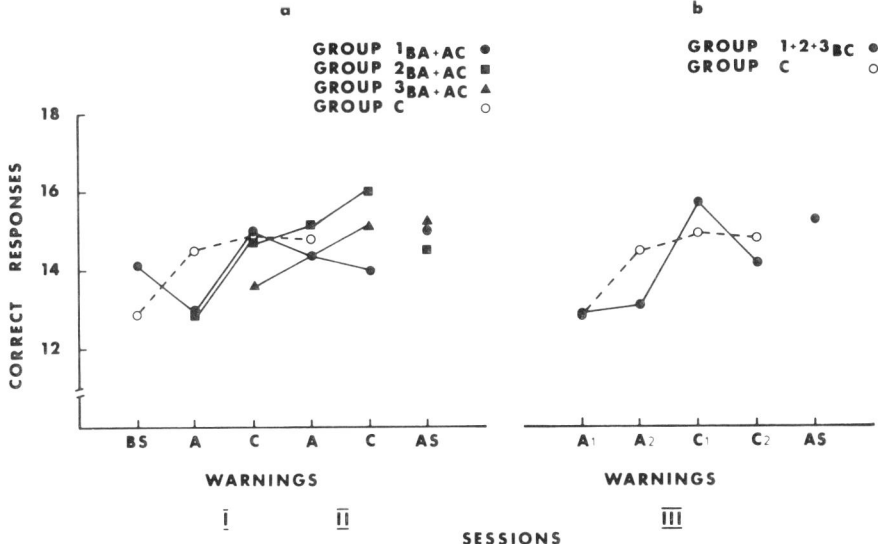

FIG. 10.2   Means of correct responses for Task A according to groups, sessions, and warnings: (a) Sessions 1 and 2; (b) Session 3.

$1/26$, $p < .05$.[2] No differences were found between groups or between warnings, and none of the interactions were significant. A comparison of Groups 2 and 3 on performance during Warning C in Sessions 1 and 2 again revealed a significant effect for sessions only, $F = 7.50$, $df = 1/26$, $p < .05$. No differences were found between groups, and no interaction was found between groups and sessions. These results suggest that performance on Task A under stress is not influenced by differential amounts of training.

As our control group performed less well on its first trial as compared to Group 1, it is difficult to assess the effects of stress on Task A performance. Comparing, however, the first performance of the three experimental groups showed no differences among them, $F < 1$, nor was a significant difference found between first and second performance on Group 1, $t = .90$, $n = 14$. Thus, these results suggest that performance on Task A is not sensitive to effects of stress. This conclusion is also supported by the findings concerning effects of false alarms on Task A performance.

Turning to FAEs, we first compared performance of Group 2 on Warning A, Session 1, with first performance during Session 3. No differences were found between the two groups, $F < 1$. In a comparison between performance of Group

---

[2]Means standard deviations of performance, and tables of analyses of variance are presented in Appendix E.

C and performance during Session 3, no differences between groups were found, $F < 1$.

To sum up, when using correct responses as the measure of performance, the systematic search required in Task A was found to be insensitive to effects of stress, differential effects of training, and FAE.

Speed. Average performance according to groups, sessions, and warnings is presented in Fig. 10.3. The pattern of results using speed as the measure of performance is quite similar to that of correct responses. However, it seems that the differences between the groups are more accentuated. Thus, analysis of variance performed on Group 1 and 2 scores revealed a significant effect for session, $F = 11.50$, $df = 1/26$, $p < .01$, and two interactions were significant: the interaction between groups and sessions, $F = 5.94$, $df = 1/26$, $p < .05$, and between sessions and warnings, $F = 7.75$, $df = 1/26$, $p < .01$. Improvement in performance from Warning A to C is greater in Session 1 and in 2. In addition, Group 2 performs on Session 2 much better than on 1, whereas in Group 1 there is only a limited improvement between sessions. Comparing Group 2 and 3 performance again revealed the significant effect of sessions only, $F = 16.48$, $df = 1/25$, $p < .001$.

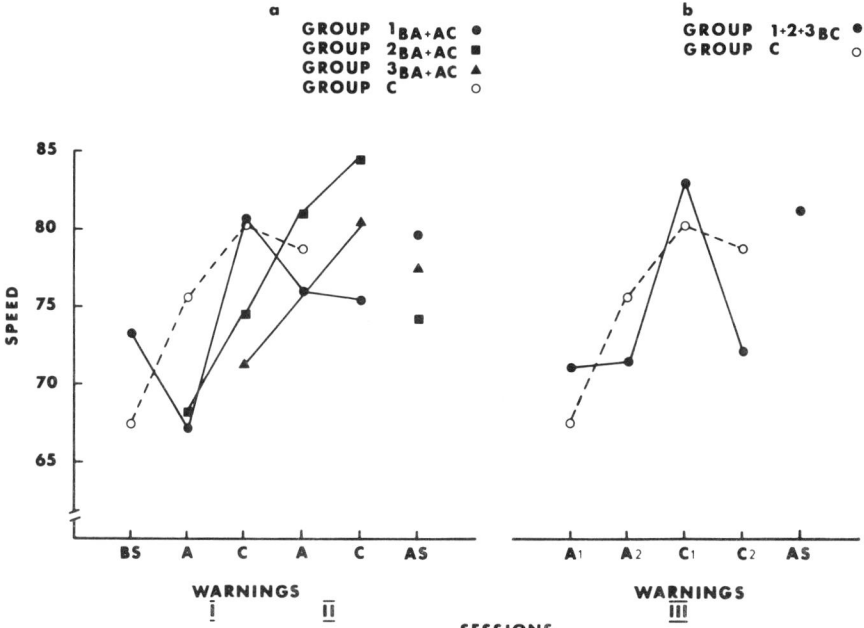

FIG. 10.3 Means of speed measure for Task A according to groups, sessions, and warnings: (a) Session 1 and 2; (b) Session 3.

RESULTS 141

Comparisons between Group C and Groups 1 and 2 on their first four trials show similar results to those obtained with the measure of correct responses. Thus, the results of the two measures are quite similar. This is not surprising in light of the high correlations between the two measures throughout the experiment, $r = .68–.90$.

Errors. Errors in this task are exclusively errors of omission (i.e., skipping the target number). Generally, only a few subjects made a few errors. Comparisons among groups on the number of errors made in each stage of the experiment did not reveal any significant effect, nor were any differences found between experimental groups and Group C.

Task B (Nonsystematic Search)

Average performance for each experimental group (and Group C) at each stage of the experiment in which the task was performed is presented in Fig. 10.4. The comparison between Groups 1 and 2 on performance during Warnings A and C, Sessions 1 and 2, revealed a significant effect for groups, $F = 6.12$, $df = 1/26$, $p < .05$. Thus, Group 1, which had one training trial before performing under stress, performed better under the stressful condition than did Group 2.

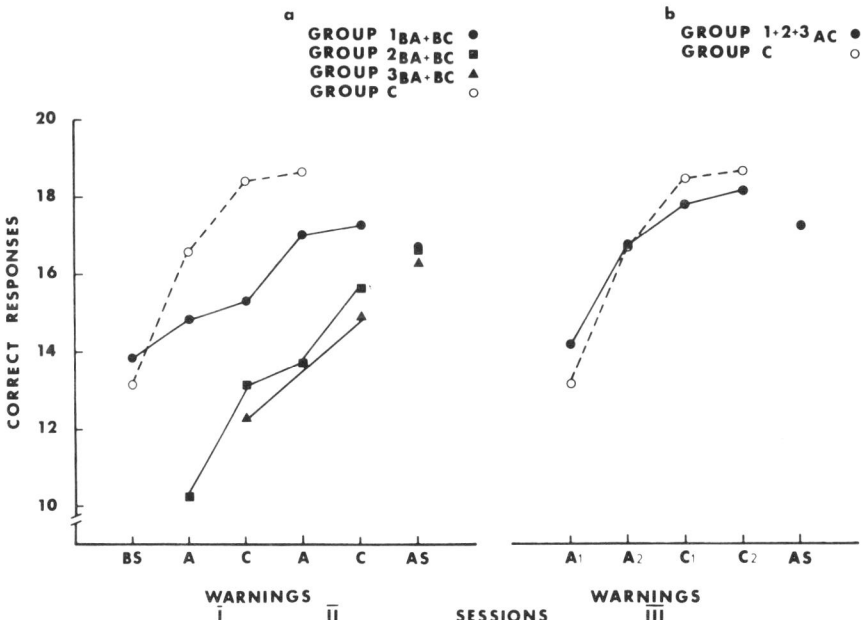

FIG. 10.4 Means of correct responses for Task B according to groups, sessions, and warnings: (a) Sessions 1 and 2; (b) Session 3.

The effects of sessions and warnings were also found to be significant, $F = 21.67$, $df = 1/26$, $p < .001$; $F = 13.89$, $df = 1/26$, $p < .005$, correspondingly. Thus, the two groups performed better on Session 2 than 1, and on Warning C than A. The interaction between groups and warnings, however, was also found to be significant, $F = 7.68$, $df = 1/26$, $p < .05$. Thus, subjects in Group 2 perform better during Warning C versus A as compared to subjects in Group 1. No other significant interactions were found, $F < 1$.

The comparisons between experimental groups and Group C support these results. Comparing Group 1 and Group C performance on the first four trials revealed a significant effect for trials only, $F = 11.67$, $df = 3/450$, $p < .001$, but no difference was found between groups, $F = 2.07$, $df = 1/150$, n.s.. In contrast, the comparison between Group 2 and Group C revealed apart from the effect of trials, $F = 18.88$, $df = 3/450$, $p < .001$, a significant effect for groups, $F = 12.08$, $df = 1/150$, $p < .001$.

FAEs are evident in the performance of Task B. The comparison between first performance in Session 3 and first performance of Group 2 has shown a significant difference between the two groups, $(F = 9.36$, $df = 1/26$, $p < .01$. No differences were found between Group C performance and performance during Session 3, $F < 1$, and there was no significant interaction between groups and trials.

Task C

Average performance for each group at each stage of the experiment in which the task was performed in presented in Fig. 10.5. Analyses of Task C results indicated that it is insensitive to effects of training, stress, or false alarms.

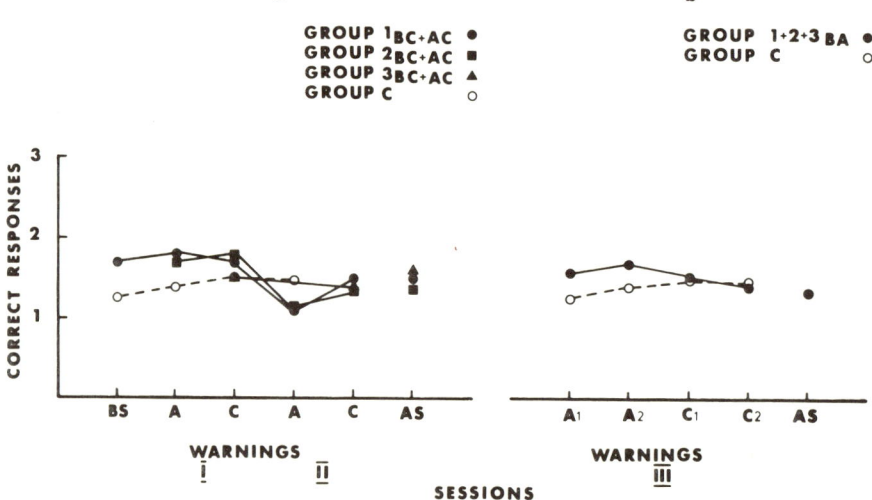

FIG. 10.5 Means of correct responses for Task C according to groups, sessions, and warnings: (a) Sessions 1 and 2; (b) Session 3.

Summary of Results on Task Performance

1. Systematic search, as required by Task A, did not benefit from training. Performance on this task was also unaffected by the induction of anticipatory stress. The relatively simple nature of this task as well as its routinization make it relatively resistant to both positive manipulations (training) and negative ones (stress). A well-developed routine by necessity reduces the intersituational variability, with the possible exception of speed of performance, as suggested by our results. Needless to say, performance that is essentially unsensitive to stress cannot at the same time be meaningfully influenced by the FAE.

2. By contrast, Task B performance was facilitated by training, if done under the relatively relaxed conditions prior to the onset of the threat. Training under stress did not lead to better performance. This fits well with the finding that stress had a clear detrimental effect on Task B performance. The impending danger impaired the "spontaneous" screening process, perhaps by narrowing the subjects' attention (Wachtel, 1967) or reducing their ability to make quick, fine discriminations (Kahneman, 1973). This negative effect of stress on performance is analogous to "suppression" of responses as reported in studies of punishment (Deese & Hulse, 1967). While the stress is operative, the performance level is reduced, and its termination leads to a return to the earlier prestress levels. Training under relatively relaxed conditions also protects the performance from the deleterious effects of stress to some extent.

3. Task B performance increased due to the FAE following the cancellation of the anticipated danger. The by now well-documented reduced fear reaction following a cancellation leads to reduced stress and consequently to better performance.

4. The foregoing results and discussion indicate that it may be useful to categorize tasks according to their intertrial lability and sensitivity to situational and motivational requirements. High sensitivity implies the possibility of both facilitation through training and performance decrement due to stress. Tasks that stand to gain the most by training are, in my view, also the candidates for a major deficit due to stress, and vice versa. It appears that in order to be relatively protected from the negative effects of stress, tasks should be *highly routinized*. Although not all tasks lend themselves to high levels of routinization, the possibility of increasing the routine elements should always be explored if the risks of exposure to stress are reasonably high.

The Effects of Task Performance on Fear Reaction

Before embarking on the analysis of the potential impact of task performance on fear reaction, a word of caution is needed. When studying performance, which implies arousal, the usage of psychophysiological indexes as sole indicators of

144 10. PERFORMANCE, TRAINING, PROTECTIVE BEHAVIOR

stress is particularly problematic. In their paper on the role of activity in anticipating stressful situations, Gal and Lazarus (1975) stated this danger explicitly: "the elevated physiological reactions exhibited by the active subjects can be interpreted as reflecting merely the body arousal that accompanies any overt activity [p. 11]."

The effects of task performance on fear should thus be tested using the entire spectrum of response channels available to us. The analysis proceeds in two stages. First we utilize the information based upon the three groups of subjects tested in Part One of this experiment, and then we proceed to look into the effects of task performance by utilizing all comparable groups tested so far.

Heart Rate

To increase the comparability between groups, we computed the Heart Rate High (HRH) minus HRH during the base-line period (HRH-BL). Figure 10.6 presents means of HRH-BL for each group according to sessions and warnings.

The results of analysis of variance with repeated measures on sessions and warnings are presented in Table 10.3, which shows that although there are no overall differences between the three groups, there is an interaction between groups, warnings, and sessions. Inspection of Fig. 10.6 reveals that subjects in Group 1 during Session 1, Warning A, are more aroused than subjects in Group 2, who are more aroused than those in Group 3, and in Warning C, subjects in

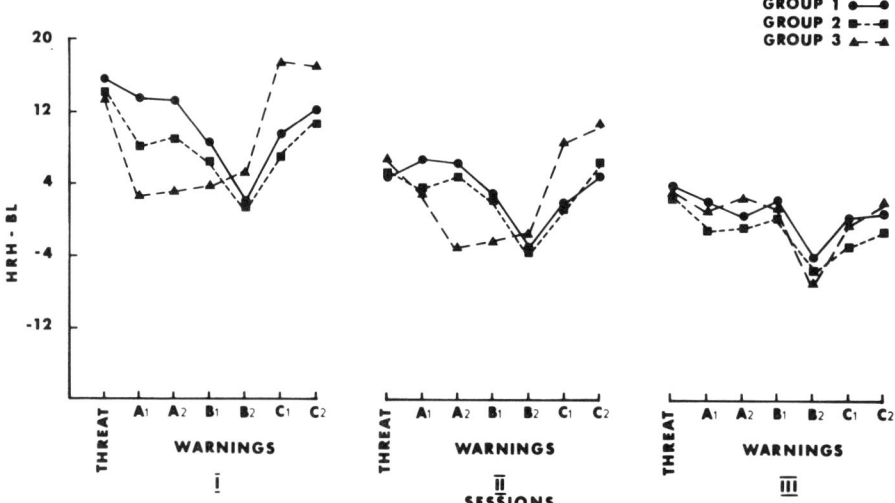

FIG. 10.6 Means of heart rate high—heart rate high base line for experimental groups according to sessions and warnings.

RESULTS

TABLE 10.3
Results of Analysis of Variance on HRH-BL

	df	MS	F	p
Groups	2	350.99	<1	
SwG	60	1430.67		
Sessions	2	9621.63	110.80	<.001
Groups × Sessions	4	50.60	<1	
Sessions × SwG	120	86.84		
Warnings	6	1783.47	48.33	<.001
Groups × Warnings	12	342.60	8.65	<.001
Warnings × SwG	360	39.60		
Sessions × Warnings	12	181.53	7.53	<.001
Groups × Sessions × Warnings	24	120.26	4.99	<.001
Sessions × Warnings × SwG	720	24.11		

Group 3 are most aroused. A similar but reduced effect is seen in Session 2, whereas in Session 3 there are no differences between the three groups. Thus it would seem that amount of training before stress elevates arousal under stress.

In order to obtain additional information about the possible functions involved, we ran an additional group of seven subjects (Group C_{BA}) who performed exactly like Group 1, subgroup BA, but without the threat of impending shock. The results of this group and of Group 1_{BA} are presented in Fig. 10.7. As can be seen the patterns of response of the two groups are very similar, apart from the fact that Group 1_{BA} is higher than Group C_{BA} at all stages of the experiment. Thus it appears that arousal during the experiment is a simple

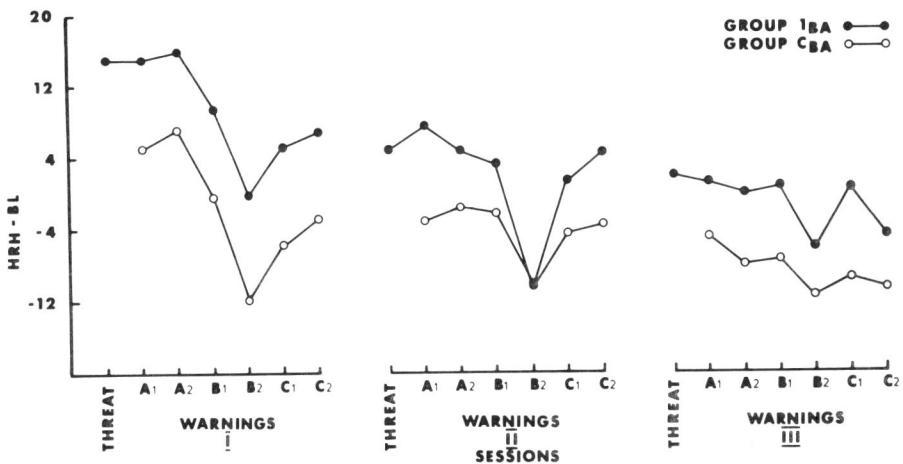

FIG. 10.7 Means of heart rate high—heart rate high base line for Groups 1_{BA} and C_{BA}.

summation of two effects: fear reaction stemming from threat of impending shock and arousal due to performance of the task. This last point is best observed when comparing the level of arousal during Warnings A and C, which include task performance, with arousal during Warning B when no task is performed.

It is conceivable that training reduces the attentional demands, and hence the subjects' preoccupation with the task, and leads to increased attention to the threat of impending shock. By contrast, subjects who are less familiar with the task are more task oriented than danger oriented.

This explanation is particularly plausible in view of the fact that the arousal component reflecting task performance should *decrease* following training on the task. The finding that the heart rate *increases* more in groups that experienced prior training thus cannot be accounted for within the context of task-related arousal and reflects the threat-related fear reaction. Because we have no way to measure these two components independently, we can only assume that the growing danger orientation and its consequent increased fear reaction following training with the task are actually higher than observed in our data.

Comparison Between Groups with Task and Without Task

In order to measure the possible effects of task performance on the various response channels, it is worthwhile to combine the data from all the groups studied so far. Thus, we have twelve groups that provide data relevant to our question. Out of those twelve groups, eight participated in the experiment without performing any task during the anticipation proper, whereas four had to perform a visual search task while waiting for the threatened danger to materialize. Even though the various groups differ from each other on many dimensions, which have been analyzed earlier in this book, there is an advantage in grouping them together and testing for the difference due to task performance, because only if there are robust effects, which distinguish between these two broad categories, would they be able to overcome the other factors. This is not a "clean" way to investigate the impact of task performance on fear or protective behavior, but it might very well be the most economic one. If in spite of all the differences between these groups a clear-cut phenomenon can still be discovered, this would make it worthwhile to invest further in this direction.

The effect of task performance on heart rate was tested by calculating the net heart rate for all subjects for the various sessions and warnings. These net scores were obtained by taking the heart rate high for each session and warning and deducting from it the highest heart rate obtained during the prestress instructions base line. Analysis of variance between groups with task and groups without task established that on the whole the net heart rate is higher when there is a task to perform. This difference reaches significance particularly during the last segment of each session, namely, Warning C. Table 10.4 presents the data, which clearly

TABLE 10.4
The Effect of Task Performance on Net Heart Rate During Warning C

	Session 1				
	Mean	*sd*	*MS*	*F*	*p*
Task	13.46	11.68	1222	7.98	<.01
No Task	8.73	12.73			

	Session 2				
	Mean	*sd*	*MS*	*F*	*p*
Task	7.32	10.12	2067	17.00	<.001
No Task	1.16	11.49			

	Session 3				
	Mean	*sd*	*MS*	*F*	*p*
Task	1.95	9.41	981	8.46	<.01
No Task	−2.29	11.43			

indicate that the heart-rate channel is positively influenced by the introduction of task performance. In this connection, it should be mentioned that the now classical findings of Lacey, Kagan, Lacey, and Moss (1963)—that attention to external cues reduces heart rate—are not in conflict with our findings. Whereas heart-rate deceleration is typically obtained a few seconds prior to an anticipated stimulus, the acceleration reported here refers to the entire period during which subjects are preoccupied with the task. This is in line with Gal and Lazarus' (1975) analysis of the effects of performance on physiological responses. The task performance itself increases the heart rate without implying that this is necessarily an additional source of stress.

Indeed, if one takes the subjects' subjective report concerning the effect of task performance on fear, an entirely different picture emerges. In the postexperimental questionnaire, which we usually give following the last cancellation of the threat, a specific question was introduced dealing with the subjects' own ideas about the possible interrelations between task performance and fear reaction. Subjects were explicitly asked whether performance reduces fear, increases fear, or does not affect it in any way. Another question dealt with the influence of fear on performance: whether fear enhances performance, decreases it, or does not affect it in any way. Table 10.5 presents the distribution of responses to these

TABLE 10.5
Frequency of Answers to Postexperimental Questions Concerning
Fear, Protective Behavior, and Performance

Question				χ^2	df	p
7. performance influence on fear	more fear 5	no change 35	less fear 23	21.71	2	<.01
8. fear influence on performance	better 4	no change 42	worse 15	37.02	2	<.01

two questions. It shows that from the subjective point of view of subjects who participated in this experiment, not only does fear significantly reduce performance, but performance is seen as significantly reducing fear. Thus, the conclusion whether performance increases or decreases fear reaction depends on the particular response channel that is being used to measure the effect. Whereas in the heart-rate channel there was an increase due to performance, the subjective evaluations tend to indicate a decrease. Differences in reported tension during the various stages of the experiment also tend to indicate that task reduced the

TABLE 10.6
The Effect of Task Performance on Distraction

	Session 1				
	Mean	*sd*	*MS*	*F*	*p*
Task	59.35	32.42	23,461	25.78	<.001
No Task	37.01	28.75			

	Session 2				
	Mean	*sd*	*MS*	*F*	*p*
Task	64.72	31.96	17,759	21.06	<.001
No Task	45.67	27.36			

	Session 3				
	Mean	*sd*	*MS*	*F*	*p*
Task	64.38	33.72	6630	6.66	<.01
No Task	52.72	30.29			

subjective tension, even though these differences did not reach statistical significance.

In order to explicate this problem further, we have looked into the responses concerning distraction. The reader may recall that there were specific questions in which the subjects were asked to estimate the percentage of time during which they did not think of the approaching danger while they were waiting for the threat to materialize. These measures of distraction should be related to task performance. If the additional cognitive load requiring the subjects to attend to the task increases their task orientation, and consequently decreases the danger orientation, this should be reflected in responses to the distraction questions. Because task performance required attention, and thus produced distraction of its own, subjects should be expected to report that more time was spent thinking of issues unrelated to the danger in groups that performed the task than in groups that did not. Table 10.6 provides the analysis of variance for these data. The table indicates that the effects on distraction of the introduction of task performance are highly significant for all three sessions and are in line with our previous reasoning. This finding adds plausibility to the notion that task performance competes with the threat instructions for the attention of the subjects in our experiments.

TABLE 10.7
The Effect of Task Performance on Time Estimation

	Session 1				
	Mean	*sd*	*MS*	*F*	*p*
Task	2.67	2.75	340	5.58	<.05
No Task	1.84	2.33			

	Session 2				
	Mean	*sd*	*MS*	*F*	*p*
Task	3.05	2.99	733	12.22	<.001
No Task	1.81	2.26			

	Session 3				
	Mean	*sd*	*MS*	*F*	*p*
Task	2.92	3.00	718	11.65	<.001
No Task	1.79	2.18			

Another indirect way to study this effect is provided by information about subjective time estimation. Following Ornstein's (1969) analysis, we have postulated elsewhere in this volume that time estimation should reflect the amount of information that was processed during the period that is being judged. It follows that if task performance acts as a distractor from the main threat, it ought to provide information that is processed by the subject anticipating the danger. The need to process this additional information should lead to overestimation of the durations involved compared with subjects who were not preoccupied by this additional task requirement. The information on time estimation appears in Table 10.7, which clearly lends support to the foregoing analysis. Although the mean estimated durations are on the whole below the actual time (3 minutes), there are significant differences between task and no-task groups. Those subjects who had to attend to the additional task perceived the duration of time spent while anticipating the danger as much longer than those who did not have the task. Thus, the task can be seen as a distractor and as an attentional focus that reduces the danger orientation.

TABLE 10.8
The Effect of Task Performance on Credibility of the Threat

	Session 1				
	Mean	sd	MS	F	p
Task	.37	1.31	15.24	11.04	<.001
No Task	.90	1.09			

	Session 2				
	Mean	sd	MS	F	p
Task	−.39	1.20	9.16	6.84	<.01
No Task	.03	1.14			

	Session 3				
	Mean	sd	MS	F	p
Task	−.73	1.26	0.36	<1	n.s.
No Task	−.65	1.19			

TABLE 10.9
Probability of Protective Behavior According to
Groups and Sessions

Sessions	1	2	3
Group 1	.38	.33	.33
Group 2	.24	.24	.24
Group 3	.33	.29	.29

One of the consequences of this process is that the credibility of the threat itself is reduced by the introduction of the task. Inasmuch as the subjects are less attentive to the threat and less frightened of the impending danger, the preoccupation with the visual search task reduces the credibility itself. Table 10.8 provides information for the three sessions. The effect is significant in the first two sessions. Following two false alarms, the credibility of the third threat is so low that the additional impact of task performance does not reach statistical significance. This supports the notion that by introducing the task into the anticipation period proper, the overall impact of the danger is significantly reduced. The fear reaction is lower, there is more distraction and subjects can spend more time thinking of other things, the subjective tension is somewhat reduced, the time seems longer, and the credibility of the threat itself is perceived as smaller. All these are indexes of essentially the same basic effect, namely, that subjects orient themselves to the task rather than to the danger.

This now brings us to the issue of the impact of task performance on protective behavior. If the analysis is theoretically sound thus far, we should predict that task orientation by reducing the danger orientation should also lead to a reduction in protective behavior itself.

TABLE 10.10
Means of Amplitude of Protective Behavior According to
Groups and Sessions

	All Subjects				Protective Behavior > 0 Only		
Sessions	1	2	3		1	2	3
Group 1	6.19	4.95	4.57	Group 1 ($n=9$)	14.44	11.56	10.67
Group 2	6.38	5.81	4.86	Group 2 ($N=5$)	26.80	24.40	20.40
Group 3	5.76	4.14	3.81	Group 3 ($N=7$)	17.29	12.43	11.43

TABLE 10.11
The Effect of Task Performance on Probability of Protective Behavior

Session	Task	No Task	p
1	.37	.74	<.01
2	.31	.71	<.01
3	.33	.63	<.01

The Effects of Task Performance on Protective Behavior

After the experiment, when subjects were asked whether the task had any influence on their tendency to reduce the intensity of the shock, 93% of the subjects claimed that no such influence took place. The remaining 7% were equally distributed between those who claimed that task performance should increase protective behavior and those who thought the opposite. Thus, contrary to our earlier issue here, our subjects' intuitive theory does not predict any effect at all. With this in mind let us now look at the actual behavior. Table 10.9 presents the distribution of the probability of protective behavior according to groups and sessions, and Table 10.10 provides the means of the amplitude of protective behavior for all subjects and for those that engaged in protective behavior only.

Although no significant differences between Groups 1, 2, and 3 can be seen, both the probability of protective behavior and its amplitude in all three groups

TABLE 10.12
The Effect of Task Performance on Amplitude of Protective Behavior

	Session 1				
	Mean	sd	MS	F	p
Task	19.24	11.29	1175	5.87	<.05
No Task	26.82	14.69			

	Session 2				
	Mean	sd	MS	F	p
Task	17.32	11.61	920	4.91	<.05
No Task	24.42	14.06			

	Session 3				
	Mean	sd	MS	F	p
Task	14.61	9.25	1271	7.21	<.01
No Task	22.89	14.06			

are strikingly low. Thus, in order to gain additional information about the impact of task performance on protective behavior, we must now compare all groups that were given task performance with all those that were not. Table 10.11 presents information concerning the probability of protective behavior; Table 10.12 presents information concerning the amplitude of protective behavior for subjects who engaged in it.

The results are clear: The introduction of a task into the anticipation of danger reduces the tendency to engage in protective behavior. This finding is in line with our reasoning based on the assumption that task performance reduces the danger orientation and, consequently, all aspects of behavior related to the danger proper. Returning to Fig. 10.1, the basic competition between the two behaviors (viz., protective behavior and task-oriented behavior) has now been established and by increasing the one, the other is necessarily reduced.

The conflict between protective behavior and task performance can further be analyzed by looking more closely into the actual correlation between protective behavior and task performance across subjects. As subjects usually engage in protective behavior during Warning A, and in this experiment some of them had to perform a task during that warning, we should expect a negative relationship between the two behaviors at this stage. In contrast, those who protected themselves should have performed better during Warning C, because by reducing the intensity of the danger they could concentrate better on the task to be performed. The correlations between amplitude of protective behavior and task performance during Warnings A and C of each session are presented in Table 10.13. Consid-

TABLE 10.13
Correlations Between Protective Behavior and Performance

	Session 1	Session 2	Session 3	
	Warning A	Warning A	Warning A_1	Warning $A2$
Task B Correct Responses	−.22 (n=28)	−.08 (n=28)	.37	.47* (n=14)
Task A Correct Responses	−.21 (n=28)	.00 (n=28)	−.60**	−.31 (n=21)
Task A Errors	.10 (n=28)	−.08 (n=28)	.11	.47* (n=21)
Task A Speed	−.33* (n=28)	.03 (n=28)	−.69**	−.05 (n=21)
Task C Correct Responses	−.31* (n=28)	−.28 (n=28)	−.45*	.08 (n=21)
	Warning C	Warning C	Warning C_1	Warning C_2
Task B Correct Responses	.24 (n=41)	−.17 (n=41)	.42*	−.12 (n=14)
Task A Correct Responses	−.09 (n=42)	.23 (n=42)	.01	.25 (n=21)
Task A Errors	.43* (n=42)	.33* (n=42)	.15	−.27 (n=21)
Task A Speed	.29* (n=42)	.49* (n=42)	.00	.00 (n=21)
Task C Correct responses	−.33* (n=42)	.00 (n=42)	.04	.32 (n=21)

*$p < .05$ (one-tailed test).
**$p < .01$ (one-tailed test).

ering the fact that very few subjects engaged in protective behavior in the first place, the data in this table are based on a very limited pool of subjects. And yet, as can be seen, the significant results are in agreement with our main hypothesis. This is clearly illustrated with data concerning the speed of performance of Task A. Subjects who protected themselves during the first warning perform faster on subsequent tasks. Because both types of behavior compete for the subject's attention, the solution seems to lie in doing first the one and only later the other. Thus, for instance, subjects who engaged in protective behavior during the first warning (A) could concentrate better on subsequent tasks.

PART TWO:
TRAINING OF PROTECTIVE BEHAVIOR

We view training and false alarms as being on essentially the same plane. Whereas through false alarms people learn that the threats are less serious than they anticipated, through training they learn that the demands posed upon them are less severe than they originally thought. In the context of task performance, training consisted of previous exposure to essentially similar tasks. Moving now to the issue of training of protective behavior, we are confronted with the question of how to translate it into operational terms.

As was stated earlier in this chapter, the simplicity of the protective behavior itself left very little about it to be trained. Thus, we have opted for the introduction of a routine checklist of all the features of the apparatus related to the protective behavior. Such a checklist provides the opportunity to become familiarized with the various components of protective behavior, and at the same time it reduces the need to invest attention in planning the behavior itself. At the termination of the routine, the subject is ready to engage in protective behavior should he so desire. Following our earlier analysis, we posit that by training the protective behavior itself subjects will be able to invest more attention in the task in front of them. Thus, training of protective behavior by reducing the cognitive and attentional demands on protective behavior should increase the task orientation. In order to be able to test the impact of this manipulation on task performance, it was essential that at least two different groups of subjects be tested: one that has to perform the task during anticipation of the danger, and the other without task performance.

METHOD

Design

This part of the experimental design consists of two groups of 21 subjects each, identical in stress, in false alarm conditions, and in protective behavior training. The two groups differed on task performance only, as indicated in Table 10.1. Thus, Group 4 was trained in active coping and, in relation to task performance, was identical to Group 1. Group 5, on the other hand, though trained in active coping, did not have any task to perform and was identical to Group C.

Procedure

The experimental procedure for Group 4 was identical to that used for Group 1 except for the addition of the advance-routine checklist requirements. Following stress instructions, instead of practicing avoidance as usual, the subject was told that before he was able to reduce shock intensity, he would have to perform a series of apparatus checks in order to insure that the apparatus was in good working condition. He was then given an advance-routine checklist and was asked to perform each check according to experimenter-monitored instructions and report in the exact words appearing on the list. The dialogue went as follows:

Experimenter:	Can you hear me well?
Subject:	I hear you well.
Experimenter:	Right foot near the pedal.
Subject:	Right foot near the pedal.
Experimenter:	Five pressings of pedal with right foot.
Subject:	[Following pressing] Right pedal is OK.
Experimenter:	Left foot near the pedal.
Subject:	Left foot near the pedal.
Experimenter:	Five pressings of pedal with left foot.
Subject:	[Following pressing] Left pedal is OK
Experimeter:	Illumination of shock intensity scale.
Subject:	Scale is well lighted.
Experimenter:	Counter condition.
Subject:	Counter is OK; set on 50.
Experimenter:	Apparatus is in working condition ready for operation

The avoidance-routine checklist was trained twice and was performed once before the beginning of warning A in each session. Subjects in Group 5 were also trained on avoidance routine, but no reference to task performance was made during instructions. Following the last cancellation of threat and the 5-minute relaxation period, they performed the tasks one after the other while still connected to the polygraph.

RESULTS

The Effect of Training of Protective Behavior on Task Performance

By comparing performance of subjects in Group 4 with those in Group 1, we could ascertain the impact of training of protective behavior itself. On the systematic search required by Task A, it was found that there were no differences in the number of correct responses, but significant differences emerged in the speed of performing the task. Figure 10.8 presents the average performance according to groups, sessions, and warnings. Analysis of variance indicates a significant difference between groups, $F = 5.18$, $df = 1/26$, $p < .05$. It seems that training of protective behavior leads to faster performance on Task A. This finding is in line with our theorizing about the competition between danger orientation and task orientation.

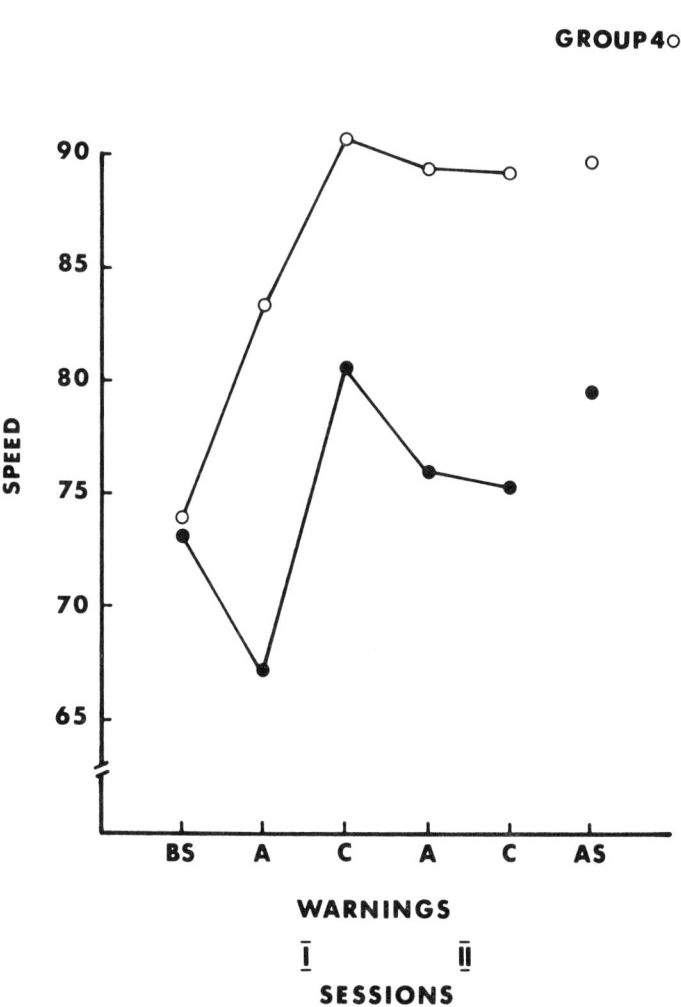

FIG. 10.8 Means of speed measure for Task A according to groups, sessions, and warnings.

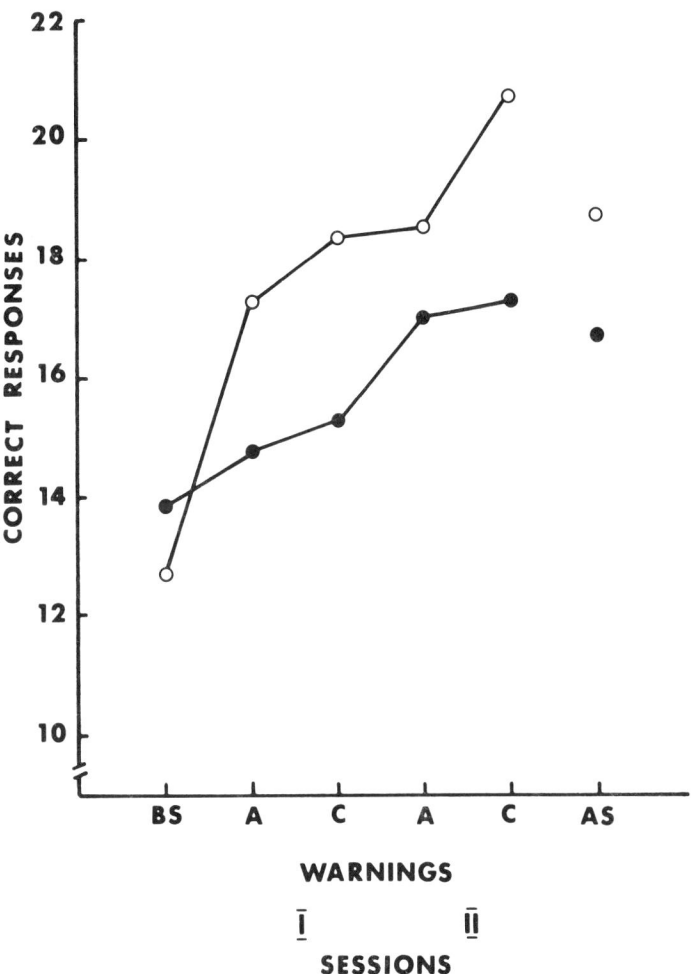

FIG. 10.9 Means of correct responses for Task B according to groups, sessions, and warnings.

The results on the nonsystematic search required by Task B are also significant and in the same direction. Figure 10.9 presents the mean number of correct responses according to groups, sessions, and warnings. Comparing the two groups on the first performance before stress conditions revealed no significant difference. Analysis of variance done on performance during Sessions 1 and 2, Warnings A and C, indicated a significant difference between groups, $F = 6.62$, $df = 1/26$, $p < .05$. Thus, once more, subjects in Group 4 performed better than subjects in Group 1.

The Effect of Training of Protective Behavior on Protective Behavior

Table 10.14 presents the probability of protection of Groups 4 and 5 versus Groups 1 and C, respectively. The results indicate that training of protective behavior reduces the tendency to engage in that behavior. This is in addition to our earlier finding that the introduction of task performance tends to reduce protective behavior. The table illustrates both of these findings. Thus, the impact of the task itself is seen by comparing Groups 1 and 4 to 5 and C, whereas the impact of protective behavior training is seen by comparing Group 4 to Group 1 and Group 5 to Group C. All these comparisons support our analysis. It should be mentioned that Group 4, which combines both effects through having the task requirements as well as training of protective behavior, exhibits the lowest probability of active coping of all the groups tested so far. Essentially the same results are obtained by looking at the amplitude of protective behavior.

The training of protective behavior acts like a "safety valve"; its very existence reduces the need for it. By increasing the easiness and availability of self-protection, the need for it has been substantially reduced. This may be due in part to the reduction of the danger orientation and in part to the stress-reducing effects of the training itself. The increased availability of protective behavior may have indeed reduced the impact of the threat itself.

The theoretical and practical implications of these findings are varied and far-reaching. Some have already been mentioned, and several others are briefly dealt with in the concluding chapter of this volume. The following paradox may

TABLE 10.14
The Effect of Training Protective Behavior on the Probability of Its Occurrence

Sessions	1	2	3
Group 1	.38	.33	.33
Group 4	.29	.19	.24
Group 5	.33	.43	.43
Group C	.87	.80	.70

suffice to illustrate the potential richness as well as the complexity of our formulation and results. Training of protective behavior increases the task orientation and task performance, whereas training of the task performance itself increases the danger orientation. Thus, an attempt to enhance task performance under stressful conditions may perhaps gain more by investing in the training of protective behavior than by investing directly in task performance. In any event, because both cannot be tackled jointly, the training of protective behavior may well turn out to be the best way to begin.

The paradoxical effect of increase in danger orientation due to growing mastery of the task is well illustrated in the classic studies of American pilots during World War II. The fliers reported that as their combat experience increased, their fears of personal failure were replaced by fears of being killed or wounded (Shaffer, 1947). A similar picture emerged in studies of infantry soldiers (Dollard, 1944).

11 The Role of Personality Differences in the False Alarm Situation

The stage in which the investigation of individual differences becomes most appropriate in any research program is a continual dilemma in behavioral research. On the one hand, there are scholars who argue that individual differences are not only a legitimate venue of research in all stages of an attempt to solve a particular problem, but that neglecting them would probably result in misleading conclusions. More specifically, it is often argued that certain components of lawfulness cannot be discovered precisely because individual-differences variables are neglected. On the other hand, there are many proponents of the two-stages strategy of research, which first attempts to discover the main effects and then studies individual differences. Although it would be presumptuous to make a clear-cut choice between these two points of view, the logic of the experimental effort described in this volume goes hand in hand with the second approach. In other words, the sequence of experiments reported here attempts to investigate the false alarm effect in a progressively complex context starting from a rather simple "basic threat" situation all the way to the complex interaction between fear reaction, protective behavior, task performance, and so forth. The intensity of the manipulation itself plays a major role in our attempt to discover the underlying main effects, which account for much of the variance in the false alarm situation. As Lazarus (1966) pointed out, the stronger the situational demand of a particular stress situation, the greater are the chances that individual differences will not play a major role. Thus, we have clearly followed the second approach by first trying to explicate some of the reliable main effects concerning the FAE. Only now, after some of these have been clearly demonstrated, are we ready to look into some of the individual-differences variables. Our approach appears to be vindicated in view of the relatively strong and reliable effects that have been found so far. It is on this foundation that we proceed to look into personality characteristics that may play a role in the false alarm situation.

Among the situational components in which individual differences may be of particular interest, we may list the following:

1. The amount of fear experienced by the subject, both in terms of the psychophysiological index of heart rate and the subjective account of the experience.
2. The willingness of the person to invest in protective behavior.
3. The dilemma of task orientation, in case a task performance is included in this situation, versus the danger orientation. In other words, what are some of the individual differences in the motivational and attentional preferences or tendencies considering these two opposing orientations?
4. Last but not least, the question of learning from the false alarm experience itself is of paramount importance. Stated differently, one can ask which subjects have a stronger FAE than others.

There is no attempt to treat all of these research possibilities exhaustively in this volume. All that could be done up to this point is to try a very simple and minimal approach to the broad issue of personality characteristics and their potential role in the false alarm situation by exploring some of the more obvious variables that lend themselves to standard psychological research. However, even this minimal approach was carried out in addition to the ongoing experimental program, not as research on its own. Thus we gave our regular subjects personality inventories. These were usually filled out after the termination of the experiment proper, and the data were compared with our other indexes such as heart rate and protective behavior. In the case of subjects who were also required to perform a visual search task, we could compute the correlations between the personality inventories and task performances as well.

A word of caution is necessary at this point. Not only were the personality inventories added following the experimental treatment, but not all the subjects went through exactly the same experiment in the first place. Thus, when we try to analyze individual differences, we are actually combining information taken from different experiments for the sake of this particular analysis. It should be mentioned, however, that such a procedure by necessity introduces a major element of noise into our data base thus making it more difficult to discover a systematic relationship between personality and other facets of behavior in the false alarm situation. If in spite of this a reliable result could be obtained, it would add an additional element of robustness.

In the context of the present research three personality traits were chosen as candidates for our preliminary study: anxiety, locus of control, and social desirability. Spielberger (1975) has suggested drawing the distinction between anxiety as an emotional state and trait anxiety. Anxiety as an emotional state is characterized by perceived feelings of tension, apprehension, and nervousness, and it may vary in its intensity and fluctuate over time. Trait anxiety, on the other hand, refers to stable differences among people in the tendency to perceive a situation as threatening and to respond to it with elevation in state anxiety. It is thus the predisposition to respond to a threatening situation with high anxiety. It is maintained that persons high and low in trait anxiety do not differ in their reactions to threats emanating from physical danger, but they are supposed to differ in regard to task performance (i.e., the more anxious person should perform simple tasks better than the less anxious one as opposed to complex tasks; see also, Spence, 1956). Anxiety is thus seen as a drive that affects performance. Therefore, the inclusion of the anxiety measure was thought worthwhile, particularly in terms of characterizing the psychological demands of the various tasks used. In addition, the relationship between anxiety, protective behavior, and the FAE could also be investigated. Highly anxious persons are supposed to perceive greater danger in threats to self-esteem. Protective behavior in situations of danger could be seen as such a threat.

Locus of control (Rotter, 1966) is a personality trait referring to the way people perceive the amount of control they have over events occurring in their lives. Internal control refers to the belief that reinforcements are contingent upon behavior, capacity, or attributes. External control refers to the belief that reinforcements are under the control of powerful others, luck, chance, fate, and so on. We may thus predict that the more external the person is, the less he believes in his ability to cope with the demands imposed upon him in the stress situation. Consequently, protective behavior and task performance should be reduced, whereas fear should be elevated.

Social desirability as defined by Crowne and Marlowe (1960) refers to a person's need to obtain approval by responding in a culturally appropriate and acceptable manner. Here our predictions are clear-cut. Because protective behavior is regarded by many subjects as a sign of cowardice, we would predict that the greater the person's need for social approval, the less willing he would be to engage in protective behavior.

In addition to these three personality inventories, two additional characteristics were tested using behavioral measures. The first was a measure of intolerance of ambiguity. Here we have followed Smock (1955) and presented our subjects with incomplete pictures, which they had to recognize. With each additional card they received additional input allowing for better recognition. The various measures indicate the ability of a subject to withhold judgment in a situation of ambiguous information. The exact test and the indexes derived from it are detailed in a later section of this chapter.

Last but not least, we were interested in testing the characteristic of risk taking in our subjects. Risk taking as a trait was investigated by Slovic (1964) using various measures including response sets, confidence levels, gambling procedures, and questionnaires. For the present research, we chose a gambling situation in which subjects' decisions were assumed to reflect risk-taking tendencies. It was essentially a game of roulette in which subjects were free to decide on what probability of gain or loss they are willing to play and what amount of money they were willing to allocate for this purpose. A detailed description of the risk-taking procedures and measures follows shortly.

The main rationale for including a measure of intolerance of ambiguity lies in the analysis of the false alarm situation itself. Following the cancellation of a threat, the subjects in our experiments are threatened once more by the instructions of the experimenter. This typically produces an ambiguous situation par excellence. On the one hand, there is the experience gained by the false alarm itself, namely, that the threat need not be taken seriously. On the other hand, the instructions of the experimenter indicate that there is a new session beginning and that the danger is real. It is not at all clear whether to put more emphasis on the present instructions or on the past experience and in what degrees. These conflicting messages thus produce an ambiguous situation, and the extent to which the FAE itself is operative depends on the ability of the person to integrate the past experience into the present threat.

The issue of risk taking as an important characteristic in the false alarm situation is almost self-evident. In all our analyses of protective behavior, we have pointed out that by engaging in protective behavior one is actually reducing the amount of personal risks. Thus, it is of some interest to study the effect of precisely this characteristic on protective behavior as such. We would hypothesize that subjects high on risk taking would be less prone to make use of the protective behavior option.

METHOD

Following the entire experimental sequence, including the filling in of the postexperimental questionnaire, subjects were given the three standard personality inventories: State-Trait Anxiety Inventory, The Locus of Control, and Social Desirability. The behavioral measures of intolerance of ambiguity and risk taking were obtained in the following manner.

Intolerance of Ambiguity

The test consists of series of 15 cards each. The first card has only a few elements of a complete picture on it, but each consecutive card provides additional cues for recognition of the picture, which appears in its complete form on the fifteenth card. The subject was told the purpose of the task is to see how soon he is able to recognize the picture. Three series of 15 cards each were selected from Smock (1955) and administered according to complete counterbalanced order across subjects. Prior to administering each set of cards, subjects were shown six

164   11. THE ROLE OF PERSONALITY DIFFERENCES

possible goal responses for 10 seconds. The correct response was always one of the first three on the list. In addition, a sample of four cards was prepared for demonstrating the complete experimental task. The complete instructions appear in Appendix F. The test allows for several measures: the serial number of the card to which the first response was given, the serial number of the card to which the first correct response was given, the serial number of the card to which the final correct response was given, the total number of responses given in each series, and the difference between the first serial number and the first correct serial number. According to Smock, threat conditions will elevate intolerance of ambiguity, and this would be expressed in early responding, but the same condition should also cause retarted recognition, which can be expressed in the delay of correct responding.

Risk Taking

Subjects were presented with a roulette wheel and a gambling chart. The rules of the game were explained in detail (see Appendix G). The first part of the experiment included four trials. On each trial the subject was allowed to bet one chip, which was the equivalent of five Israeli pounds, but was free to choose the probability of winning–losing, which ranged between ½ and 1/36. The first trial was self-paced, that is, the subject was given all the time he needed to make a decision. The additional three trials were limited by time. There were three conditions of time pressure: 5, 10, and 20 seconds. The order of time pressure conditions was completely counterbalanced across subjects. The second part of the experiment also included four trials. In this part the subject was allowed to bet only according to a probability of 1/2 but was given 20 chips on each trial and could choose the amount he would gamble with. As in the first part, the first trial was self-paced in terms of time, but the additional three bets were made under time pressure. Two different measures of risk taking could be utilized: probability (the lower the probability chosen by a subject, the higher the risk he takes in gambling) and amount (the higher the amount a subject gambles with, the higher the risk he takes at gambling).

RESULTS

The number of possible analyses between the various measures that were taken is practically unlimited, but in this chapter we concern ourselves primarily with the relationships between the various measures of individual differences and the most important of those indexes that were used throughout this volume in an attempt to describe the false alarm situation. Thus, we do not concern ourselves with the intercorrelations between the various measures that were used; rather we see whether a certain amount of the variance in protective behavior, fear reaction, and the FAE as such can be accounted for by these measures of individual differences.

Protective Behavior

No significant relationships were found between state anxiety, trait anxiety, locus of control, and either the probability of protective behavior or its amplitude. This is of some interest in view of the fact that a naive interpretation of protective beahvior might have suggested that high-anxious subjects would be more willing to invest in self-protection than low-anxious subjects. This issue, however, lies at the heart of the entire complexity of the relationship between protective behavior and fear. We have already seen that there is a certain amount of desynchrony between these two, a point which is taken up further in the next chapter. Furthermore, it is not at all clear whether a certain predisposition for anxiety should affect protective behavior directly or only via a more intense fear reaction. In any event, the negative finding is thus of special interest because it again illustrates that whether a person engages in self-protection or not is a highly complex issue depending on a multitude of different factors.

The lack of relationships between locus of control and protective behavior is likewise interesting. Because protective behavior implies "taking one's fate into one's own hands," it is legitimate to expect that subjects whose orientation to life is primarily that of internal locus of control would be more willing and more highly motivated to protect themselves than those who view the world and its impact on themselves as primarily outside of their control. That such is not the case can be due to the possibility that the decision to refrain from protective behavior can be seen as much a decision of internal control as the opposite. In this respect, the option of protective behavior is essentially neutral, and the subject may decide either to take advantage of it or not. In both instances, he is demonstrating internal control.

However, the situation is quite different when we come to the characteristic of social desirability. Here we have found that the probability of engaging in protective behavior is negatively related to social desirability. In other words, subjects high on the social desirability dimension are less prone to protect themselves. This finding relates to the probability of self-protection only; there were no such findings concerning the amount of self-protection. Thus, we once again have the indication that these two decisions—namely, Should I protect myself? And if so, how much?—are indeed separate and reflect different psychological processes.

Because the decision whether to protect oneself or not is dichotomous, the data testing for the impact of social desirability on protective behavior were analyzed in the form of t tests between subjects who protected themselves and those who did not. Table 11.1 presents the data for all four variables and indicates that subjects who engaged in protective behavior are significantly lower on social desirability than those who did not. This relationship holds well

TABLE 11.1
t Tests on the Effects of Personality Characteristics on Protective Behavior (First Session)

	Social Desirability					
Protective Behavior	n	Mean	sd	t	df	p
Yes	46	15.98	5.3	2.97	119	.004
No	75	18.80	4.9			

	Locus of Control					
Protective Behavior	n	Mean	sd	t	df	p
Yes	44	7.25	4.0	.77	115	ns
No	73	7.82	3.9			

	State Anxiety					
Protective Behavior	n	Mean	sd	t	df	p
Yes	46	29.33	6.1	.37	117	ns
No	73	29.82	7.8			

	Trait Anxiety					
Protective Behavior	n	Mean	sd	t	df	p
Yes	46	35.04	7.9	.48	117	ns
No	73	35.81	8.7			

throughout the three trials of the experiment. The direction of this relationship is particularly striking, because it indicates that subjects who worry more about the impression they make on others (i.e., high on social desirability) are less willing to use the protective behavior option. This would suggest that, at least for some subjects, the main reason for not protecting themselves is not necessarily a lack of fear, but rather the fear of losing status. We have already suggested that subjects may feel threatened not only by the impending danger, but also by anything that may suggest to other people that they are indeed afraid. Inasmuch as protective behavior can be interpreted by them as a clear indication of their own fear and worry, some may prefer to subject themselves to the highest intensity of pain rather than give an indication of their fears and worries.

This finding points out the importance of social pressures and modeling in any attempt to induce people to protect themselves in the face of danger. If there is a norm suggesting that by not taking self-protective measures the individual exhibits greater personal courage in the face of danger, then the chances that people will protect themselves, even if such behavior is clearly rational, are rather limited. Needless to say, such group norms are particularly necessary in situations of false alarms. It is precisely under these circumstances that those individuals who appeared to be externally brave by withholding any self-protective action are ultimately vindicated when the danger does not strike. This puts those individuals who engaged in protective behavior at a double disadvantage: On the one hand, they appeared to be less courageous; on the other, their behavior proved to be totally unnecessary. The finding that no relationship between social desirability and amount of protective behavior could be found in our research lends further support to the foregoing analysis. It is the lack of any indication or symptom of personal "cowardice" that is at the heart of the matter from the point of view of those subjects. Once they are willing to indicate that they are sufficiently scared to invest in protective behavior, how much they are willing to invest becomes relatively unimportant.

Of the remaining indexes based on the two tests of intolerance of ambiguity and risk taking, the only one that was found to relate systematically to protective behavior was the amount of risk. More specifically, subjects who did not engage in protective behavior were found to take greater risks and play for higher stakes. The results indicate, however, that in order for this tendency to reach statistical significance, subjects must have relatively enough time to ponder their betting behavior. In other words, the relationship between protective behavior on the one hand and risk taking on the other was found to reach statistical significance during that trial on which subjects were given the longest time to think about their behavior. This finding was repeated systematically for the three sessions. Table 11.2 presents the analysis of variance for each session separately. The findings indicate that subjects who do not invest in protective behavior are higher risk takers than those who do. This makes sense in view of the fact that if in the face of danger a person is not protecting himself, even though it is possible for him to do so, he is in fact taking a greater personal risk. Thus, we can say that our data showed that there is a greater tendency of those who are risk takers in a betting situation to also be risk takers in the danger situation and vice versa. Risk taking is thus a personality variable that clearly influences protective behavior.

Of special interest is the fact that this tendency is more marked when there is sufficient time for deliberation. We have seen in previous chapters in this volume that decision time can have a major influence on protective behavior. More specifically, the reader may recall that we found that when there is very little time given for subjects to decide whether they want to take advantage of the protective behavior option, all of them do so. In other words, time pressure leads to smaller risk taking. A similar finding was also reported by Ben-Zur and Breznitz (1981). Whatever risk-taking tendencies are operative can find expression and influence the subject's behavior only when time pressure is some-

TABLE 11.2
Amount of Risk Taking According to Protective Behavior and Decision Time

First Session

	Protective Behavior			
Decision Time	Yes	No	F	p
Self-Paced	12.69	9.10	3.19	ns
5 Seconds	13.00	14.34	0.63	ns
10 Seconds	12.54	15.24	1.86	ns
20 Seconds	11.77	15.69	5.72	<.05

Second Session

	Protective Behavior			
Decision Time	Yes	No	F	p
Self-Paced	10.31	10.17	0.00	ns
5 Seconds	12.15	14.72	2.42	ns
10 Seconds	11.62	15.66	4.40	<.05
20 Seconds	10.77	16.14	12.27	<.01

Third Session

	Protective Behavior			
Decision Time	Yes	No	F	p
Self-Paced	11.00	9.82	0.33	ns
5 Seconds	12.71	14.54	1.23	ns
10 Seconds	12.21	15.50	2.93	ns
20 Seconds	11.43	16.00	8.60	<.01

what reduced. This is in line with the present findings, which show that what was discovered as a between-groups manipulation also holds true for within-group individual differences.

An interesting feature of Table 11.2 is that there seems to be a difference between betting behavior when it is self-paced and when it is under the time pressure of the experimenter. In fact, the lowest amount of risk taking is obtained by subjects who did not engage in protective behavior in the self-paced condition. Additional research may shed some light on this unexpected result. It is quite conceivable that subjects high on social desirability, as indeed those subjects tend to be, subjectively interpreted the self-paced condition more stringently in terms of available time than the other group did.

Fear Reaction

Analysis of the heart-rate channel did not indicate any significant relationships with the personality measures that were investigated in this study. Considering it was found that subjects who engaged in protective behavior respond differently than those who do not on some of the tests, it was thought worthwhile to analyze the relationships between the various measures and heart rate separately for these two groups. This attempt was more than rewarded by the results. Once again, it was the social desirability variable that turned out to be the focus of the relationships.

It was found that the relationships between heart rate as the psychophysiological index of fear reaction and social desirability are negative in the case of subjects who engaged in protective behavior and positive in subjects who did not. It was no surprise, therefore, that no clear relationships could be found with the entire pool of subjects. The specific results indicative of the entire list of heart-rate measures appear in Table 11.3, which suggests that those subjects who engaged in protective behavior are drastically different from those who did not. It is as if we had two entirely different subpopulations in the same sample. Thus, fear reaction is related to social desirability but in a very complex fashion. One way to look at these results is to assume that subjects in our experiment are afraid of two different and conflicting threats. On the one hand there is the threat of pain due to the stress instructions; on the other hand there is the threat of loss of status, which is asociated with protective behavior. In fact, it can be suggested that theirs is essentially an *avoidance-avoidance conflict*. Subjects are caught between these two conflicting tendencies, and their behavior depends on the predominance of one over the other. If the fear of shock is higher than the fear of

TABLE 11.3
Correlations Between Social Desirability and
Heart Rate According to Protective Behavior

Social Desirabilty With	Protective Behavior	
	Yes	*No*
Base Level	−.30	.18
Threat$_1$ H	−.13	.26
Threat$_1$ L	−.30	.18
Warning A$_1$ H	−.13	.27
Warning A$_1$ L	−.35	.22
Warning B$_1$ H	−.29	.22
Warning B$_1$ L	−.24	.21
Warning C$_1$ H	−.26	.19
Warning C$_1$ L	−.24	.22

170   11. THE ROLE OF PERSONALITY DIFFERENCES

losing face, subjects engage in protective behavior. But if the fear of losing face is greater, subjects refrain from using the protective behavior option. The relationship between these variables and social desirability is schematically presented in Fig. 11.1.

The figure illustrates that high fear reaction can be the outcome of two entirely different factors. In the lower spectrum of social desirability it can be the outcome of high fear of shock, where as in the higher spectrum it can be the outcome of high fear of losing face. The results reported earlier in this chapter justify the assumption that most of the subjects who refrained from protective behavior are clustered in the upper portion of the social desirability dimension, whereas most of those who engaged in it are in the lower portion. The very fact that psychophysiological indexes such as heart rate are not threat specific and can reflect the entire spectrum of stressors operative at any given point of time makes it, of course, almost impossible to distinguish between the various components mentioned here. However, this problem illustrates the importance of such mediating variables as social desirability, which can explicate some of these intricate relationships.

The function as described in Fig. 11.1 can account for the results obtained in Table 11.3 in the following manner. Looking at the left-hand position of the figure (i.e., at subjects who protected themselves), we find that as social desirability goes up, fear (of shock) goes down. Within the right-hand section of the figure (i.e., subjects who did not protect themselves), the relationship between social desirability and fear reaction is a positive one.

Fear reaction as measured in the subjective tension scores presents a different picture. Here we find systematic negative correlations between social desirability

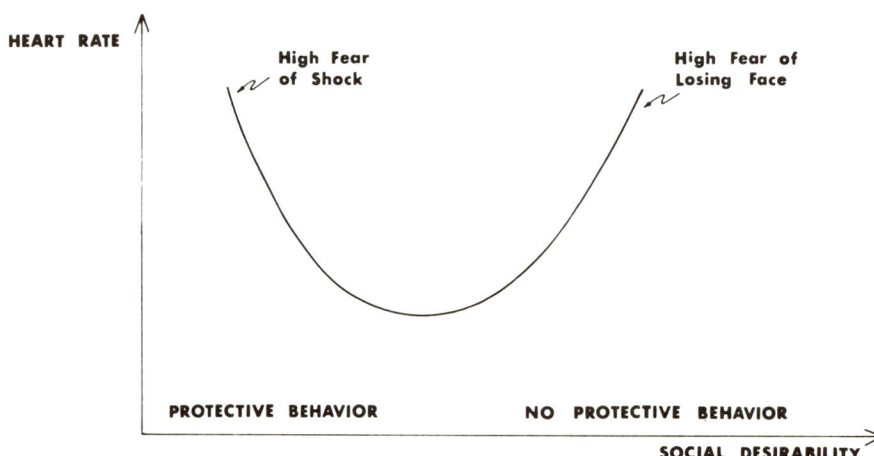

FIG. 11.1 Relationships between fear, social desirability, and protective behavior.

TABLE 11.4
Correlations Between Social
Desirability and Subjective
Tension

Social Desirability With	Correlation
Warning A_1	−.21
Warning B_1	−.17
Warning C_1	−.19
Warning A_2	−.20
Warning B_2	−.21
Warning C_2	−.25
Warning A_3	−.18
Warning B_3	−.20
Warning C_3	−.18

Note: All correlations are significant at least at the .05 level.

and reported tension. Table 11.4 presents the data, which indicate that subjects high on social desirability report being less afraid of the danger. This is in line with the obvious fact that both measures are to some extent subjective reports under the control of the respondent. Thus, those subjects high on social desirability, who care about the impression they make on other people, are less willing to report being afraid of the impending danger. It should be remembered that no such control is possible when dealing with the autonomic nervous system as indicated by the heart-rate results.

Subjective reports of tension are also sensitive to the state and trait anxiety measures. This can be clearly seen in Table 11.5, which presents the correlations involved. The table indicates that high-anxious subjects report a higher subjective experience of fear during the various segments of anticipation. To some

TABLE 11.5
Correlations Between State Anxiety, Trait
Anxiety, and Subjective Tension

Tension	State Anxiety	Trait Anxiety
Warning A_1	.25	.23
Warning B_1	.17	.18
Warning C_1	.24	.23
Warning A_2	.19	.19
Warning B_2	.22	.23
Warning C_2	.20	.21
Warning A_3	.15	.17
Warning B_3	.16	.23
Warning C_3	.17	.24

Note: All correlations are significant at least at the .05 level.

extent this is almost tautological in view of the direct questions involved in measuring state and trait anxiety. It is worth mentioning that in terms of the internal logic of the state-trait distinction, the state measures should have been more highly correlated with subjective reports of tension than the trait measures. This, however, was not the case. There are no systematic differences between these correlations.

The relationship between state anxiety and heart rate is once again complicated by the moderating variable of protective behavior. Whereas the correlations between the two for the entire sample of subjects tested with both are minimal and in no instance significant, a different picture emerges once we distinguish between those subjects who engaged in protective behavior and those who did not. Table 11.6 presents the results, which clearly indicate that whereas in the group that did not engage in protective behavior there is no correlation between heart rate and state anxiety, a different picture emerges in the other group. Thus, looking only at those subjects who took advantage of the protective behavior option, we find that the higher the state anxiety, the greater is the fear reaction measured by the heart-rate index. Furthermore, closer scrutiny of the table indicates that the correlations are particularly high when using the lowest heart rate in any given segment of the experimental sequence. This would imply that high state-anxiety subjects had greater difficulty in recovering from the stressful impact of the various warnings. These results suggest that state anxiety, which is assumed to measure the amount of apprehension felt in the experiment proper, is a sensitive individual-differences variable primarily among those subjects who consider physical threat the major component of stress in the experimental situation. By comparison, those who are more concerned with saving face (as indicated by refraining from engaging in protective behavior) are less influenced by this variable. It is quite conceivable that when subjects are taking the

TABLE 11.6
Correlations Between State Anxiety and Heart Rate According to Protective Behavior

State Anxiety With	Protective Behavior	
	Yes	No
Threat$_1$ H	.30*	.18
Threat$_1$ L	.33*	.18
Warning A$_1$ H	.33*	.05
Warning A$_1$ L	.44*	.13
Warning B$_1$ H	.32*	.04
Warning B$_1$ L	.49*	.11
Warning C$_1$ H	.22	.04
Warning C$_1$ L	.36*	.08

*$p < .05$.

state-anxiety inventory, they are more aware of the physical danger made explicit through the instructions of the experimenter than the social threats implied by loss of status. These implied social threats were less visible, and perhaps subjects were not directly aware of them. This would lend further support to our interpretation that state anxiety is a meaningful individual-differences variable only for subjects whose prime concern is the physical danger of shock.

Locus of control is negatively related to heart rate, especially among those who refrained from protective behavior. Table 11.7 presents the correlations, which indicate that subjects with internal locus of control (those with lower scores) are more afraid of the shock than those with external locus of control. This relationship holds only for the group of subjects who refrained from protective behavior. One possible explanation of this interesting finding is that internal control, though often the better of the two alternatives, is particularly conducive to producing strong stress reactions in situations in which the subjects are objectively helpless. Paradoxically, such situations are easier for external control individuals, who depend to a greater extent on both positive and negative events coming from outside the realm of control and intervention. By contrast, those individuals who have a high tendency to control a situation are more threatened when such control is impossible.

The reader may correctly argue that the situation in this experiment is not one of objective helplessness, because it allows self-protection. To some extent this is true, and it is precisely why the finding holds only for those who willingly gave up on that option. For a variety of reasons, some of which were mentioned already in this chapter, these subjects chose to turn what is essentially a controllable situation into an objectively helpless one by refraining from using the protective behavior option. Once they made this decision, however, it is for all practical purposes a helpless situation; thus, those who are used to and perhaps in

TABLE 11.7
Correlations Between Locus of Control and
Heart Rate According to Protective Behavior

Locus of Control With	Protective Behavior	
	Yes	No
$Threat_1$ H	.06	−.22*
$Threat_1$ L	−.01	−.24*
Warning A_1 H	.00	−.29*
Warning A_1 L	.16	−.29*
Warning B_1 H	.10	−.23*
Warning B_1 L	.00	−.24*
Warning C_1 H	.11	−.23*
Warning C_1 L	.03	−.27*

*$p < .05$.

greater need of internal control find it more difficult to bear than those who rely on external intervention.

We submit that the important psychological variable of helplessness, which has received quite extensive treatment following Seligman, 1975, can profit from considering this additional aspect. In other words, whereas simple experiments tend to present simplistic, clear-cut dilemmas between control and lack of control, more complex experimental situations (and of course, real life) often allow a sequence of decisions that may ultimately lead to either control or objective helplessness. Thus, we can argue that individuals may have control over decisions that may ultimately lead them to objective helplessness. Stated differently, we can decide whether we want to be helpless or not, but once that decision is made, it can turn out to be irreversible and its consequences have to be borne out to the full. Our results indicate that individuals high on internal control of reinforcements may find such objectively helpless situations, whether imposed from the outside or entered voluntarily, more difficult to bear than external control individuals. This is reflected in the amount of fear reaction exhibited by these subjects.

Before leaving the issue of fear reaction, there is one additional finding that deserves to be mentioned. It was found that trait anxiety was negatively correlated with the subjects' ability to distract their minds from the impending danger. Thus, the correlations between trait anxiety and reported distraction were for the first session $-.25$, for the second session $-.22$, and for the third and last session $-.18$. All these correlations, though relatively low, are significant at the .05 level. It is conceivable that the attentional demands imposed by the threat instructions on individuals high in trait anxiety are greater than those lower in trait anxiety. Basically, we may actually be dealing with one of the major components of trait anxiety itself, namely, the aspect of worrying (Breznitz, 1971). The cognitive monopolizing of attention to threatening information and the inability to distract one's mind from it may turn out to be one of the most typical features of highly anxious individuals.

Individual Differences in the False Alarm Effect

Which subjects have stronger FAEs? Who are those that learn more from the cancellation experience than others? Analysis of the various personality inventories used in this research indicate that with the exception of two, no significant relationships with the FAE could be discovered. The exceptions, however, are interesting in their own right. The more important one involves intolerance of ambiguity. Thus, we found that subjects high on intolerance of ambiguity exhibit a stronger FAE as measured in the heart-rate channel. In other words, if we look at the difference between heart rate during the first and second sessions, we find that this difference, which indicates the extent of the FAE, is significantly correlated with some of the indexes of intolerance of ambiguity. The correlation is highest when we consider the serial position of the last correct recognition. Thus, the correlation between this index and the FAE in highest heart rates in the first and second sessions = .45, $p < .01$, and the FAE between the two lowest heart rates correlates .38, $p < .05$.

This finding can be understood in the context of viewing the false alarm situation as producing an ambiguous message. The subject is confronted with an experience that taught him the threat need not be taken seriously, but at the same time there is the second threat, which raises the possibility that this time it will materialize. Those subjects who are less able to tolerate this ambivalence tend to put a greater premium on the false alarm experience. In many ways this fits in with the literature on intolerance of ambiguity, which tends to emphasize its relationship to the authoritarian personality (Adorno, Frenkel-Brunswick, Levinson, & Sanford, 1950). The authoritarian personality is likely to view the world in a yes–no, black–white manner. Within the context of our experiment, the subjects high on intolerance of ambiguity prefer to analyze the credibility issue in such crude yes–no terms; in other words, they believe the threat either will materialize or not. A false alarm experience may thus lead them to put great emphasis on the credibility loss and dramatically reduce the subjective probability of the next event.

It could be argued that in principle the crude categorization of subjective probabilities in terms of the yes–no dichotomy could lead to exactly the opposite result as well. In other words, subjects could choose to stick to the original credibility and disregard the false alarm altogether. The fact that such is not the case suggests that the FAE obtained after one cancellation of the threat is sufficient to carry the credibility of those subjects across the highest uncertainty point of .5 and thus closer to 0 than to the original 1. A weaker FAE would thus, following the foregoing argument, produce a negative correlation between intolerance of ambiguity and the FAE. Our manipulation, however, was apparently too strong to allow the testing of this theoretical possibility.

The practical implications of our finding are far-reaching, and are treated more specifically in the last chapter of this volume. However, at this point, it should be mentioned that in situations in which people are threatened, there often evolves a psychology of mass behavior, which has some elements of the authoritarian personality. Thus, typically in disaster situations involving a large number of people, it is conceivable that superimposed on such a psychological background the FAE will tend to be magnified beyond its original proportions.

Last but not least, we found that subjective credibility loss due to the false alarm as measured by the postexperimental questionnaire was negatively related to state anxiety, $r = -.20$, $p < .05$. This finding indicates that high state-anxiety subjects have smaller FAEs than low state-anxiety subjects as measured by a subjective report of credibility. There can be many different explanations for this finding, and the present research cannot distinguish among them. Thus, for instance, it is possible that high state-anxiety subjects learn less from the experience than those with lower state anxiety. This would indicate that high-anxiety, detrimental to all learning, can also disrupt the learning involved when drawing the right conclusion from the cancellation itself. A totally different interpretation can emphasize the situation during the second threat. In this case one can argue that high state-anxiety subjects are more prone to be afraid, even though they have experienced the FAE, and thus, the difference between the two would be minimized. Whatever the explanation or explanations are, it should be emphasized that because we are dealing primarily with stressful situations, the chances that state anxiety will play a role in the false alarm experience are relatively high. This, of course, should be qualified in view of the fact that the only index that demonstrates this relationship is a single question on the postexperimental questionnaire.

Concluding Remarks

Our venture into the explication of some of the individual-differences variables that may play a significant role in the false alarm situation cannot be considered anything but a pilot project. At the same time, however, the results of this limited approach are quite rewarding. More specifically, it appears that social desirability plays a major role in a situation in which there is a dilemma as to whether it is worthwhile to engage in protective behavior. The protective behavior itself was found to be a central moderator variable. Subjects who engage in protective behavior behave quite differently than those who decided not to do so. Moreover, the impact of the various personality characteristics measured in this research was different in those two groups. If anything, our results suggest that protective behavior, in addition to its practical value, also has a major *diagnostic value*. A substantial amount of further theoretical and empirical work is necessary to explicate some of the intriguing results obtained in this research.

12 The Three Systems Analysis of Fear Reconsidered

Fear as a psychological variable has received a substantial amount of experimental treatment and theoretical analysis. This is not surprising in view of the central position that the concept of fear occupies in many attempts to give a satisfactory account of such diverse phenomena as panic, courage, phobic reactions, and avoidance behavior, to mention just a few. The prevalence of fear in all its manifestations makes it undoubtedly a major representative of all emotions and the analysis of fear is thus at the core of the psychology of emotions in general.

It is in this context that the experimental and clinical evidence pointing to the fact that the various aspects of fear do not always correspond to each other in a perfect manner raised serious doubts about how fear should be understood. Rachman (1978), more than anybody else, addressed himself to this set of issues. He describes the problem: "People can experience subjective fear but remain outwardly calm, and, if tested, they show none of the expected psychophysiological reactions. We also receive reports of subjective fear from people who make no attempt to escape from or avoid the supposedly frightening situation [pp. 4–5]." Case studies (Rachman, 1978) indicate essentially the same thing: "Self-reports of fear correlate well with each other; they correlate moderately well with the ratings of fear made by external judges and also with the avoidance behavior observed in a fear test; self-reports correlate modestly with physiological indices of fear; physiological indices of fear correlate modestly with each other and hardly at all with muscle tension [p. 20]." This can be seen as a fair summary of a relatively extensive effort to describe the results of clinical studies (e.g., Becker & Costello, 1975; Hepner & Cauthen, 1975; Hersen, 1973; Lader & Marks, 1971; Leitenberg, Agras, Butz, & Wincze, 1971; McCutcheon & Adams, 1975).

Peter Lang (1970), who in many ways can be seen as the father of the three systems analysis of fear, argued that fear responses, although related to each other, are also partially independent. Thus, in one of his experiments he obtained a correlation of .41 between the subjects' ratings of fear and their avoidance behavior. In the same experiment the correlation between the questionnaire responses and the fear overtly expressed in the avoidance test was only .04. To add to this confusion further, it was also found that many patients exhibit improvement following behavior therapy in one channel, without corresponding improvement in the other channel. Thus, for instance, patients can improve in their behavior without at the same time reporting concurrent, subjective relief.

On the basis of these and other indications, Rachman (1978) found it useful: "to think of fear as comprising three main components: the subjective experience of apprehension, associated psychophysiological changes, and attempts to avoid or escape from certain situations. When the three components of fear fail to correspond, as they commonly do, problems arise [p. 4]."

This lack of correspondence, or desynchrony, poses major problems for the theoretician. Although Hodgson and Rachman (1974) attempted to integrate some of the findings about desynchrony, this is still very much uncharted territory. Its exploration promises great rewards both in terms of theory of emotions and specifically in terms of practical implications concerning the understanding and treatment of certain phobic reactions. Our own systematic experimental program sheds some light on these problems. We have already mentioned desynchrony in various points of our discussion, and we now turn the focus of this chapter to the explication of some of these problems. More specifically, we believe that the research on false alarms can contribute to the understanding of desynchrony between the various components of fear.

DESYNCHRONY AS A GOAL

Rather than viewing desynchrony as the necessary outcome of an imperfect world, in the context of our analysis we have considered it as a goal to be pursued by various means. From the point of veiw of an effective warning system, desynchrony between the behavioral component (i.e., self-protection) and the fear component (e.g., subjective experience of tension or the psychophysiological index of heart rate) provides the opportunity to establish rational self-protective behavior without at the same time experiencing fear of too high an intensity. The reader may consider once again the simple typology that appeared in Chapter 7. Let us present it briefly once more. For the sake of simplicity, let us view both dimensions as dichotomies rather than as continuous systems, which they actually are. Table 12.1 presents the types. Although the three systems analysis of fear would suggest a three dimensional table for a variety of reasons, some of which have already been mentioned and some which follow shortly, we have

TABLE 12.1
The Four Response Types

	Protective Behavior	
Fear	High	Low
High	A	B
Low	C	D

chosen to neglect the difference between the subjective experience of fear and the psychophysiological index and concentrate on the difference between those two and the behavioral component.

In a situation where we start with a highly credible warning system, individuals may be assumed to have the Type A response; namely, they experience a high level of fear and act accordingly. With each false alarm, assuming there is no desynchrony between the two components, there ought to be a transition from Type A to Type D response. Stated differently, the false alarm effect would be expressed in the relatively positive reduction of fear and at the same time with the rather negative reduction of protective behavior. Thus, the goal of a rational warning system would be to produce the most effective kind of Type C behavior. In that situation the person is willing to invest in protective behavior, while at the same time being relatively free of fear. His protective behavior is thus not under the control of the fear reaction, but rather under the control of some other factors such as the understanding of its importance. Needless to say, Type B behavior is the least effective of all, and it can be labeled as neurotic in the sense that a person experiences a high level of fear without at the same time engaging in the behavior that might be instrumental in reducing it. We can thus see that desynchrony is a necessary condition in any attempt to shape the course of transition from A to D. More specifically, it raises the chance to establish Type C behavior, while at the same time there is the danger that Type B would develop. Because false alarms are one of the main reasons for the transition from Type A to Type D, the amount of desynchrony and its control become a major consideration for any effective warning system.

The foregoing analysis is to some extent diametrically opposed to that which is appropriate in the context of phobic reactions. There, instead of assuming an objectively justified danger, the situation often indicates that the self-protection is totally unnecessary. In other words, the heart of the therapeutic program is the reality testing involved. The client has to find out that his behavior is unnecessary. In other words, what is needed is to overcome the experience of fear and approach the frightening situation in order to find out that it is essentially harmless. Some patients indeed have the ability to act bravely and confront the frightening situation in spite of high levels of fear and anxiety. This, too, happens primarily because there is a certain amount of desynchrony between these various components of fear. Thus, in Rachman's works, these clients experience courage, which like all courage can best be defined as a situation of desynchrony. More specifically, it involves acts of approaching a frightening situation in spite of the experience of fear.

Any systematic attempt to take advantage of desynchrony in order to produce one of the asymmetrical types—in the instance of effective warning systems, Type C, and in the instance of behavior therapy with phobic patients, Type B— must look for variables that affect the different systems at different rates. In other words, if a certain kind of desynchrony is the goal in its own right, the means to bring it about ought to be studied directly, rather than left to chance, or to noise due to lack of understanding of the relationships involved. In the previous chapters, several such attempts found to be successful were reported. Thus, for instance, we have found that when a person anticipating danger is given a very limited amount of time to decide whether to take advantage of the protective behavior option or not, the chances are good that he will do so. The time pressure in this situation is an additional force toward Type C behavior. In yet a different experiment we have seen that by explaining the causes of false alarms after they have taken place, it is sometimes possible to restore the credibility as it affects protective behavior, without at the same time restoring the level of fear. It was found particularly effective when the explanation involved some indication that the cause of the false alarm was detected and measures were taken to change the weak link in the warning system proper.

In the preceding chapter we have seen that certain individual-differences variables also tend to be associated with desynchrony. Thus, social desirability, anxiety, and risk taking were all found to affect behavior in a very complex manner in which protective behavior functions as a moderator variable. In no instance were the relationships between these personality characteristics and the three systems of fear exactly identical, nor were they necessarily in the same direction.

However, these are relatively minor issues when considering the major finding reported in Chapter 7, which sheds some light on what might very well turn out to be one of the main reasons for desynchrony. The reader may recall that we have found that the relationship between protective behavior and heart rate depends primarily on the timing of the person's decision about whether to engage in protective behavior, and if so, how much. In other words, subjects who decide at a later stage of the anticipation sequence exhibit a positive correlation between fear and protective behavior, which indicates that their self-protection may indeed be under the control of the amount of fear that they are experiencing. But, those individuals that decided in advance how much they are willing to invest in self-protection produce a negative correlation between self-protection and fear. This follows logically in view of the fact that self-protection reduces the objective threat in the context of the present experiment. Moreover, because neither self-protection nor fear reaction can typically be seen as a single discrete event, but rather should be viewed as a continuous multistage sequence, we submit that the dual relationship between protective behavior and fear is probably present at least to some extent in all real-life situations.

This argument is schematically presented in Fig. 12.1. Diagram A of the figure presents the essential argument concerning the three systems analysis of fear. Thus, we see that the three systems are positively related to each other, yet at the same time this relationship if imperfect, with each system being under the separate influences of so-called "random shocks." These random shocks can be

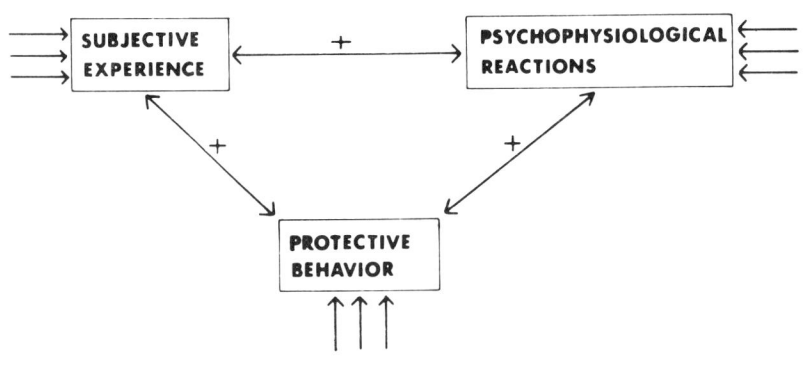

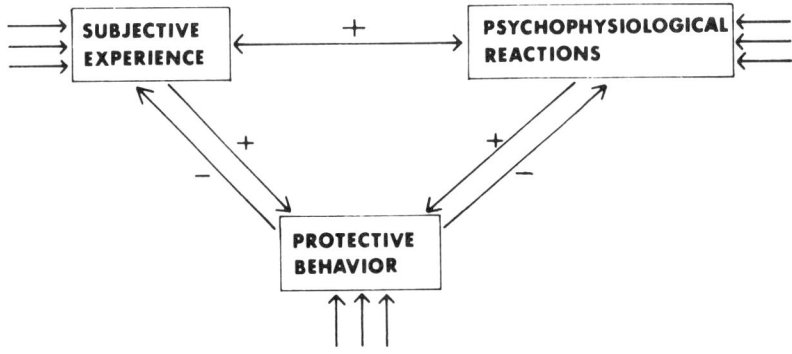

FIG. 12.1 The three systems analysis of fear.

viewed as the unexplained variance in this particular universe of discourse. Although empirically desynchrony happens to be the prevalent case, there is no argument that it must be so in principle. A more thorough understanding of these random shocks may indeed explain away at least certain elements of desynchrony.

However, Diagram B of Fig. 12.1 presents a rather different picture. Here we are drawing on our own results, which force us to introduce into the assumed relationships between the various components one of the major sources of desynchrony. Thus, whereas the relationship from fear to protective behavior is positive, there is a negative relationship when going in the other direction (viz., from protective behavior to fear). Thus, even without relying on the many obvious random shocks, we can predict that desynchrony will be the rule rather than the exception in many situations. It is operative within the three systems themselves, rather than being the outcome of forces from outside. Inasmuch as temporal factors are present in any situation, this dual relationship between protective behavior on the one hand and subjective experience and psychophysiological reactions on the other is a critical feature whenever fear is evoked.

The evidence from the effect of early decision on the negative relationship between protective behavior and fear has already been presented in various chapters of this volume. The importance of this effect can be further illustrated by analyzing the relationship between the amount of protective behavior and the latency of the first response. The reader may recall that protective behavior in these experiments was carried out by the subject pressing his right foot any number of times to reduce the anticipated intensity of the shock by 1 point. One way to distinguish between those subjects that decided ahead of time whether they are going to use the protective behavior option or not is to look at the latency of the first such action, calculated from the beginning of the first warning, which allows the subjects to protect themselves. Although it is difficult to predict what the exact reaction time under such circumstances ought to be, we tried the arbitrary cutoff point of 1.5 seconds following the beginning of the warning signal. Thus, all subjects who engaged in protective behavior were divided into two groups: those who started responding before 1.5 seconds and those who started responding later. Table 12.2 presents the t tests for the three sessions, and it indicates that there is a highly significant difference between the two groups. Thus, those subjects that decided ahead of time that they were going to use the protective behavior option used it in a greater amount than those who did not necessarily decide in advance. We have no direct evidence about the decision process itself, but it is still possible that some of those subjects whose latency was longer than 1.5 seconds also belong to the group that decided ahead of time but for some reason were not quick enough to begin their action. Possible overlap between these two groups makes it even more difficult to obtain such highly significant differences as the ones reported here.

There is of course an alternative explanation that may account for these results. Thus, we can argue that the causal relationship does not go from early

TABLE 12.2
The Effect of Latency of First Response on the Amplitude of
Protective Behavior

First Session

Latency	n	Mean	sd	t	p
Up to 1.5 secs.	65	31.5	13.7	6.11	.000
Longer	74	18.3	11.8		

Second Session

Latency	n	Mean	sd	t	p
Up to 1.5 secs.	64	29.3	14.0	4.86	.000
Longer	69	18.6	11.3		

Third Session

Latency	n	Mean	sd	t	p
Up to 1.5 secs.	54	25.4	14.8	3.17	.002
Longer	65	17.8	11.3		

decision to amount of protective behavior, but rather the other way around. In this case we would argue that all subjects decided ahead of time how much they were going to protect themselves, and those that knew they were going to use a greater amount of the protective behavior option started earlier. One can even argue that they had to start earlier because they could not know whether they would have sufficient time to carry out their intentions to the full. Although such an alternative explanation is in principle conceivable, the assumption that all subjects decided ahead of time how much they were going to use the protective behavior option does not fit data reported earlier in this volume. Furthermore, whatever the causal relationship between the two, there is an obvious indication that temporal considerations affect protective behavior in a significant manner. These considerations, which are not necessarily related to fear, thus contribute to the amount of desynchrony between the two. Before leaving this highly significant result, it should be mentioned that when trying other arbitrary cutoff points—ranging all the way from 1 second, 1.5 seconds, 2 seconds, 2.5 seconds, up to 3 second—the results were essentially the same, although not as significant. By choosing the 1.5 cutoff point, we achieve a certain amount of maximization of this effect, but it cannot be seen as an artifact of a totally arbitrary and random parameter.

Another important source of desynchrony is the fact that not all systems are continuous to the same degree. Thus, whereas psychophysiological reactions such as conductance, GSR, or even heart rate are for all practical purposes continuous, the behavioral component need not necessarily be so. In the preceding chapters we have seen that even within the context of protective behavior itself there is a need to distinguish between the dichotomous decision to use it or not to use it, and if so, how much. Such decisions are obviously discrete, and the number of different categories would necessarily be smaller than those that could be used in a truly continuous dimension. A similar problem exists in the attempts to measure the subjective experience of fear. As stated by Rachman (1978): "Subjective reports of fear also tend to be of limited value in assessing the intensity of the experience because of the difficulties in translating such expressions as 'extremely frightened,' 'terrified,' and 'slightly anxious' into a qualitative scale with stable properties [p. 4]."

It should be explicated that we are not dealing only with psychometric difficulties, but with what is essentially a phenomenological problem as well. One can actually raise the question of whether individuals are able to subjectively experience different levels of fear for which they do not have the appropriate label. This would necessarily produce a situation in which one of the systems is changed smoothly and continuously, whereas the other is changed by jumps and steps, producing differential levels of desynchrony in the various stages of the sequence.

Yet another source of desynchrony that has emerged from our analysis relates to the fact that protective behavior itself can be interpreted by some people as indicating fear, which ought to be hidden from other individuals at all cost. Subjects who are high on social desirability are often more afraid of losing status by indicating their fear of the danger than of the danger itself. Thus, not only in terms of individual differences, but also in terms of the norms operative in any given situation, the forces on the various systems of fear tend to differ. This is in line with Hodgson and Rachman (1974), who argued that high levels of demand in the therapeutic situation will produce a greater amount of desynchrony between the various components. Thus, when the clients are required to face that which frightens them, they might be pressed to do so, without at the same time being less afraid; on the contrary, such pressure will probably increase their experience of fear, and thus increase the desynchrony involved.

DESYCHRONY AND THE FALSE ALARM EFFECT

FAE, due to the cancellation on an anticipated danger, is the manipulation par excellence in any attempt to study the three systems analysis of fear. The initial threat that induces fear, followed by its cancellation, provides a convenient framework for the investigation of the possible differential impact of false alarms on each of the components of fear. Once again, the experimental program described here parallels what is often found in the psychological clinic. Thus, Rachman (1978), when describing the behavior of clients subjected to behavior therapy, claims: "the different indexes of fear might show different *rates* of response to treatment—a type of desynchrony. The recognition that the patient's subjective report tends to be the slowest to change was of some relief to therapists as well as to patients. In general, the order of change in response to therapy is declining physiological reactivity, followed by behavioral improvement, and, finally, by subjective improvements [p. 17]." Translated into our situation, Rachman would thus predict that the FAE is most marked in the psychophysiological index of heart rate, followed by protective behavior, and finally by subjective reports of tension.

In what follows we show that the false alarm manipulation affects desynchrony in more than one way. Some of these effects are further elaborations of the preceding argument concerning differential rates of change, and others are additions related to other phenomena.

Differential Rates of Change

There can be many reasons leading to differential impact of the false alarm on the various response channels studied in our experimental program. Thus, for instance, the very fact that the threat is induced by *verbal instructions* makes it particularly conducive to desynchrony. Because the cognitive appraisal of the threat when presented in a complex verbal form implies a great deal of cognitive elaboration and mediation, it stands to reason that subjective experiences as reported by our subjects would be under greater control of such cognitive variables. On the other hand, the physical stimuli of the warning signals themselves as well as the general atmosphere of threat presented in the laboratory situation might have greater impact on the psychophysiological channel of responding. Protective behavior, particularly because it involves a rather difficult calculation of cost–benefit on the part of the subject, would again probably tend to be under the direct influence of cognitive factors. That such is the case was already demonstrated in our experiment concerning the explanation of the causes of false alarms which had direct impact on restoring the credibility as measured by protective behavior, without at the same time increasing the corresponding level of fear.

This general argument is directly related to a corollary concerning the subjects' theory of how they should behave and how they should feel during the various stages of the experiment. This can be well illustrated by looking at the mean subjective tension reported in the various segments of the experiment. Whereas the psychophysiological index of heart rate indicates that fear is highest during the first warning (A), a simple theory about proximity of the danger influences our subjects to report, and perhaps to feel, that the tension is highest during the last warning (C). Table 12.3 presents the results for both channels for all three sessions. Close scrutiny of the table shows that in the heart-rate channel, Warning A is always the one producing the highest intensity of fear. Then the fear is reduced during Warning B, and there is once more a smaller increase during Warning C. This typical U curve fits well with the reports by Epstein and Fenz (1965) and other studies discussed in the earlier chapters of this book.

However, the situation is entirely different in the subjective reports of tension. Here we find that tension is systematically growing from A through B to C. Thus, our subjects are either unaware of their autonomic arousal during Warning A, or perhaps their subjective reports are based on a different body of information. It could be argued that the naive theory that tension is related to the proximity of the danger played some role in affecting these responses. Another indication in the same direction was found in the study on task performance. When our subjects were asked whether they thought that engaging in task performance reduced their heart rate or increased it, they almost always claimed that task performance reduced their heart rate, whereas in reality the opposite happened. Here again, it is conceivable that our subjects responded according to the naive theory of the effect of what they considered distraction on fear.

The differential rate of change due to the false alarms can best be seen when looking at the correlations between the FAEs of the various response channels. Thus, we find that the FAE in the amount of protective behavior is negatively related to the FAE in the psychophysiological index of heart rate. The correlation for the first false alarm is $-.22, p < .01$; for the second false alarm it is $-.16$, $p < .05$. Although these correlations are relatively small, they are significant, and they indicate that those subjects whose FAE was stronger in one channel had a correspondingly weaker FAE in the other channel and vice versa. The correlations between the intensity of the FAE in the amount of protective behavior and

TABLE 12.3
Mean Heart Rate (High) and Subjective Tension According to
Warnings and Sessions (N = 240)

Heart Rate (H)	*First Session*	*Second Session*	*Third Session*
Warning A	107.3	102.0	98.0
Warning B	104.8	98.4	96.3
Warning C	106.3	99.2	95.1

Tension	*First Session*	*Second Session*	*Third Session*
Warning A	3.80	3.11	2.79
Warning B	3.90	3.28	2.86
Warning C	4.26	3.86	3.39

reported tension tend to be positive, but they are significant only for the second false alarm. Thus, we find that the correlation between the intensity of the FAE in the amount of protective behavior and reported tension in the first warning is .33, $p < .001$, with the reported credibility loss .23, $p < .01$, and with the increased amount of ability to distract one's mind .17, $p < .05$.

It is of some interest to report that within the subjective report as such, there is no clear-cut synchrony between the various aspects of the experience. Thus, there is no significant correlation between the amount of reported credibility loss and the amount of reported tension reduced. All of this suggests that the FAE has a differential impact on the various components of fear and its consequences, thus leading to a substantial amount of desynchrony. Another way to look at this problem is to consider the fact that in the case of protective behavior, the false alarm demonstrated that it was a wasted, unnecessary effort and perhaps a loss of money. In the case of fear reaction, the false alarm demonstrated that it was wasted fear, which was unnecessary. The loss involved in each case is of a totally different kind, and perhaps one need not expect that the impact of both would be the same.

Sequential False Alarm Effect

If, as was shown in the previous paragraph, the FAE does not take place simultaneously in the various channels, how then does it take place? It is suggested that the FAE takes place in stages; namely, at each stage a different aspect of the situation is particularly affected. Fortunately, in our experiments we have two FAEs, and thus some of the implications of the foregoing hypothesis can be tested.

Let us begin by looking at the intensity of the FAE within the same channel for the two false alarms. Table 12.4 presents the correlations between the consecutive FAEs for the various indexes. The results indicate that with the single exception of distraction, all the response channels show either zero correlations or significant negative correlations between the intensity of the two consecutive false alarms. This, combined with the earlier data, suggests that following the cancellation of a threat some of the response channels are significantly reduced, with the others remaining the same or being reduced in only a minor fashion. Then, when the second cancellation takes place, they switch positions; namely, those that were already reduced stay put, and the others are now reduced more significantly.

Figure 12.2 presents the pattern of FAEs of a few subjects on the two dimensions of the highest heart rate during the last warning (C) and protective behavior, correspondingly. Although the illustration cannot be seen in any way as representative of the entire population of our subjects, it demonstrates the main theme of our argument. Thus, the FAEs tend to go in straight lines either vertically or horizontally. Very few subjects indicate the FAE simultaneously in

TABLE 12.4
Correlations Between the Intensities of the First
and Second False Alarm Effects

Index	Correlation	p
Heart Rate		
Threat	−.28	<.001
Warning A	−.19	<.001
Warning B	−.25	<.001
Warning C	−.23	<.001
Tension		
Warning A	.00	
Warning B	.00	
Warning C	.00	
Credibility	−.26	<.001
Distraction	.17	<.01
Protective Behavior	.00	

both channels in equal measure. This illustrates essentially that the transition from high credibility, Type A response pattern in Table 12.1 to low credibility (i.e., Type D) tends to progress through either Types B or C rather than directly from A to B. This is essentially at the heart of the desynchrony argument. The FAE thus operates in discrete steps moving from one channel to another.

There is, however, an interesting constraint to the freedom of movement of the various channels. This constraint is directly related to the negative relationship between amount of protective behavior and fear reaction. Thus, if a subject experiences a strong FAE in the protective behavior channel, he may reduce the amount of protective behavior to such an extent that his fear would actually increase. It can be suggested, therefore, that following an experience of false alarm this would be a very rare occasion indeed, and thus the amount of FAE allowed in the protective behavior should not reach the point at which fear reaction would increase.

This paradoxical outcome of a false alarm is an extreme case of desynchrony. It is illustrated by Subject G in Fig. 12.2. This subject engaged in protective behavior, which reduced the anticipated intensity of the first shock by 20 points. At the same time his heart rate during the last stage of the anticipation was 96. Following the cancellation of the first threat, he reduced the protective behavior from 20 to 9. Judging from the increase in heart rate, which was elevated from 96 to 102, the FAE on protective behavior was apparently too big. Following the second cancellation, this subject did not further reduce his protective behavior; actually, he increased it from 9 to 10, and this time the heart rate was reduced from 102 to 98. Subject G is a very rare exception to the rule, but he illustrates some of the constraints on the sequential process of the FAE due to the asymmetric relationships between fear and protective behavior.

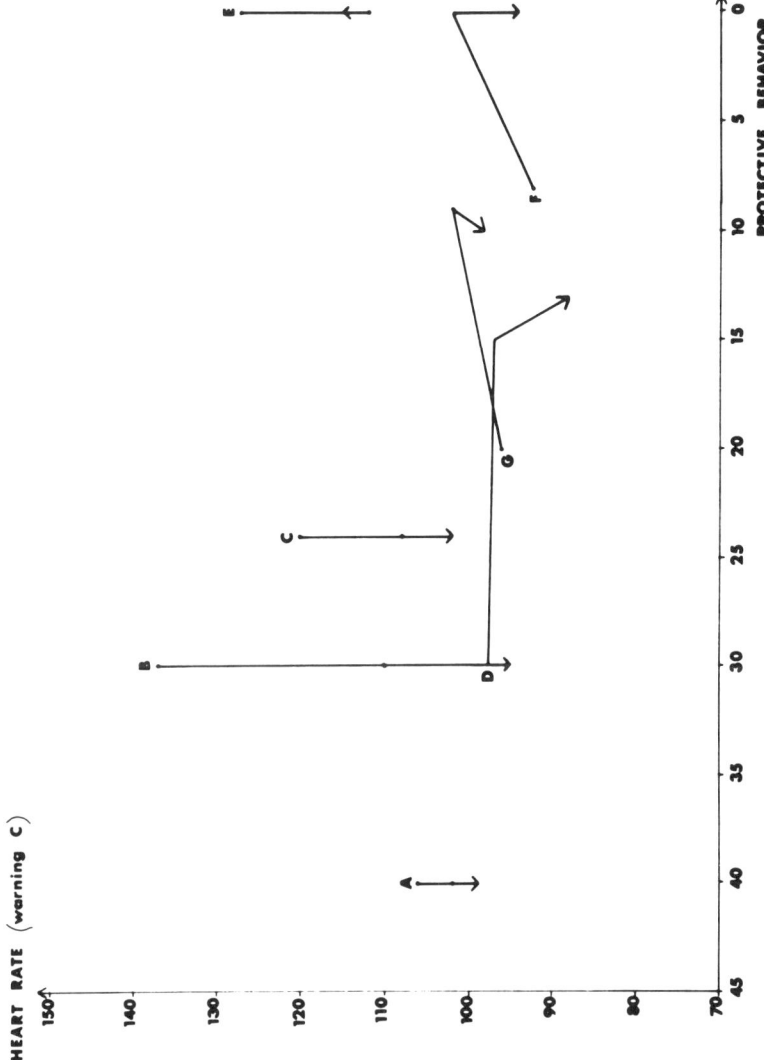

FIG. 12.2 Sequential FAEs.

Learning from Experience and the Similarity of Conditions

The FAE is seen as a case of learning from experience. The individual experiences a threat followed by its cancellation, and thus when a similar situation arises in the future, he draws conclusions about the credibility of the threat, and this produces the FAE. Central to this argument is the similarity between the two consecutive threats. It is precisely because the second threat appears to be very similar to the one that was canceled that the experience with the first becomes relevant.

There are many features of a particular situation that determine the amount of similarity between it and another situation as perceived by the individual. In our experiments we have deliberately tried to keep the similarity as high as possible. There is, however, at least one feature of the situation that is under the control of the subject himself, namely, the amount of protective behavior. Thus, whether the two situations are similar or not depends to some extent on whether the subject engages in the same amount of protective behavior in both instances. This may appear as if we are begging the question, for the very fact that the subject engages in a certain amount of protective behavior may already be the outcome of the perceived similarity or dissimilarity with the previously canceled threat. Although this is obviously the case, when focusing on the other indexes of fear, the foregoing becomes a critical factor. Stated differently, we predict that if the subject engages in exactly the same amount of protective behavior, he is producing a greater similarity between the two occasions and thus increasing the chances of the FAE in the other channels of behavior. This argument is, of course, totally symmetrical in the sense that if the subject experiences the same level of fear in both instances, this, too, increases the similarity between them and may affect protective behavior, among other things. Because fear reaction as measured by the heart-rate channel is a more continuous variable, more difficult to categorize into a few discrete simple categories than protective behavior, we have chosen to test the aforementioned hypothesis in one direction only. Thus, we can divide our subjects into three different groups: (1) subjects that refrained from using the protective behavior option on both trials; (2) subjects that used it in exactly the same amount on both trials; (3) subjects that used it in different amounts on both trials. Because this last group actually demonstrates the FAE, we usually find that the amount of protective behavior on the first trial is higher than on the second trial.

It is now possible to look at the impact of this self-imposed similarity between the situations on the fear reaction as measured in the heart-rate channel. More specifically, is there a difference in the amount of the FAE as indicated during the last warning between these three groups? If our argument is correct, we should predict that there will be a difference with a higher FAE in those groups that maintain the same amount of protective behavior in both trials Table 12.5

TABLE 12.5
The Effect of Similarity in Protective Behavior on the FAE in Heart Rate (Warning C)

Protective Behavior	Mean	sd	t	p
Session 1 = Session 2 > 0	8.32	8.74	2.28	<.05
Session 1 > Session 2	4.63	8.70		
Session 1 = Session 2 = 0	7.51	8.27	2.08	<.05
Session 1 > Session 2	4.63	8.70		
Session 1 = Session 2 > 0	8.32	8.74	0.58	ns
Session 1 = Session 2 = 0	7.51	8.27		

presents the data. Starting with the mean intensity of FAE, we find that the reduction in heart rate during the last warning is most pronounced in the group comprised of subjects who engaged in protective behavior on both trials using exactly the same amount. Next comes the group of subjects who refrained from using the protective behavior option on both trials. Last are those who protected themselves more on the first trial than on the second. It is interesting to note that the difference between the two groups in which the amount of protective behavior (whether higher than 0 or 0) is the same in both sessions and the group in which the amount differs is statistically significant. The data thus give support to our analysis. When the amount of protective behavior is the same, there is a slight tendency toward higher FAEs in cases when the protective behavior is greater than 0, but this effect does not reach statistical significance.

The analysis of the FAE in terms of sequential stages as presented in the preceding pages rests on essentially the same empirical basis. What is presented here is another way to look at the desynchrony between heart rate and protective behavior, an analysis that is in line with our current understanding of learning processes. Thus, any attempt to decrease the FAE should utilize discriminative cues as one way to reduce the tendency to learn from the false alarm experience. This idea, which has some practical value, is pursued further in the last chapter.

False Alarm as a Reinforcer

From the point of view of the credibility of a warning system, a false alarm experience is essentially quite dangerous because it tends to reduce the credibility of subsequent threats. But from the point of view of the individual experiencing the cancellation of a threat, there are certain positive elements involved. Thus, for instance, it stands to reason that subjects who were quite threatened by the impending danger and experienced a substantial amount of fear feel relieved when they learn it is all over and there will be no shock. This relief can function as a positive reinforcer of the behavior that preceded it, if subjects perceive the cancellation to be contingent on their own behavior. Although from the point of view of the design of our experiments such perception of contingency is faulty, some subjects can still perceive the situation differently. Thus, instead of viewing the danger as naive and totally independent of their own actions, they may perceive it as cynical and act accordingly. In order to gain some information about this possibility, in several of the last experiments reported here we asked our subjects specifically to what extent the cancellation of the threat was contingent on their own behavior. About 20% of the subjects who were asked this question answered affirmatively. Although this is a small minority, it indicates that the psychological analysis leading to such an interpretation of the cancellation is in principle possible. Once such an interpretation takes place, the cancellation can serve as a reinforcer leading to an increased probability that subjects on the second trial will repeat their behavior from the first trial. This is particularly relevant when considering protective behavior, which is under total control of the subjects.

The false alarm thus produces an interesting dilemma. It should lead to a decrease in the amount of protective behavior due to the FAE itself, but if the situation is interpreted as one of a cynical danger, it may lead to a tendency to repeat as closely as possible the behavior from the earlier trial. In view of our analysis of the sequential stages of FAEs and the impact of self-produced similarity, we would submit that one of the main consequences of such an interpretation would be a higher FAE in the other response channels. This is possibly the basis of the finding reported in Table 12.4 that the FAE as evident in the amount of distraction is positively related between the two cancellations. In other words, it is possible that subjects who did not think about the approaching danger and distracted their mind were reinforced by the cancellation and proceeded to do more of the same on the next trial. Whatever the exact process involved, it illustrates the enormous complexity of the underlying mechanisms that operate in the false alarm situation. A great deal of additional research is required to allow more refined analysis of these phenomena.

Let us consider for a moment the difference between those subjects who engaged in protective behavior, and after the cancellation of the threat learned that it was unnecessary, and those that refrained from self-protection, and after the cancellation were vindicated. Which kind of experience is more potent in influencing subsequent behavior? Who learns more from the experience, those who were right or those who were wrong? Here the data are clear: The positive experience of being vindicated is more influential than the negative one. This is evident from the fact that practically none of the subjects who refrained from self-protection and were then confronted with the false alarm used self-protection on subsequent trials. On the other hand, many of the subjects who engaged in protective behavior continued to do so even following the cancellation of the threat, although often on a more reduced scale. This asymmetry in terms of the informational value of positive and negative information is not unlike the phenomenon discovered in many learning experiments. Specifically, the very fact that it is possible to teach a correct response, even when using a partial reinforcement of 50% or less, indicates that the positive information in the reinforced trials is greater than the negative information present in the nonreinforced or extinction trials.

Protective Behavior in the Absence of Threat

At an earlier stage of our discussion, we had a chance to deliberate on the problem of cynical dangers that are omnipresent and await the opportunity to strike. One illustration was the danger of a traffic accident. Here we are confronted with a situation in which there is no clear-cut threat; that is, there is nothing specific that necessarily indicates the proximity of the danger. At the same time, however, the very fact that there is not clear signaling of the danger does not necessarily indicate that the danger is remote. On the contrary, it is primarily through the self-protection of a driver who follows routine precautions that the danger is not greater. When the extent of self-protection and caution is reduced, for a variety of reasons, this necessarily increases the threat of an accident.

One process that may systematically reduce the alertness of the driver is the fact that nothing very frightening is happening. Thus, through minute discrepancies between optimal behavior and actual behavior, the driver may find out that there is no need to take precautions and that, even if he travels at a faster speed and less carefully, nothing much happens. Nothing much happens, that is, until it does. But it might very well be the case that earlier experiences taught the driver that he can get away with a certain amount of carelessness. Thus, we have a situation of a series of small false alarms, which are contingent on the reduction of protective behavior. This process can be seen as similar to the one of shaping, but in this case it is self-shaping. Such self-shaping can produce a gradual drift from careful self-protection to certain forms of neglect. If at any point during this process the driver experiences a near miss, this may restore the credibility of the threat and restore the motivation for self-protection. If a near miss does not take place, however, over relatively long periods of time, the danger of a true accident grows continuously.

Needless to say, this type of situation presents a form of desynchrony par excellence. After all, there is a need to engage in protective behavior without at the same time experiencing fear. It is precisely the induction of fear through a near miss experience that somehow restores the balance into this basically asymmetric relationship among the various systems under consideration. Although self-protection need not be under the control of fear, it is very difficult to maintain it for long durations in the total absence of fear.

FOUR SYSTEMS ANALYSIS OF FEAR

Before concluding this analysis, the possibility ought to be raised that the analysis of fear reaction can profit by the includsion of yet another system, namely, task performance. The discussion in Chapter 10 indicated that when individuals in a situation of threat have to engage in performing a task that is irrelevant to the threat itself, this poses a major demand on their attention. We have seen that there is a basic dilemma between the danger orientation and the task orientation. Because in terms of attention the channel capacity of individuals is finite, these two orientations are negatively related to each other; the more an individual attends to one, the less he or she can attend to the other.

The results reported in Chapter 10 also indicated that any manipulation that makes it easier for people to perform a task would actually relieve them to pay more attention to the danger and vice versa. This surprising, and at first glance paradoxical, outcome can best be understood in the context of a four system analysis of fear assuming partial independence among the various components.

Such a four system analysis would not be alien to traditional psychological treatment of behavior. More specifically, it could be argued that there is an interesting overlap between the various systems discussed and the classical division of behavior into its conative, cognitive, and affective aspects. Thus, the psychophysiological system is closely associated with the affective component, subjective experience with the cognitive component, and avoidance (or protective behavior) with the conative or motivational component. We suggest adding task performance as the representative of the fourth component, namely, that of attentional demands. Although these are not necessarily simple parallels, modern psychology cannot be satisfied with emotion, cognition, and motivation, without at the same time inquiring about the role of attention in any complex behavior. Needless to say, desynchrony among these four components, or some of them, is probably the rule rather than the exception. Even a relatively simple simulation of the FAE cannot, however, be satisfactory without explicitly paying attention to these complex interrelationships.

13 Some Clinical and Theoretical Issues

The preceding discussion of the false alarm effect and the three systems analysis of fear paves the way to the present attempt to tackle three particularly complex issues. First among them is the suggested distinction between avoidance and protective behavior. It touches upon some central difficulties in a variety of real-life settings, which defy adequate reality testing. The second issue, namely, the distinction between fear of danger and fear of fear, bears directly on some clinical problems pertinent to anxious and phobic patients. Finally, the last section of this chapter attempts to account for the FAE itself by resorting to some of the relevant psychological mechanisms.

AVOIDANCE AND PROTECTIVE BEHAVIOR

There are many reasons why the distinction between avoidance behavior and protective behavior needs to be made. Chief among them in the context of our present chapter is that Rachman (1978) and others who discuss the three systems analysis of fear relate to avoidance behavior, particularly as exhibited by phobic patients, as one of the central components. It can actually be said that avoidance behavior in those patients is their main problem. According to the prevalent theorizing in this area, it is precisely because of their tendency to avoid what is essentially a harmless situation that they are unable to discover for themselves that there is nothing to be afraid of. Traditional psychological experimentation also relates to avoidance learning as one of the most important elements of behavior in which fear and anxiety may play a role (e.g., Mowrer, 1960; Solomon & Wynne, 1954). Thus, one of the central issues to emerge from this tradition of research is the robustness of the avoidance phenomenon, namely, its resistance to extinction procedures.

The central element common to both the clinical and the experimental research traditions is the fact that when animals or people engage in avoidance behavior, there is no way for them to find out whether that behavior was actually necessary. In other words, there is built-in protection of the credibility of the threat, which induces such behavior in the first place. This is why it is so difficult to extinguish and why phobic patients maintain their avoidances even though they may be very costly to them personally.

Protective behavior as defined in our experimental program concerns the attempt of the individual to reduce the intensity of the damage that is anticipated in a threatening situation. Specifically, in our case it is the reduction of the intensity of the anticipated pain produced by the shock. However, a central element in this arrangement is that in no case can our subjects reduce the intensity to 0 and thus actually avoid the pain altogether. Protective behavior as used here thus deals with the intensity of the threat rather than its probability. This was, of course, necessary in our case in order to be able to study the effects of false alarms. If through instrumental behavior our subjects could change the situation to such an extent that there would actually be no chance of experiencing the shock, there would have been no way of knowing whether their behavior was necessary. In such a case the absence of shock could have been the outcome of two separate causes: (1) it could have been simply the effectiveness of the avoidance behavior that eliminated it; (2) it might have been a true false alarm. In the absence of independent information extrinsic to the warning system itself, there would have been no way to distinguish between the two. Furthermore, all available psychological knowledge would clearly suggest that the first of these two explanations would be the preferred one from the subjective point of view of the individuals concerned. Whether one would use the theory of cognitive dissonance (Festinger, 1957), reinforcement theory, or other notions such as the search for mastery, self-efficacy, projection, or delusion, the temptation to attribute the positive outcomes of one's effort to these actions is too great to resist.

The evidence for this should be clear; after all, in any avoidance situation the two logical possibilities do exist in principle. In other words, even phobic patients could in principle interpret the fact that a particular danger did not materialize due either to their own avoidance behavior or to the absence of the danger. That such is practically never the case (and that is why phobic patients are patients) indicates the strength of the first interpretation. From their point of view the credibility of the danger is protected from the FAE because of the avoidance behavior, which does not allow testing the credibility in the first place.

We thus posit that there is a major theoretical and practical difference between avoidance behavior and protective behavior. We suggest using the latter when the intensity of the danger rather than its probability is affected. Thus, logically, all avoidance behavior is at the same time protective behavior, but not the other way around. By this measure, protective behavior is never fully effective.

For the same reason, however, it is also more sensitive to demands presented by objective reality. Thus, people often take precautions that turn out "unnecessary" once the threat becomes a false alarm. In such a case protective behavior is not resistant to extinction; on the contrary, following a sequence of false alarms it is often drastically reduced. Put upside down, this argument can serve as a suggestion for a method to protect a warning system from the necessary credibility loss due to a false alarm. Thus, if it is possible to introduce avoidance proper into the situation, the individuals who experience the cancellation of the threat may be unable to distinguish between false alarm and successful avoidance. This, however, can turn out to be a mixed blessing indeed. Cynical dangers in particular provide the occasion for this form of protection of credibility, provided there is no extrinsic information about the threat.

When protective behavior is only *partially effective* in reducing the threat, it poses special problems of its own. If people are aware of the fact that the coping activity at their dispoasal is not sufficiently effective to eliminate a powerful threat totally, but only reduce it, they often act in what seems to be a paradoxical, irrational way. Whereas in principle partially effective protection is, of course, better than the alternative of no protection at all, certain individuals under highly threatened conditions prefer to refrain from self-protection altogether. It might very well be that this is to some extent based on one's attempt to maintain a sense of invulnerability at all costs. Protective behavior, particularly if it does not hold the promise of 100% protection, also serves as a reminder of the problem itself, and thus is sometimes avoided. Leventhal (1970) found that many of the people most in need of the preventive action refuse it in an attempt to maintain their illusion of personal invulnerability. Among a group of smokers encouraged to have chest X-rays, 53% of those with moderate levels of fear were willing to do so, as compared with only 6% of those with high fear, demonstrating that those with the greatest fear were *not* the ones most likely to take action to safeguard their health. In a recent volume on the denial of stress, Breznitz (1982) presents a more thorough analysis of this phenomenon in a variety of situations. Among the most dramatic circumstances where such denial is operative is the case of patients who recently suffered a heart attack. The prescribed regimen involving such things as diet, exercise, and so forth does not insure safety for the future and often serves as a reminder of the threat itself. Under these circumstances many patients prefer, for psychological reasons, to refrain from these activities altogether. This quest for invulnerability can very well lie at the core of backsliding into undesired forms of behavior by individuals who seek change but find difficulties in achieving it (Janis, 1982).

It is tempting to overstress the effectiveness of protective measures that are not 100% foolproof. Such "promise" often motivates individuals to invest in self-protection more than they would otherwise. This is particularly important when there is relatively low motivation for self-protection or when the behavior in question is costly in terms of time and effort. Thus, one sometimes finds that the army is tempted to promise that if the soldiers follow a particular self-protective routine exactly, they do not have to worry about being hit by the enemy. Naturally, such a presentation of the case of protective behavior increases the motivation to learn it, train it, and engage in it more thoroughly. But problems arise when evidence indicates that it was a false promise. Once that happens, the credibility of the controlling agency is dramatically reduced, and there is a great danger that the protective behavior will be abandoned or neglected altogether. It is only when the chances of putting it to test are minimal that one may encourage the overstatement of self-protection.

To illustrate again from the situation of cardiac patients following a heart attack, there might be a temptation for medical authorities to present the effectiveness of the various behaviors that the patient is encouraged to perform as greater than it truly is. Thus, rather than saying to patients that if they control their weight, exercise, eat proper foods, refrain from smoking, and so on, the probability of another heart attack would be substantially reduced, they might be told that if they do all of these things they have little to fear. Short-term considerations will thus be traded for long-term considerations; patients would be more willing to invest in changing their life style in accordance with the medical advice, but the realization that another patient who did exactly this experienced another heart attack, or even died, may have shattering consequences. However, a more balanced presentation of the effectiveness of self-protection would still have to deal with the attempt to deny the threat and one's personal vulnerability. Thus, even if the patients are explicitly told the truth, they may reinterpret the information in a way that will suit their own needs and put greater weight on the perceived effectiveness of these protective measures. These defensive tendencies are sometimes so powerful that no matter how reality is presented, it can be construed in a totally biased fashion.

FEAR OF DANGER VERSUS FEAR OF FEAR

Not only is fear an unpleasant experience, it is a threat in its own right. Thus, when confronted with a situation in which the individual anticipates his or her own fear reaction, that element adds to the apprehensions involved. We may thus claim that not only the anticipation of danger can be problematic, but the anticipation of the fear reaction that will develop is an additional psychological burden. This idea is, of course, the central element in Mowrer's two stage theory of avoidance conditioning, as well as other formulations in this area. Animals and people are assumed to be motivated to reduce the fear reaction as such, the successful reduction of which becomes a positive reinforcement (Mowrer, 1960).

In Chapter 8 we reported a surprising finding, which we attempted to understand in the framework of this analysis. Subjects who could protect themselves only during the last warning prior to the materialization of the danger were very rarely using the protective behavior option. One possible explanation for this rested on the idea that because the fear was already experienced, they had less to gain by protecting themselves at this late sequence of anticipation. In other words, protective behavior is assumed to serve two separate functions: It reduces the anticipated intensity of pain, but it also reduces the fear during the anticipation stage proper. Though logically interrelated, these two functions can to some extent be independent psychologically. We have shown that it is possible to manipulate the one without necessarily affecting the other.

Let us now try to carry this argument one logical step further. In the same manner that fear can be concerned with either the objective danger or with the experience of fear itself and in the same manner that protective behavior can be used either to reduce the objective intensity of the danger or the intensity of the experienced fear, so must any attempt to reduce either fear or protective behavior address itself to the foregoing distinction. This point is well illustrated when considering the role of *reality testing* as a means to extinguish a phobic reaction.

We submit that phobic patients are not so much afraid of the objective danger in the particularly frightening situation, but rather of their own panic reaction, which they know ahead of time that they will experience. Furthermore, we claim that the avoidance of the situation is an attempt to cope primarily with the fear itself, rather than with any objective danger. These patients often know perfectly well that their fears are irrational, yet they cannot help themselves. The reason for these fears is immaterial in terms of our analysis; we suggest that the most frightening element for these patients is their own experience of fear and anxiety. By avoiding these situations, they are able to avoid their own emotional reactions, often at great cost to quality of their lives. The notion that through reality testing these patients will be able to overcome their fears rests on the assumption that what is needed is for them to discover that the danger is objectively not present. If we are right, however, this is a faulty assumption. For many of these patients the reality that is threatening is the experience of their own fear and anxiety, and thus, by exposing them to the situation—a procedure that always involves the experience of the fear reaction itself—their fears are always vindicated. For them, the frightening reality is the experience of fear, and thus any reality testing that evokes these fears only reinforces this process.

The FAE is based on the cancellation of an objective danger. Therefore, it cannot directly affect phobic patients for whom the objective danger is of secondary importance. They are in possession of extrinsic information indicating that the danger is not objectively real, but yet at the same time it is psychologically very real. The discovery that the danger did not materialize—a typical false alarm—need not, therefore, contribute much to the extinction of the phobic reaction itself. This is particularly so if there was an intense subjective experience of fear in the process. A host of research with clinical populations indicates that when the patients are able to approach the frightening situation, the fear itself is not reduced, but actually increases. This is the necessary outcome of desynchrony and particularly of the negative relationship between protective behavior and fear as emphasized in our research. One should bear in mind that from this point of view protective behavior is never truly wasted in the sense that even if the alarm turns out to be a false alarm, a certain amount of fear is saved. Even when fear turns out to be unjustified, given the fear, any behavior that reduces it is always justified.

FALSE ALARM EFFECT: HABITUATION, EXTINCTION, OR WHAT?

Our attempt to reconsider the three systems analysis of fear in view of the FAE brings us to the question of the theoretical status of the FAE itself. After demonstrating its significance and trying to understand some of the parameters involved, the psychological process responsible for the credibility loss and its manifestation should be further elaborated. Up to now our position was that the FAE is due to "learning from experience." In other words, we see in the false alarm situation essentially a learning situation, which ought to follow the same rules that have been discovered in the general framework of learning.

Psychological theory suggests two different concepts that may account for the reduction in the various indexes of fear due to cancellation of a threat: *habituation* and *extinction*. Although the two have a great deal in common, they are basically different psychological processes.

In one of the earlier, and by now classical, discussions of this problem, Janis (1962) used the term "emotional adaptation." He claimed:

> In its most general form, the "emotional adaptation" hypothesis asserts that the vigilance tendency aroused by any warning concerning a familiar source of danger will be dampened if the recipient has previously been exposed to one or more warnings pertaining to the same threat, provided that the warnings do not add any new information about increased vulnerability to the danger. Little experimental evidence is available as yet, but field studies of disaster behavior provide some preliminary support for this hypothesis (see Janis, 1951; Janis, 1959, pp. 227–229; McCarthy, 1943 [p. 81].

It is our hope that this book furnishes the experimental evidence that Janis refers to, but the exact mechanism through which emotional adaptation is achieved is far from being self-evident. Because this issue, in addition to being of major interest in its own right, is also directly relevant to the problem of desynchrony between the various components of fear, we should now address ourselves to it.

Mackworth views habituation as a "decrease in sensitivity to stimulation and a decrease in readiness to respond" (1969, quoted from Rachman, 1978, p. 201). According to Groves and Thompson (1970), habituation is assumed to be determined largely by stimulus repetition. Extinction, on the other hand, is viewed by psychological theory as a manipulation in which a previously reinforced response is now emitted without being followed by the reinforcer.

In his attempt to analyze the processes involved in the fear reduction of a phobic patient, Rachman (1978) likewise raises the two concepts of habituation and extinction as possible candidates of explanatory value. He makes the point that the assessment of the possible role of these processes has been hampered by the question of whether they can in principle be distinguished from each other: "Both are decremental processes and the repeated presentation of the fearful stimulus is the central operation in both. They also share some parametric properties such as the duration of presentations, intervals between stimuli, and so on [p. 273]." As one of the differences appears to be that habituation is a temporary decrement, whereas extinction tends to be stable, the absence in our experimental program of trials after a relatively long interval following the false alarm experience makes it impossible for us to determine exactly whether habituation is indeed operative or not. The logic of the arguments presented in the preceding pages of this chapter, as well as most of the data, would suggest the possibility that the different response channels may be under the control of different psychological mechanisms responsible for fear reduction. We agree with Rachman (1978), who suggests that perhaps: "The physiological component may be particularly susceptible to habituation, and the avoidance behavior to extinction. The subjective components seem open to both processes, habituation and extinction, although the extinction hypothesis might not explain adequately what the relevant reinforcement is [p. 277]." This implies that one major source of desynchrony in the false alarm situation can be that the different systems are differentially influenced by these two psychological mechanisms of response decrement.

This raises a host of new problems and issues. Thus, we ought to consider the question of whether credibility can be extinguished because it is not conceived of as a response, but rather as an expectation or belief. Another related issue would be the unitariness of the credibility. If carried to an extreme, the three systems analysis would make credibility a useful concept void of much meaning. Is there one credibility, or do we need the concepts of psychophysiological credibility, experiential credibility, and so forth? What is the role of labeling in this situation? Is it not conceivable that by labeling the threat as either credible to a certain extent or not credible our subjects introduce a certain amount of coordination between the various response channels leading to greater synchrony and covariance.

The particular experimental analogue of warning systems used in our research, and quite probably in many real warning systems as well, adds additional complexity to this analysis. It is clear that neither habituation nor extinction can account for certain features that play an important role in the false alarm situation. This makes it necessary to introduce additional explanatory devices into this context.

Consider, for instance, the fact that protective behavior is only partially effective and, unlike avoidance, makes it possible for the person to get direct evidence about its necessity. This feature leads to two important consequences. On the one hand, those subjects who engaged in a substantial amount of protective behavior may following the cancellation of the threat find out that it was wasted effort on their part and thus reduce it on subsequent trials. Such relatively quick response reduction is impossible in case of complete avoidance. On the other hand, those individuals who did not take major protective action, or no protective action at all, are vindicated by the cancellation of the threat, and their earlier decision is thus further reinforced. Thus, another possible explanatory mechanism for the FAE, as well as desychrony, is the positive reinformcement that we have just described. This is surely different from any extinction procedure.

However, this is all a minor complication considering the one to be raised at this point. We refer to the fact that instead of a conditioning paradigm, which is based on a series of repetitions, both the induction of the threat and its cancellation are based on single-trial verbal instructions. Thus, how can one speak of the extinction of responses that were never reinforced in the first place: What is the status of verbal instructions coming from either the experimenter or from some formal source representing a warning system? Furthermore, the very fact that we are dealing with single-trial learning indicates that our subjects never really experienced a similar threat, not to mention its actual materialization. This would increase their dependence on the exact words used by the source of information, and its credibility would be judged purely on evidence available in the present experimental context, rather than relying on prior experience. Seligman (1971) makes the distinction between fears transmitted indirectly through information and those that are "prepared phobias" (i.e., experienced directly). He suggests that the first have a larger cognitive element, implying that they can be more readily acquired and reduced by cognitive manipulation.

The results of our experiments suggest some similarities between verbal instruction and the extinction paradigm. In view of the phenomenological difference between the two, these similarities are particularly striking. Let us mention two:

1. The greater resistance to extinction of responses acquired under a partial reinforcement schedule is a well-documented phenomenon. It is thus of some interest to note that low-probability threats, when canceled, produce a smaller FAE. This finding, which was elaborated in Chapter 6, illustrates the type of morphological equivalence between the two paradigms. One can view a low-

probability threat as analogous to one acquired under a partial reinforcement schedule in a typical conditioning paradigm. The rarer and more unpredictable the occurrence of the reinforcements are, the longer it will take to extinguish their effect. In the same way, the lower the initial probability of the announced threat, the smaller will the ensuing credibility loss be when it does not materialize.

2. In Chapter 5, when discussing the effect of pacing of warnings on the FAE, we reported that by earlier cancellation of the threat the more advanced warnings are protected from credibility loss. It is because they do not appear that they are thus protected, very much like the case of extinction procedure, when the absence of a response protects it from extinction.

Analogues to habituation proper can also be found in our data. Thus, we have seen that whereas each onset of a warning raises the heart rate of our subjects, immediately following the warning, as long as no new information comes in, there is a gradual relaxation of the psychophysiological response. Furthermore, the mere repetition of the stimulus situation between trials leads almost automatically to reduction in heart rate, as well as in reported tension. Thus, whereas the FAE in the protective behavior channel seems to be under a substantial amount of control from cognitive factors, the mere repetition of similar stimulus components on the second and third threats appears to be sufficient to explain the FAE in some of the other response channels. Habituation can also be seen as the major element in the self-shaping phenomenon discussed earlier. We have suggested the possibility that in certain situations of cynical danger, when there is a need for protective behavior in the absence of any clearly signaled threat, there is a danger that due to frequent small false alarms the level of protective behavior will gradually be reduced. Such self-shaping might very well be the outcome of habituation to what is essentially a seemingly harmless repetitive situation.

Side by side with these analogues, however, there are also certain features in our data that do not fit easily into the existing explanatory frameworks. Thus, for instance, the fact that probability of engaging in protective behavior is unrelated to the amplitude of that behavior indicates the central role of cognitive mediation. Furthermore, the centrality of temporal considerations concerning the decision related to protective behavior likewise suggests cognitive mediation. The various manipulations reported here by which we reduced the FAE or reinstated lost credibility indicate that the FAE is at least partially under the control of an elaborate decision-making process. Such a process cannot be exhaustively described by either habituation or extinction. It is a separate process of its own, deserving special attention. These additional complexities do not, however, detract from the main argument that desynchrony can be the outcome of a variety of psychological mechanisms involved in the FAE. On the contrary, the cognitive elements, which we submit cannot be subsumed under either habituation or extinction, further contribute to the asymmetries involved.

14 Toward a Theory of Credibility of Warning Systems

We have reached the point in our analysis where a certain amount of integration seems warranted. The remaining two chapters attempt to put all the experimental evidence into perspective. Thus, in this chapter we attempt to formulate some basic theoretical propositions that may account for much of what has been discussed so far. In the last chapter we attempt to translate some of these ideas into more concrete suggestions concerning application.

Inasmuch as all our work deals with the credibility of warning systems, it would be presumptuous and unjustified to attempt any generalization beyond that frame of reference. Whatever is said about credibility should therefore be seen in the context of credibility of warning systems only. But at the same time, the possibility exists that if our formulations hold true in one relatively important area of experience, they ought to be tested in other areas as well. My personal opinion is that at least some of the propositions concerning credibility are of more general value, but this is something only the future can decide. I hope that kind readers are not too harsh in their criticism when the temptation to suggest such broader lawfulness becomes too great to resist.

Because warning systems are primarily concerned with predicting something about the future, their credibility is likewise concerned with that future. It can be seen as a belief or a set of beliefs concerning the nature of a threat associated with the particular function of a warning system. Credibility is related to information, and consequently, its status is changing as new information becomes available to the receiver. We have already seen that it is important to distinguish between two different sources of information: intrinsic information coming from the warning system itself and extrinsic information coming from sources other than the warning system. Both have important implications to the credibility of the warning system at any point in time, although their exact status differs in many respects.

THE LAW OF INITIAL CREDIBILITY   205

This implies that credibility cannot be viewed as a discrete phenomenon, but rather must be seen as a dynamic, continuously changing belief. The dynamic factor is further enhanced due to the fact that credibility has implications for action; once a particular action is taken, however, that in itself may change the credibility of the warning system.

Credibility is always subjective. As a belief, or set of beliefs, it does not and cannot have an objective status. Objective events can, of course, be systematically related to credibility, but phenomenologically, they do not constitute the credibility, nor can they replace it. The subjective nature of credibility also implies that individuals may differ in their perception of the same set of "objective events," and therefore their beliefs about future threats may differ as well. The experimental program reported in this volume followed precisely this logic. We attempted to investigate the various objective features of information management in the case of false alarms in order to be able to specify the relationships between these events and credibility. At the same time, however, we began the investigation of individual differences in the experimental situation in order to be better able to explicate some of the between subjects variance.

Credibility is a theoretical construct. We never measure it directly, but only by resorting to a set of indexes that are presumably related to it and affected by it. Whereas in principle it could be possible to relate the various objective manipulations to the set of objective indexes that are the outcomes of these manipulations, we suggest that this would not be the best advised course of action theoretically. Credibility of warning systems, although ascertained only indirectly, can help us better analyze the many forces operative in any given situation and introduce more meaningful order and lawfulness into the complex interactions involved. Needless to say, even though we prefer to consider credibility as a theoretical construct, this does not preclude the possibility that individuals actually experience the beliefs involved and respond to them.

Of the many types of information that influence the status of the credibility of a warning system, one particular kind stands out as most important, namely, the extent to which the anticipated future as described by the warning system materializes or not. This relates to both positive and negative outcomes. Thus, a warning system that predicts a particular danger will materialize at a particular time in a particular way gains a great deal of credibility if such indeed happens to be the case. In the same way, although probably to a smaller extent, if a warning system predicts a particular danger will not strike, and it does not, this also adds to its credibility. Taken to its absurd extreme, one can assume that as long as nothing happens, and indeed there were no warnings, this, too, should add to the credibility of a warning system. Nonevents are, however, psychologically very tricky in more than one way, and it is not at all clear whether we are able to address them meaningfully.

At the same time, two important mistakes or failures of a warning system can drastically reduce its credibility. On the one hand, we have the false alarm situation implying that a warning was issued, and it did not materialize; on the other hand, there is the surprise of a danger that strikes without prior warnings. Whereas this volume is concerned primarily with the first kind of failure, there is little doubt that a warning system which failed to provide information about an impending danger must by virtue of its raison d'etre lose credibility. Such is the fear of a surprise danger that warning systems tend to respond to relatively weak signals indicating its approach, thus producing many false alarms. On the other hand, our research indicates that a few false alarms are sufficient to set the stage psychologically for a surprise of this sort. The FAE is a powerful decrease in the credibility of a warning system, which dramatically reduces its effectiveness in spite of accurate detection and information management.

Paradoxically, if after a few false alarms a warning system predicts a danger, which is not taken seriously by the receiver due to the credibility loss based on the recent history of the warning system, and if that new danger happens to materialize, the warning system may regain a great deal of credibility. This can, to some extent, start the cycle of credibility loss all over again.

THE LAW OF INITIAL CREDIBILITY

Most of the information gained in the experimental program reported in the preceding chapters can be integrated under two broad theoretical statements. The first of the two is *the law of initial credibility*. In its exact form it reads: "The amount of credibility loss of a warning system following a false alarm is a positive function of the initial credibility of the warning system prior to the information concerning the cancellation of the threat."

The law of initial credibility posits that a warning system that enjoyed high credibility will lose more credibility following a false alarm than one whose credibility was lower in the first place. Stated differently, it suggests that those people who took the threat more seriously will have a greater amount of credibility loss following the false alarm information than those who took it less seriously.

Although our experimental work did not test the impact of a true alarm, we suggest that the same law of initial credibility holds for threats that do materialize and increase the credibility of the warning system. This hypothesis, which ought to be tested in separate research, would read: "The amount of credibility gain of a warning system following a true alarm is a negative function of the initial credibility of the warning system prior to the information concerning the materialization of the threat."

This hypothesis states that warning systems that enjoy a relatively high level of credibility will gain less by a successful prediction concerning a danger than those that are less credible. It should be noted that in the case of credibility loss we speak of credibility change being a positive function of the initial credibility, whereas in the case of credibility gain the function is assumed to be negative.

Although the logic of the arguments in both instances is essentially the same, our research provides the evidence for only the first instance (i.e., the effect of false alarms). Let us now recount the findings that support this broad theoretical statement.

Between-Groups Manipulations

The experiment concerning the effect of pacing of warnings on the FAE, as reported in Chapter 5, gives clear support to the law of initial credibility. The data indicate that the arrival of information concerning the cancellation of the threat during a more advanced stage of warning leads to a greater amount of credibility loss than if the cancellation takes place in the earlier parts of anticipation. It should be recalled that as the danger comes closer, it is taken more seriously by the subject, increasing the subjective probability that the threat will materialize. By contrast, if the false alarm takes place during the very first stage of warning, the damage to the credibility of the warning system is smaller as the danger appears at this point to be still rather distant.

The research on stated probability of the initial threat as reported in Chapter 6 gives clear evidence supporting the law of initial credibility. Thus, it was found that the higher the initial probability, the greater the amount of the FAE following the cancellation. Subjects who were given the initial probability of 1.0 indicated greater credibility loss than those who were given the initial probability of .5, with the subjects who were given the probability of .05 showing the smallest credibility loss of all.

It should be stated that the between-groups manipulations mentioned here, as well as other possible manipulations along similar lines, are essentially under the control of the information-management subsystem of any warning system. Thus, one way to reduce the amount of credibility loss would be to translate the implications of the law of initial credibility into a policy of information management. The possible applications of such a policy are further elaborated in Chapter 15.

Within-Group Variance

The law of initial credibility can be analyzed on the individual-differences level as well. It specifically suggests that whatever the particular group treatment, those individuals that take the threat more seriously should have a greater amount of credibility loss following the cancellation of the threat. We can thus look into individual differences as a source of additional information concerning the validity of the preceding theoretical formulation.

In its most general form, the foregoing suggests that positive correlations should be found between all measures of credibility or fear reaction and the amount of reduction in that credibility or fear reaction following the false alarm.

Such positive correlations were found on all indexes measured, most of them being relatively high and statistically significant. But there is a difficulty because the correlations between an initial score and a difference score would always be positive for mathematical reasons. Cronbach and Furby (1970) address themselves to the issue of measuring change and the mathematical and statistical problems it raises. There are, unfortunately, no simple ways to overcome this problem, and thus even when a relationship is a true finding, there is a great difficulty in distinguishing between it and a mathematical artifact. In order to gain some insight into the law of initial credibility on the individual level, we thus had to resort to more complex statistical procedures. These procedures did not, unfortunately, allow us to analyze the entire spectrum of responses available in our studies; the only response channel that could have been treated in this manner was the psychophysiological index of heart rate.

Our first analysis is based on the experiment that investigated the effects of probability on the FAE. The 56 subjects in this experiment were divided into three different groups, but for the purposes of the present analysis they were all grouped together. The main reason for choosing this experiment as the beginning of our analysis was that the heart-rate data in these early experiments were analyzed differently than in those that followed. The reader may recall that initially we counted every single heartbeat during the various stages of the experiment, and only later did we switch to the more economic sampling of the highest and lowest heart rate as representative of the various segments studied. We have thus opted for the more conservative approach of coding the heart rate as providing the suitable basis for the preliminary testing of the law of initial credibility on the individual level.

Specifically, we have computed for each subject: (1) the heart rate during the last minute of anticipation, namely, during Warning C in the first session; (2) the amount of FAE in the heart-rate channel by deducting from the foregoing the heart rate during the last warning of the second session (C12); (3) the net heart rate during the last warning of the first session by deducting from it the initial base line that was measured on the entrance to the experimental room; and (4) the base line itself. Table 14.1 presents the means, standard deviations, and the intercorrelations between these four measures. The table indicates that the amount of FAE is, as predicted, positively related to the heart rate during the last warning of the first session. At the same time, however, it is important to note that the correlation with the net increase in heart rate during that warning is even higher. This definitely cannot be accounted for by mathematical artifacts. No correlation was found between the base level and the amount of the FAE.

Now our problem is to find a way to extricate the artifactual component of the correlation, which is due to the fact that both C1 and C12 share a common element (i.e., C1). In order to achieve this purpose we have performed a step-wise multiple regression analysis with the FAE as the dependent variable. By forcing C1 to enter first into the equation, it is possible to compute the partial

THE LAW OF INITIAL CREDIBILITY   209

TABLE 14.1
Indexes of Initial Fear Reaction (Heart Rate) and Credibility Loss
($N = 56$)

Variable	Mean	sd
Base	75.96	13.24
C1	77.95	13.34
C1NET	1.99	9.84
C12 (FAE)	2.02	5.26

Intercorrelations

	Base	C1	C1NET	C12
Base	1.00	.75	−.36	.05
C1	.75	1.00	.38	.42
C1NET	−.36	.38	1.00	.51
C12 (FAE)	.05	.42	.51	1.00

correlation of C1NET. That correlation was found to be .42, $f = 11.24$, $p < .01$. Thus, we see that the relationship between the net increase in heart rate and the amount of FAE is not explained entirely by the intensity of fear reaction on the first trial. Solving the entire stepwise multiple regression, we find that the BETA for C1 is .27, and for C1NET it is .41. This, too, suggests that it is the increase in heart rate rather than its actual value that has a major impact on the amount of the FAE.

In order to gain a better picture of the interrelations among these four measures, a path analysis was performed with the FAE (C12) as the dependent variable. Figure 14.1 presents the results. The estimates of the various forces playing a role in determining the actual simple correlation between the various variables are quite surprising. Thus, we find that there is actually a negative influence of the base level on the amount of the FAE. This suggests that those individuals with lower base levels, as measured in the context of this experiment, subsequently have a higher FAE than those who start on a higher level of fear

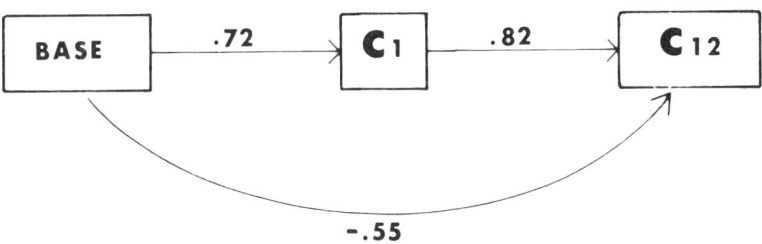

FIG. 14.1 Path analysis on the effects of initial fear reaction on credibility loss ($N = 56$).

reaction. This important and unpredicted finding should be further elaborated as our analysis evolves.

In order to test for the robustness of these results, we have proceeded to analyze these relationships for the entire sample of our subjects who participated in all of the experiments. Here our sample consists of 239 individuals, and instead of the total number of heartbeats for any critical time period, we are using the highest heart rate recorded during any such period. This is clearly visible in the actual means of heart rate, which are now of course much higher than in the previous analysis. Table 14.2 presents the means, standard deviations, and intercorrelations between the relevant variables for the entire sample of subjects. Once again we can see that there is a significant and high correlation between the FAE and the amount of fear reaction during the last warning of the first session. This time there is also a small positive correlation between the base line, as measured by the highest heart rate during the period preceding the stress instructions, and the FAE. The results of path analysis appear in Fig. 14.2. The data of the path analysis based on the entire sample of subjects are essentially very similar to those reported in Fig. 14.1. Again we see the negative influence of base line on the FAE.

Last but not least, we have tried to test the law of initial credibility by selecting out of the entire pool of subjects only those who demonstrated the mean heart rate during the last warning of the first session. This total restriction of range makes it impossible to explain the remaining variance in the FAE in terms of the shared element of C1. More specifically, because we found that the mean highest heart rate during C1 is 106, we selected all subjects whose highest heart rate during that period ranged between 103 and 109. This consists of 1/6 of one standard deviation from each side of the mean. There were 23 individuals who

TABLE 14.2
Indexes of Initial Fear Reaction (Heart Rate) and Credibility Loss
($N = 239$)

Variable	Mean	sd
Base (H)	95.86	14.48
C1 (H)	106.25	17.48
C1NET	10.39	12.55
C12	7.07	8.06

Intercorrelations				
	Base (H)	C1 (H)	C1NET	C12
Base (H)	1.00	.71	−.17	.21
C1 (H)	.71	1.00	.58	.51
C1NET	−.17	.58	1.00	.47
C12	.21	.51	.47	1.00

THE LAW OF INITIAL CREDIBILITY 211

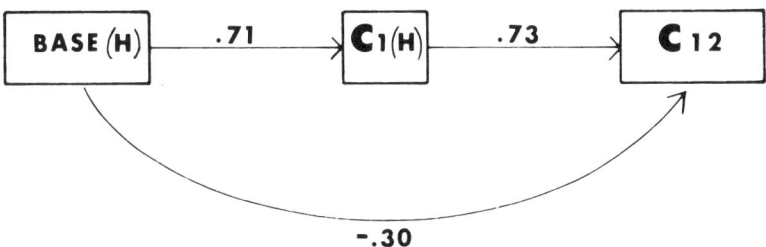

FIG. 14.2 Path analysis on the effects of initial fear reaction on credibility loss ($N = 239$).

met this rather harsh criterion, and the analysis was performed on them. Table 14.3 presents the means, standard deviations, and intercorrelations between the four relevant variables for this group of subjects. The positive correlation between C1 and C12 was obviously wiped out by this selection, and we have actually found a small and insignificant negative correlation between the two. After partialing out the effect of C1 on C12, we found that the contribution of C1NET and of the base line is actually increased to .34 and −.34, correspondingly. (The reader should be aware of the fact that after partialing out C1, the contribution of C1NET and of the base line must actually be the same, but in a different direction.) Of main interest is the finding that the base line is negatively correlated to the amount of FAE as would have been by now expected on the basis of our previous analysis. This negative correlation, which could be seen in the path analysis described earlier, could surface, however, only by controlling for the impact of C1 through the selection procedure that we have used. There is in principle a difference between statistical control of a variable through partial

TABLE 14.3
Controlling for C1 (H) and the FAE (C1H>103 and C1H<109)

Variable	Mean	sd
Base (H)	94.52	8.80
C1 (H)	106.04	1.74
C1NET	11.52	9.01
C12	6.65	8.26

Intercorrelations				
Base (H)	1.00	−.02	−.98	−.33
C1 (H)	−.02	1.00	.22	−.20
C1NET	−.98	.22	1.00	.28
C12	−.33	−.20	.28	1.00

correlation procedure and control through particular selection of subjects, which makes it impossible for a certain variable to affect the difference. It is important to note that those procedures yielded essentially the same results.

In trying to summarize these analyses, the law of initial credibility appears to hold not only on the intergroup level, but also on the intragroup or individual level. Thus, we see that it is not the amount of fear reaction during the first session as such that is positively related to the FAE, but rather the amount of increase in fear from base line to the last warning of that session that can explain a significant amount of the variance in the FAE itself. Furthermore, we have seen that the fear reaction as measured by the psychophysiological index of heart rate prior to the impact of the first threat is negatively related to the FAE. This is in addition to the aforementioned finding, and it constitutes a different psychological element, which ought to be taken into consideration.

Needless to say, the base lines recorded in this study are not true base lines. Our subjects are aroused by the various procedures prior to the announcement of the first threat, as the relatively high heart rates indicate. The baseline label is therefore quite misleading. It would be more appropriate to think in terms of a general disposition toward fear reaction prior to specific information about the nature of the threats. Such dispositions may in turn be related to certain personality characteristics, such as state and trait anxiety, locus of control, social desirability, and others, some of which have been discussed in Chapter 11.

There appears to be an interesting distinction between a phasic increase in fear—as measured by C1NET—and a more "chronic" high level—as measured by the base line. They influence the FAE in opposite directions; namely, whereas the amount of the phasic reaction is positively related to the FAE, the chronic level is negatively related to it. In simple psychological terms this would imply that:

1. The higher the increase in fear due to the impact of the threat, the greater is the credibility loss following its cancellation.
2. The higher the chronic level of fear, the smaller is the FAE. In other words, those who are more frightened "in general" remain more frightened of the second, postcancellation threat as well.

As these two measures are intricately related to each other, it is only through indirect means that their separate impact can be properly ascertained.

A POSSIBLE EXPLANATION OF THE LAW OF INITIAL CREDIBILITY

Although our experiments helped us discover the law of initial credibility, they cannot provide an adequate explanation for it. In order to take that additional step, specific studies will have to be carried out attempting to test for specific elements in the law of initial credibility which might favor one explanation relative to the others. Until this research is forthcoming, it may be of some use to put forward what appears at this stage to be one possible explanation of this reliable phenomenon.

In its broadest form the explanation can be seen as resting on the principle of *minimization of regret.* Following the cancellation of the threat, individuals realize that because they have taken the threat seriously they invested in effort that turned out to be unnecessary. The greater the amount of initial credibility, the greater the amount of investment that individuals are willing to make under these circumstances. Consequently, after the cancellation of the threat, the greater is the disappointment or regret about their own behavior.

Considering the various facets of behavior analyzed in our experimental program, let us be more explicit. The waste can occur on several levels:

1. Protective behavior may be perceived as wasted effort leading to unnecessary precautions at some cost to the individual.

2. From the hindsight of the false alarm the fear reaction itself can be perceived as wasted emotion. This was clearly indicated in our study about the timing of protective behavior (Chapter 8) where we found that subjects who could not protect themselves until the very last stage of the anticipation did not find it worthwhile to invest in protective behavior at that late stage. It was argued that the reason for this is that the fear experience during the anticipation proper is already a thing of the past and could not be reduced or saved by protective behavior. Subjects who experienced high fear during the first session, when told that the threat would not materialize, may have felt fooled by the experimenter or by the warning system and that their fear was unwarranted by reality.

3. By taking a particular threat seriously, individuals required to perform an unrelated task could not attend to it properly. Thus, the high initial credibility of the threat led to decrement in task performance or to wasted attention. In Chapter 10 we saw the extent to which the danger orientation and the task orientation compete for the attention of the individual in this kind of situation; by investing in one, the other is neglected. High initial credibility of the threat leads to greater investment in the danger orientation with consequent performance decrement. From the hindsight of the false alarm information, this again could be perceived as waste.

4. We have already discussed at some length the notion of loss of face, which is of concern to our subjects from the point of view of unnecessary self-protection. This, too, suggests that when the initial credibility is high, the chances for losing face in front of the experimenter or meaningful others are higher than when the initial credibility is small.

The perception of wasted effort is proportional to the amount of initial credibility, thus producing the effect described here. When the next threat comes, individuals want to protect themselves from additional waste, or stated differently, they want to insure that they will not again regret their behavior. Although there is no guarantee that this time the alarm would be a false one, on the basis of previous experience there is a fair chance that circumstances will repeat themselves. It is on this basis that the perception of wasted effort is superimposed and amplifies the FAE.

The law of initial credibility, particularly if the foregoing explanation of it is valid, thus appears to work contrary to what one would predict on the basis of the theory of cognitive dissonance (Festinger, 1957). This theory, as well as its subsequent developments, would predict that the greater the effort spent, the greater the commitment to do likewise in the future. There is, however, a very good reason for this discrepancy. In order for the cognitive dissonance argument to be relevant, it is essential that the individual is not aware of any unnecessary effort on his or her part. The classical experiments on cognitive dissonance all had to insure that subjects who gain less for the same behavior are unaware of the fact that others gain more. In the absence of explicit information of this nature, cognitive dissonance appears to play a major role in motivating people to maintain their initial commitment and to justify it by all means. It might indeed be the case that in situations which allow for total avoidance of danger something similar may play a role in maintaining that behavior. But such is not the case in situations like ours, which contrary to avoidance allow only protective behavior of a certain degree. Thus, there is clear evidence that it was unnecessary, leading to the law of initial credibility. The prophecy of the warning system clearly failed, and so did those who believed in it.

THE LAW OF INTERWARNING SIMILARITY

The second organizing principle based on our research relates to the stimulus properties of the information coming from the warning system. When a warning system issues a warning, it does so in a particular way. Receivers process that information and compare it to other experiences which they have had with the same warning system. Thus, if a warning did not materialize and if the next warning is issued in very much the same manner, the perceived similarity between these two warnings increases the FAE. In other words, the amount of generalization from the false alarm experience to the next warning is increased by the similarity between the two warnings. This surely is a simple notion taken from the psychology of perception and learning. Stated more explicitly in the present context, it reads: "The greater the similarity as perceived by the receiver between a warning which turned out to be a false alarm and a subsequent warning, the greater the credibility loss."

The law of interwarning similarity is also concerned with the subjective perception of the receiver. Even though similarity can clearly be manipulated by objective factors of information management, the critical factor remains the subjectively perceived similarity rather than the objective one. For a variety of reasons these two levels, although obviously highly correlated, may sometimes lead to important discrepancies; there are also reasons individuals may perceive sequential warnings as more or less similar than they actually are, leading to important psychological consequences. The law of interwarning similarity relates to two consecutive warnings. Although there may be a gradient of influence of a false alarm beyond a single step, we do not know anything about this possibility at this point. All our research was based on the immediate-recency effects of the canceled threat on a subsequent similar one.

Experimental Evidence

Throughout this volume we have met evidence relevant to the law of interwarning similarity. Let us mention here only the most important findings:

1. In Chapter 6 we analyzed the question of the extent to which the FAE is entirely determined by reactions to the threat that was later canceled or also by reactions to the subsequent threat. We found that although a great amount of the FAE is indeed determined by behavior to the initial, canceled threat, it is not exclusively so. To some extent, the amount of the FAE depends on the information presented during the second threat. The reason is clearly that only when the second threat takes place can individuals learn to what extent they can rely on their recent false alarm experience. The greater the similarity between the new threat and the canceled one, the greater the FAE. The law of interwarning similarity does not allow the drawing of conclusions on the basis of the initial threat alone; it must be compared to the second one.

2. The data concerning postcancellation explanations are particularly relevant to this issue. As we saw in Chapter 9 the attempt to regain lost credibility by explaining that the new information, unavailable during the issuing of the threat, justified its cancellation, does not restore any credibility. This, too, is to some extent the outcome of the law of interwarning similarity. The receiver understands why the warning system failed, but when the next threat is issued, the warning system and its information are essentially the same as they were on the first trial; thus, there is no reason to assume that this time they will not fail. It is only by changing some vital element in the warning system itself, such as the decision maker in charge of the information processing, that the similarity between the two occasions is reduced, and the second threat is to some extent treated as a new one. As we saw in Chapter 9 this can restore a certain amount of lost credibility, particularly in the protective behavior channel.

The law of interwarning similarity can be the basis of additional deductions that could be tested in the laboratory directly. One such possibility would be the effect of certain stimulus properties or labels on the FAE. These can be changed and manipulated at relatively little cost and grant the warning system a certain amount of credibility even if there was a false alarm experience. This is further analyzed in the last chapter of this book.

Implications

The law of initial credibility implies that credibility loss is a negatively decelerating function. The FAE should be highest on the occasion of the first cancellation, with subsequent cancellations reducing the credibility in increasingly smaller amounts until a bottom plateau is reached. The first few trials of a warning system thus become particularly important.

The foregoing implication suggests that the various response channels form a Guttman scale. If indeed they measure various aspects of credibility each on a unidimensional scale, the highest intensity should occur on the first trial, with the next highest intensity on the second trial, and so forth. With only very few exceptions, the intensity in each of the various response channels should be either reduced or stay the same. These essentially are the requirements of a Guttman scale. We have tested for scalability of the various indexes, and the statistics appear in Table 14.4. The data indicate that all indexes without a single exception form almost perfect Guttman scales as predicted by our analysis. The high coefficients of reproducibility imply that by knowing the scale score, it is possible to reconstruct the specific responses on each of the three sessions almost

TABLE 14.4
Testing for Guttman Scales (Session 1 > 2 > 3)

Index	Coefficient of Reproducibility	Coefficient of Scalability	Division Point
Protective Behavior Probability	.98	.96	Yes/No
Protective Behavior Amplitude	.96	.92	25 points
Heart Rate			
Warning A (H)	.96	.90	107
Warning A (L)	.96	.92	77
Warning B (H)	.96	.90	105
Warning B (L)	.96	.92	76
Warning C (H)	.97	.90	106
Warning C (L)	.98	.92	78
Distraction[a]	.96	.90	40% of time
Subjective Tension			
Warning A	.98	.94	4
Warning B	.96	.91	4
Warning C	.93	.85	4

[a]On this item, Session 3 > 2 > 1.

perfectly. There are, of course, a host of practical implications to both the law of initial credibility and the law of interwarning similarity. These are further elaborated in Chapter 15.

POSITIVE ASPECTS OF FALSE ALARMS

Until now we have been preoccupied primarily with the negative consequences of false alarms. By taking the point of view of a warning system that tries to maintain its credibility or restore it to some extent after it is lost, we have seen that false alarms are a major danger. This is so primarily because there is no way to entirely protect a warning system from the FAE. Being essentially a case of learning from experience, this is inevitable.

However, all is not entirely negative. We have seen that a false alarm experience reduces the fear reaction of the receiver. At the same time, it may or may not reduce the protective behavior that he or she is willing to take. The whole issue of desynchrony between the various components of fear suggests the possibility that the ideal Type C, (viz., low fear and high self-protection) may in some cases be achieved via a false alarm experience. If the various forces that determine pattern of transition from Type A to Type D can be better understood and taken advantage of, false alarms can very well turn out to be one of the means of producing the ideal Type C behavior pattern. The research reported here already suggests some promising manipulations in this direction.

There is, however, yet another positive aspect of false alarms. Some dangers may be extremely rare. If there are frequent warnings threatening these very rare dangers, it is precisely because of false alarms that individuals will learn not to take these threats too seriously. Protective behavior against these extremely low-probability events is truly a matter of waste, and a few false alarms may provide sufficient experience to save the individual from a great deal of unnecessary effort. It is this last point which I believe is the basis toward the understanding of the highly reliable and intense FAE. One could pose the question: Why is it that people developed such a strong tendency to reduce the credibility of a warning through one or two false alarms? Taking an evolutionary point of view, one would look for a function of a strong FAE. I submit that it is precisely the advantage of disregarding the many low-probability dangers that may have been conducive to the evolvement of the general predisposition toward quick and strong FAEs. At the cost of occasional surprise, the FAE thus plays a major role in abolishing a multitude of unnecessary fears.

THE PSYCHOLOGY OF FALSE PROMISES

False alarms and false promises have a great deal in common. They both provide information about the disconfirmation of an anticipated future. Although this book is concerned almost exclusively with false alarms, a great deal of what we have discovered could very well apply to false promises as well. We would not be surprised if a corresponding false promise effect, like the FAE, could be ascertained. Such a false promise effect, taking place when a promise did not materialize, would also automatically reduce the credibility of the source of that promise. Moreover, we submit that some of the manipulations that have been tested in our experimental program would be most relevant to the investigation of the false promise effect as well. Thus, one could investigate the impact of pacing of cues about the proximity of the materialization of the promise on the false promise effect, the impact of the initial probability of the promise being fulfilled on the subsequent false promise effect, the role of information about the causes of the promise being unfulfilled on behavior during a subsequent promise, and so forth.

The positive anticipation of a desired future may lead to emotional reaction, subjective evaluation of the promise, and a certain amount of instrumental preparation as well. We suggest that desynchrony between these various components is in principle to be anticipated, very much like in the false alarm situation. All in all, there is a need for a psychology of false promises as a necessary counterpart to the research reported here. We hope that experimental work leading to the explication of this almost entirely neglected area of behavior will be forthcoming shortly.

15 Defense Against False Alarms: Practical Implications

False alarms are powerful offensive weapons. Whether the danger is naive or cynical, a few false alarms are sufficient to increase its surprise power. Thus, intentional or not, false alarms have the power to disarm the defense against subsequent dangers. Their offensive nature is based upon history, and without an intelligent mind to take note of them, they would be entirely harmless. Whenever human decision makers and human recipients of warnings are involved, however, false alarms constitute a major threat in their own right.

There is no total defense against false alarms. At best, their impact can be reduced, their edge blunted, and the loss they produce partially restored. Any efficient warning system must be able to protect itself against false alarms; we now propose some practical steps that may help achieve this end.

The focus on false alarms as a potentially irresistible offensive weapon is the direct outcome of the development of sophisticated early warning systems. The main purpose of these detection devices was to give sufficient warning time between the threat and its materialization, and they paradoxically increased the centrality of false alarms as a potential danger in their own right. We have already seen that the more sensitive the detection subsystem is, the more false alarms it inevitably produces. By trading accuracy for warning time, the emphasis shifted from lack of information to the credibility of information. Thus, the chances that a danger will take someone by surprise because of lack of information about its approach has been greatly reduced, but at the same time, the chance that a danger will strike by surprise in spite of all the information about the threat has actually increased. There is thus a growing shift from the detection subsystem to the decision maker or evaluator of that information. Indeed, the possibility exists that in certain areas we would be better off with a less sensitive early warning device than those already in use. The explication of the long-term dangers of false alarms on the effectiveness of even the most credible warning systems would hopefully lead to the reevaluation of what constitutes the optimal sensitivity of a detection subsystem. Nothing less than the total effort to protect the credibility of a warning system should be acceptable, because once that credibility is lost, the cost of regaining it can be prohibitive, often nothing less than a major disaster.

The practical analysis of defense against false alarms should take advantage of all options, and thus be multidimensional. We propose that the defense should be on the following six levels:

1. Preventive measures of the information-management subsystem.
2. Corrective measures of the information-management subsystem.
3. Selection of individuals better able to resist the FAE.
4. Training against the FAE.
5. Provision of social norms conducive to resistance against the FAE.
6. Role definition and institutional support.

Various suggestions, most of which are directly based on the research presented in this volume, are given as a list of practical propositions. Following those propositions, which are phrased in general terms, we analyze three concrete examples of warning systems belonging to different contexts. As each warning system has some special features of its own, we have chosen three that are rather different from each other: natural disasters, the military, and warning systems concerning health.

PREVENTIVE MEASURES BY INFORMATION-MANAGEMENT SUBSYSTEMS

No preventive measure can possibly eliminate the FAE entirely. At the same time, however, certain features of information management can reduce the credibility loss following the false alarm if and when it takes place.

In manufactured warning systems the information-management subsystem controls all the intrinsic information concerning an impending threat. It is in possession of all data coming from the detection subsystem, its filtering, evaluation, and eventual distribution. The temporal characteristics of information release have a clear impact on the magnitude of the FAE.

Proposition 1. The more advanced the stage of a warning system when the cancellation of the threat takes place, the stronger the FAE.

It follows that any attempt to protect the warning system from a strong FAE should try to keep it at the lowest necessary level of alert. This logic applies not only to later warnings, but also to the first warning itself.

PREVENTIVE MEASURES BY INFORMATION-MANAGEMENT SUBSYSTEMS

Proposition 2. The warning system should attempt to delay issuing the threat as long as possible.

This proposition states that whereas the detection subsystem provides early warnings about remote threats, such information need not be automatically provided to the receiver. For any given kind of danger the minimal time necessary for taking precautions should be defined and the information delayed until such time is reached. Since by then many of the threats turn out to have been false alarms, the receivers need not be aware of them at all.

Needless to say, we are here concentrating on one particular aspect of a complex situation; namely, how to protect the long-range credibility of a warning system. There may be many other considerations, such as freedom of information, which can make the foregoing suggestions impractical in some contexts. We are not concerned with any value judgments about the relative merits of these opposing arguments; therefore, our practical suggestions are clearly unidimensional and out of context. At the same time, however, we submit that on the basis of all available evidence, these propositions as well as those that follow can increase the defensive capability of warning systems against false alarms.

Proposition 3. The more differentiated a warning system (i.e., the more discrete warnings it has ranging from the first to the last), the better it can protect the most advanced warning stages from the FAE.

Because the information released by the warning system to the receiver cannot be continuous, it can profit by increasing the number of discrete stages of alerts. Thus, the more differentiated a warning system is, the greater the chances that the cancellation of the threat in the case of a false alarm will occur prior to the issuing of the last warning. Many warning systems may profit by changing the classical three stages of alert to the more refined five, six, or even seven stages. This can be done irrespective of the pacing of protective behavior. Thus, in certain situations receivers may be urged to engage in protective behavior, which typically reflects the last stage of warning, even before issuing the last warning. This saves the last warning from a possible FAE without compromising self-protection.

Proposition 4. The lower the announced probability of the threat, the smaller the FAE following its cancellation.

This proposition implies that the information-management subsystem need not be just a simple messenger. Inasmuch as the objective probability that a particular threat will materialize is an estimate that may fluctuate and change as new information comes in, it is suggested that from the point of view of defense against false alarms, the announced probability should aim at the lowest possible estimate within a given range of probabilities at any given time. Of course, this also depends on other considerations, which may or may not allow such filtering of information and obviously on considerations of action, which are contingent on probability. Within these broadly defined constraints, however, the proposition clearly states that the lower the announced probability, the smaller the chances of a substantial credibility loss following the false alarm. The law of initial credibility implies that there may be an advantage in having warning systems that are not very highly credibile to begin with. This is clearly a paradox, for why should one attempt to protect credibility by reducing it in the first place? It is, however, possible that in the long run, following a sequence of consecutive false alarms, the credibility of a warning system that started with a relatively lower credibility will be higher than one starting with a high initial credibility. This leads to our next proposition.

Proposition 5. As long as the probability of the cancellation of a threat is relatively high, any information that implies the difficulty in forecasting the future and lowers the expectation that the warning system is infallible will reduce the FAE.

Proposition 5 is clearly a dynamic one in view of the fact that at various stages of anticipating a danger different kinds of information should be emphasized. Thus, while the possibility that the threat will be called off is still a predominant one, Proposition 5 applies. Once the probability of the danger being called off is minimal, the opposite kind of strategy would be required. Needless to say, any attempt to change the emphasis of the information systematically should be based on reliable feedback about the behavior of the recipients of the information at any given point in time. The monitoring of the impact of a warning system is thus an essential prerequisite for its effectiveness.

Proposition 6. In the event that receivers engage in substantial protective behavior, attempts should be made to perceive the danger as a highly cynical one.

This proposition takes advantage of what is often seen in the clinical context as essentially a negative phenomenon, namely, the prevention of reality testing through avoidance behavior. In the present context this phenomenon makes it very difficult for receivers to distinguish between a false alarm and a true alarm that did not materialize because of their own behavior. In the absence of extrinsic information to the contrary, a warning system can use this phenomenon to defend against the FAE. Consider the psychological situation of a highly religious person who in the face of imminent threat engages in pious prayer in the hope of revoking the danger. If the threat subsequently turns out to be a false alarm, the person may perceive it as a true alarm that did not materialize only because of his or her actions. Thus, the warning system will be spared the usual credibility loss. This is an extreme illustration of the principle behind Proposition 6, which can be highly effective in less dramatic situations.

Proposition 7. The request to engage in protective behavior should be limited by time.

The chances for encouraging protective behavior are best if that behavior must be performed immediately. The longer the time interval between the request for protective behavior and its onset, the lower the probability that individuals will engage in it. Thus, protective behavior ought to be limited also in terms of "last chance" when it can still be effective. However, such a deadline must not be too close, otherwise it could produce panic behavior. We should keep in mind that it is precisely because of protective behavior that warning systems ought to defend against the FAE. After all, the credibility loss that leads to reduced fear is not something necessarily negative. It is only the danger that when protective behavior is most needed it is least forthcoming that justifies the need for defending the warning system from the FAE.

CORRECTIVE MEASURES BY INFORMATION-MANAGEMENT SUBSYSTEMS

Following the cancellation of a threat, certain kinds of information can partially restore the credibility loss due to the FAE. Logically, the distinction between preventive measures and corrective measures is quite arbitrary, because corrective measures following one threat can be seen as preventive measures when referring to the next. At the same time, however, the kinds of information released immediately after a false alarm has taken place differ from the manipulations presented up to now.

Proposition 8. By identifying a particular segment of the warning system as responsible for the false alarm and by indicating that this segment is being corrected or replaced, the lost credibility can be partially restored.

Proposition 8 thus consists of two separate factors: the diagnosis of the source of the warning system's mistake and the indication of its being corrected. Thus, only if the mistake is of a sort that can in principle be corrected is its detection conducive to credibility restoration. Whether the mistake was due to instrument error or human error, the receiver has to be convinced that it was properly detected and corrected. (It should be mentioned that there is in principle no need for the error being a true one; as long as the receiver believes that the warning system learned its lesson and corrected itself, that is sufficient in order to reduce the credibility loss.) In this respect, therefore, finding a scapegoat to blame for the mistake can clearly be effective.

Proposition 9. Following a false alarm, any information that indicates an increase in the effectiveness of the warning system can partially restore its credibility.

This proposition indicates that even without specific diagnosis of the source of error, it is possible to restore some of the lost credibility by indicating that the warning system acquired new capabilities. What is essential, however, is that these new capabilities are clearly perceived as changes that took place after the false alarm. Only then can the warning system draw certain advantages from them. These changes, whether in hardware, software, or human resources, should not be wasted. Thus, with a long-range defense of a warning system's credibility in mind, certain increased capabilities of a warning system need not be prematurely disclosed. In other words, they should be kept in reserve for the occasion of a false alarm. This is particularly the case in view of the fact that if they were disclosed before a false alarm, the credibility loss would have been, of course, much greater. Naturally, the number of times that a particular warning system can be rescued by these means is finite, and thus they should be used with maximum discretion.

Few events restore the credibility of a warning system to the extent that a near miss does. We have defined near miss as any threat that turns out to be more serious than subjectively anticipated. This further reinforces Propositions 1 through 5, because by presenting a particular threat as distant, with a low probability of materializing, the chances that it will turn into a near miss are greater than if it is presented in more dramatic terms. There is, however, a substantial gray area between a false alarm and a near miss, particularly in view of the fact that even when the receiver did not experience the danger, others might have. This leads to our next proposition.

Proposition 10. Following the cancellation of a threat, the receiver should be given all information that indicates how close, serious, and harmful the threat was.

By providing information about the damage caused by the danger to other individuals, the warning system may succeed in turning what was essentially a false alarm into a near miss. Effective communication networks and the mass media make this proposition a workable defense measure against FAEs.

The law of interwarning similarity clearly prescribes the need for emphasizing the uniqueness of each threat. Discriminative cues make it easier for recipients to consider a threat without necessarily evoking their recent histories of false alarms.

Proposition 11. Any information that indicates the uniqueness of a threat reduces the FAE.

This proposition can be seen both as a preventive measure and a corrective measure at the same time. By stressing the uniqueness of a present threat, even if it is called off, the chances that it will be exactly similar to the next one are clearly reduced. Thus, the specific features of the threat serve as a preventive measure against future FAEs. At the same time, however, by stressing the specific features of a particular threat, its similarity to the preceding ones is also reduced, thus protecting it from generalization. Needless to say, the degree to which uniqueness should be emphasized depends on recent history. If a particular threat follows a sequence of false alarms, the present proposition is particularly valuable. If, on the other hand, it follows a series of near misses or true alarms, then generalization rather than discrimination would be called for.

There are many ways in which the uniqueness of a particular threat can be emphasized. Two threats, even if they relate to essentially the same phenomenon, need not be labeled exactly the same way. The instructions through which the threat is communicated to the recipient need not follow the same routine pattern. Even the voices of the communicators can make a difference. A sophisticated warning system alerted to the danger or false alarms should take advantage of all sensory dimensions possible to increase the interwarning differences.

SELECTING INDIVIDUALS RESISTANT TO THE FALSE ALARM EFFECT

No intelligent person can be fully resistant to the FAE, because it involves learning from experience. At the same time, however, certain characteristics make one particularly vulnerable to the FAE, and thus warning systems should be careful not to position such individuals in sensitive decision-making roles. Whenever possible, individuals responsible for important protective measures should also be selected accordingly.

Proposition 12. Individuals low on risk taking are more resistant to the FAE.

Proposition 13. Individuals high on tolerance of ambiguity are more resistant to the FAE.

Proposition 14. Individuals low on social desirability are more resistant to the FAE.

Proposition 15. Individuals high on state anxiety are more resistant to the FAE.

Proposition 16. Individuals with higher basic levels of tension are more resistant to the FAE.

Although each of these personality characteristics can be tested for separately, it is by combining some or all of them that the maximal resistance to the FAE can be achieved. Whereas Propositions 12, 13, and 14 are probably most important for decision makers within the warning system itself, Propositions 15 and 16 are more applicable to the recipients of the threat. It is of some interest to note that instruments exist to measure all of the foregoing characteristics, and thus can be used in a variety of warning systems.

TRAINING AGAINST THE FALSE ALARM EFFECT

Because false alarms can reduce the credibility of a warning system both among its own human elements as well as among the recipients at large, a comprehensive defense against this problem should attempt to train individuals to resist the effect. This can be done on two different levels.

Proposition 17. Training for the search of the uniqueness of each threat can reduce the FAE.

Proposition 18. Individuals should be given full information about the FAE and the parameters that influence its magnitude.

The specific preoccupation with discriminative cues is a particular case of the broader attempt to teach individuals as much about FAEs as possible. The continuous awareness that one is subject to an inevitable process of relying on recent experience may, to some extent, reduce the temptation to give it too much weight. A specific material illustrating the way cynical dangers may take advantage of the FAE can be particularly conducive in motivating individuals to learn how to defend against it. In the case of naive dangers one may have the illusion that because the danger lacks intelligence, one is always in full control of the decision-making process. Such an illusion is less acceptable in the case of cynical dangers, which may thus be more conducive for didactic purposes.

SOCIAL NORMS IN DEFENSE AGAINST THE FALSE ALARM EFFECT

Warning systems operate in a social context. This inevitably raises the importance of social norms as forces that may determine the actual impact of a threat. Situations in which protective behavior can be taken are particularly vulnerable to social pressures, which may induce such behavior or its opposite.

Proposition 19. A warning system should invest in developing social norms that encourage protective behavior.

Because self-protection can often be perceived by others as unnecessary, or even as an act of cowardice, this is particularly important following a false alarm. The next proposition gives one possible solution to this dilemma, which may apply to certain situations.

Proposition 20. Routines requiring protection are preferable to individuals' freedom of choice.

This proposition is clearly violating many of our most cherished values; at the same time, however, from the limited point of view of defense against false alarms, it has a substantial value. The routines that require self-protection have the additional advantage of relieving the individual from group pressure. In the absence of a viable alternative, self-protection cannot indicate too much personal concern, and therefore, does not lead to loss of face. Warning systems that do exercise such a major amount of control over the behavior of individuals should take advantage of this possibility. But like all defense against false alarms, it too, is not foolproof.

Proposition 21. The contribution of protective behavior to the welfare of others reduces the FAE.

This proposition recognizes that social norms of helping behavior may increase the willingness of an individual to engage in protective behavior even though it was found unnecessary on several occasions.

Proposition 22. Warning systems should invest in producing social norms against the upgrading of alerts.

This is a particularly difficult goal to achieve in view of the positive reasons that decision makers may have for upgrading the alert of a particular threat. It is precisely because of their dedication that individuals sometimes exaggerate a threat in order to make sure that others take it seriously and protect themselves. However, the long-range dangers of such a practice more than outweigh the short-term advantages. As it often may be the case that individuals in responsible roles will not be occupying the same positions in the future, the temptation to invest everything in the immediate present must be resisted by all means. Explicit social norms to that effect may play an important role in achieving this goal.

INSTITUTIONAL SUPPORT IN DEFENSE AGAINST FALSE ALARMS

Proposition 23. Warning systems must protect their decision makers from being personally accountable for false alarms.

Warning systems, particularly early warning systems, always operate in a situation of uncertainty. Under these conditions the decision makers must weigh the pros and cons of calling an alert, as well as calling it off. The cancellations of a threat that was taken seriously and thus leads to protective measures costly in terms of time, effort, and resources may produce strong pressures by individuals directly involved with the decision maker. He or she may be the scapegoat of what can wrongly be perceived as a wasted effort. Such pressures may lead either to their replacement and censure or to a clear warning not to repeat the same when the next danger comes. Thus, these individuals will be willing to take greater chances in the face of imminent dangers in order to protect themselves from the consequences of another false alarm. Thus, Proposition 23 calls for role definition that will protect them from such a state of affairs.

Under no circumstances should the individuals responsible for making the decision about protective behavior be directly dependent on their popularity with their recipients. Such an arrangement would almost inevitably lead to a major FAE and subsequent risk taking on their part.

Propositon 24. Warning systems should routinely replace their decision makers.

This proposition implies that experience more than anything else is the kernel of the false alarm problem. Thus, decision makers having long experience with a particular danger, even though in many ways more knowledgeable than a new person, are particularly susceptible to give their experience too much weight. Needless to say, this proposition is particularly important in warning systems that go through frequent false alarms. At the same time, however, the replacement policy should be one of routine and not contingent on any specific events. Such contingency would clearly violate Proposition 23.

Proposition 25. Warning systems should have specific roles representing both the short-term and the long-term credibility interests.

Stated differently, this proposition calls for specific advisors or deputies of the chief decision maker whose main purpose is to state the case of the short-term or long-term considerations, respectively. In other words, the defense against false alarms should have a clear champion within the institution itself. Under the pressure of an impending threat no single individual can be expected to give the long-range considerations sufficient weight, so this should be formalized in a specific role.

This list of 25 propositions bearing on the variety of methods that can be used to defend against false alarms is by no means exhaustive. We have merely mentioned the more obvious ideas that are related to the experimental evidence presented in this volume. Although this reflects a great potential for opportunities, their chances of effectively combating the FAE are at best imperfect. However, the six levels of intervention open a variety of potential approaches, all of which should be explored in the context of a specific warning system.

No two warning systems are exactly alike. Their special characteristics may to some extent determine which of the 25 propositions would be most useful and which would be inappropriate. Thus, even though we have attempted to list the propositions in the most general terms, their actual translation into action cannot be done in a theoretical vacuum. Some important features of a particular family of warning systems need be analyzed before any simple practical application of these principles can be attempted.

NATURAL DISASTERS

Natural disasters are naive dangers par excellence. As such, their main parameters are not affected by the behavior of their potential victim. Although different kinds of natural disasters such as tornadoes, hurricanes, floods, earthquakes, and the like differ from each other, they do share the characteristic of involving entire communities. It is this feature that increases the importance of social psychological factors in determining the reactions of the recipients of information concerning an impending danger to life and property. Not only social norms on the primary group level, but also the psychology of mass behavior of multitudes of people all confronted with uncertainty, often determine the course of action. Thus, under such circumstances there is a marked increase in the tendency to follow the behavioral pattern of the "authoritarian personality." This involves, among other things, the search for a scapegoat and for strong leaders. The reduced tolerance for ambiguity often leads to perception of complex issues in highly simplistic yes–no, black–white terms. This poses particular challenges to the warning system, especially if because of its credibility, drastic protective measures such as mass evacuation were taken and then proven unnecessary.

In line with Proposition 23 natural disasters call for specific measures to protect the decision maker. The famous leader of a community at a low-lying area of the Pacific Coast demonstrates this particularly well. This community received several tsunami (tidal wave) warnings following information about seismic activity at the bottom of the Pacific Ocean. Because seismic waves travel faster than tidal waves, there is a period of a few hours during which all low-lying communities can be evacuated, which is the only protection against tsunamis. The objective probability of a tsunami at a given location around the vast shores of the Pacific Ocean are practically zero, yet the decision whether to evacuate or not must be made. The story tells of the leader of a community that decided on two consecutive occasions to evacuate the entire community; fortunately both were false alarms. Unlike the situation of a hurricane or a tornado, wherein even if it changes direction one can still perceive its proximity or the damage done to other areas, in the case of tsunami simply nothing happens. It was also the case that the leader of that community was chosen by the people to that position, and it was made clear to him that he had better take care not to waste their time and resources again or else. . . . The story has it that there was another tsunami warning, and the decision maker decided not to evacuate or do anything about it. The tidal wave struck his community, which became the victim of false alarms. The total dependence of the decision maker on the support and good will of the receivers made him totally vulnerable to the FAE (Whittow, 1980).

Essentially the same point was made by participants in the regional seminar on community preparedness and disaster prevention organized by the United Nations in Tokyo during June, 1976. Considering the cyclone Grvaise, which struck Mauritius on February 6, 1975, and produced a great death toll, it was pointed out that (Proceedings of the regional seminar on community preparedness and disaster prevention, 1978): "The reluctance of the forecasters to issue warnings in good time is explained to a great extent by the attitude of the public when put to a lot of inconvenience by warnings which turned out to have been unnecessary [p. 108]."

Thus, we see that false alarms can indeed be deadly and must be defended against. Even when some precautions and measures conflict with freedom of information and freedom of speech, they should be given due consideration. Democratic societies realize there must be limits to freedom of speech, and just as one is not allowed the freedom to shout "Fire!" in a packed movie house, so must responsible warning systems be given the means to protect the people. It is of some interest to note that the danger of shouting "Fire!" in a packed movie house is twofold: There is the obvious danger of producing panic behavior with far-reaching consequences, and there is the long-range danger of a false alarm.

The ascent of the computer as a major information-processing tool holds some interesting possibilities in defense against false alarms. Thus, if a computer after evaluating all the information that the detection subsystem fed into it comes out with a clear warning and if that warning happens to be a false alarm, the computer need not be subject to the censure and displeasure of the recipients of that information. In the absence of such feedback, it will be protected against the long-term consequences of false alarms.

MILITARY DANGERS

In sharp contrast with natural disasters, military dangers are typically cynical. The "enemy" attempts to maximize its impact by monitoring the precautions taken against it. This unavoidably leads to cancellation of danger for two entirely different reasons: on the one hand, false alarms proper, and on the other hand, true alarms that were called off by the enemy in view of the protective measures taken by its potential targets. The distinction between the two can be of critical importance to any intelligent system, but the difficulty in drawing it paradoxically protects the warning system from a strong FAE. As has already been stated in Proposition 6, cancellation of threats due to false alarms can sometimes be attributed to reactions by cynical dangers. The following case of a pilot may illustrate this point.

Consider a pilot flying a sophisticated airplane that has a warning system telling him when he becomes a target for enemy missiles. He was trained to engage in a particular escape maneuver immeditely when the warning signal comes on. This escape maneuver must override any ongoing activity in order to be effective. Now consider the case in which the highly sensitive warning system flashes its signals in the absence of any real threat. The pilot terminates whatever he is doing and engages in the escape maneuver. He is successful, and after a while the warning signal stops and he lands safely in his home base. There is a clear danger that if he would have known that his escape maneuver was totally unnecessary because the warning system flashed a false alarm, he would be less willing to engage in it in the future. But in the absence of any additional intrinsic or extrinsic information to the contrary, he has no way to find out whether the threat was a false alarm or not. This arrangement protects the warning system from the otherwise inevitable loss of credibility.

Military warning systems, by being able to take advantage of most of the propositions suggested earlier, have some special problems of their own. These fall into two broad categories:

1. The particular milieu of the military encourages personal risk taking, conformity to social norms, intolerance of ambiguity and clear-cut solutions, and the authoritarian personality style. All of these increase the vulnerability of the individuals involved to the FAE.

2. The second set of problems relates to the tendency of the military to provide relatively simple and standardized routines in all its domains of activity. These routines also apply in the area of information processing and information management. As such, they increase the tendency to report on similar dangers in highly similar or even identical terms. This tendency increases the interwarning similarity and thus the FAE. It is diametrically opposed to the need to emphasize uniqueness of each threat and thus reduce the drawing on experience from similar threats.

As a measure against these two sets of problems, military warning systems enjoy a particularly high degree of control over both individuals and information. This control can more than outweigh the forgoing weaknesses in defending against false alarms. Thus, within the military context it is possible to delay the issuing of information, to control the transition from one stage of alert to another, to insure systematic debriefing procedures following a false alarm, to present information suggesting that a near miss rather than a false alarm has taken place, and so on. At the same time, the military can select individuals for particular positions in view of some of the guidelines presented in this volume. It can also train people against a FAE and insure that they are aware of most of its dangers and implications. But more than anything, it can force individuals to engage in protective behavior as part of a standard order. Such enforcement of protective behavior short circuits social pressures, which may reduce it.

WARNING SYSTEMS IN THE AREA OF HEALTH

Although threats to health abound, there are very few formal warning systems whose main goal is to alert the individual of the dangers ahead. Clearly, the most important warning system is one's own body and the messages it sends. When one feels pain or has a temperature or loss of appetite, there is surely something wrong with one's health. In this respect, there are very few false alarms indeed, and these warning systems are highly reliable and credible.

However, the situation changes dramatically when we move from slight indisposition to major threats. This is particularly the case when there are insufficient early warning signs. The case of cancer is worth mentioning. With the growing public awareness of the dangers of cancer, as well as the importance of early detection and treatment, false alarms abound. A small lump here, an undefined pain there, are often sufficient warnings to take one through a long and arduous examination with a specialist. Fortunately, most of these alarms turn out to be false. With the exception of highly anxious individuals, this is bound to reduce the credibility of the warnings themselves. Once that happens, the danger of delay in seeking medical help must be taken into consideration. In this context there is also the danger that frequent false alarms might be interpreted as a sign of hypochondria and thus increase one's inhibitions to proceed in the same way in the future. Like in other areas, routine medical checkups, which are not contingent on any particular symptom, can reduce these inhibitions substantially.

Many threats concerning one's health are after a while not taken seriously because of a continuous process of self-shaping based on false alarms. Consider, for instance, the case of smoking. In spite of all the information to the contrary, one smokes a cigarette and nothing happens. One smokes another cigarette and still nothing happens. Thus, in the absence of any clear signals that may indicate the danger involved, these threats turn out subjectively to be false alarms.

As was already mentioned in this volume, it may be worthwhile to encourage protective behavior by concentrating on its function as fear reducing rather than danger reducing. Thus, it might be worthwhile for a person to refrain from behavior that is dangerous to one's health or even go for a routine checkup not because this will reduce the danger but because there would be less to worry about. This is called for particularly when one has to anticipate the outcomes of such medical tests for a long period of time. These periods of anticipation can be emotionally quite taxing with a concomitant relief in case of a false alarm.

There is, however, no shortage of near misses and true alarms in the context of personal health, and thus the credibility of the various warnings is often restored. At the same time, however, the health agencies would be better off if the various threats were presented as less dramatic, less probable, and less immediate than they usually are. Such a procedure, in line with Propositions 1 through 5 will maintain a higher level of credibility over a period of time.

The threat of personal death itself, although highly credible in the long run, is rarely taken very seriously. This is so for a variety of reasons, denial being one of the most important ones. We submit, however, that denial itself can be particularly effective in view of the fact that death is a single-trial experience, and as long as we are alive we have been through false alarms only. The many threats that did not materilaize encourage the illusion of invulnerability so necessary to one's psychological security and well-being.

Appendix A

POST-EXPERIMENTAL QUESTIONNAIRE

You would help us a great deal by answering as truthfully as possible some questions about your experiences during this experiment. If any of the questions are not clear to you, please don't hesitate to ask.

1) Was the first session: shorter than the second
   equal in time to the second
   longer than the second
2) In terms of minutes and seconds what was the duration of the:
   first session _____
   second session _____
3) During the second session you had three warnings: A, B, and C. In terms of minutes and seconds what was the duration of:
   A _____
   B _____
   C _____
4) From the time the shock electrodes were taken off until you were told that the rest of the electrodes were going to be removed, it took _____.
5) Everybody is of course afraid during this kind of experiment. On the whole would you say that compared to other people your level of fear was:
   lower _____
   the same _____
   higher _____
6) Try to use the following scale to describe as best as you can your feelings during the various stages of the experiment.
   completely relaxed_____Very tense
                       1   2   3   4   5   6   7
   a. coming to the building _____
   b. taking the word-association test _____
   c. attachment of electrodes _____
   d. when told about the nature of the experiment _____
   e. in first session, during Warning A _____
   f.   ''   B _____

g.   "   C _____
h. in second session, during Warning A _____
i.   "   B _____
j.   "   C _____
k. right now _____
7) During the first session, how sure were you that the shock would be given?
   100% sure _____
   quite sure _____
   about 50% chance _____
   less than 50% chance _____
   sure that the shock would *not* be given _____
8) During the second session, how sure were you that the shock would be given?
   100% sure _____
   quite sure _____
   about 50% chance _____
   less than 50% chance _____
   sure that the shock would *not* be given _____
9) After the alarm was called off for the first time, what did you think?
   _____
   _____
   _____
   _____

Appendix B

ORDERED DISPLAY

22	11	01	82	69	40	41	17	43	32	57	81	94	38	15X
64	05	73	93	43	64	53	94	67	25	38	96	09	01	27
11	02	74	20	78	07	62	79	23	60	69	04	74	64	49
40	39	54	36	43	72	04	88	07	22	18	33	51	05	37
08	65	27	36	48	49	69	92	30	12	35	72	52	31	61
57	99	80	67	21	24	30	68	82	48	95	33	02	34	25
31	20	45	00	71	53	32	91	58	63	92	84	77	71	45
26	77	59	89	46	99	66	55	79	37	75	26	65	66	34
00	03	13	03	44	26	62	16	75	29	76	59	56	62	50
93	60	42	81	61	80	51	54	47	84	17	70	19	81	50
52	29	24	14	98	18	85	12	23	76	39	28	57	87	56
98	09	63	70	44	35	10	21	10	88	38	87	90	68	42
89	09	14	97	86	15	95	78	58	41	96	97	17	32	08
49	46	94	28	19	15	06	47	83	85	13	22	27	94	55
67	74	78	40	37	82	95	41	05	93	43	07	23	04	02
09	25	33	11	73	96	64	69	20	64	60	74	11	53	62
67	61	27	24	36	31	30	82	38	01	08	02	62	92	01
80	21	40	79	49	05	65	33	51	34	25	68	54	48	39
57	72	65	30	72	84	92	91	52	71	00	86	22	07	43
34	75	66	04	88	18	36	99	35	12	77	48	71	32	53
58	31	45	29	26	44	63	50	76	59	37	55	59	89	79
75	26	26	11	54	66	11	46	51	80	77	81	62	45	20
50	81	03	87	35	03	63	56	84	68	10	87	56	13	16
23	76	60	42	93	17	70	11	99	11	47	61	00	19	09

Appendix C

INSTRUCTIONS FOR THE NUMBER SEARCH TASK

The preceding pages include lists of pairs of numbers. On every page you will have to go through the number pairs and search for one given number (or pair of numbers) which will be written on the page.

The first time you find the number, write the serial number *1* on the number pair in which the given number appears. After this you will continue to search until you find the given number the second time and you will write the serial number *2* on the number pair. When you find the particular number the third time, write the serial number *3* and so on; everytime you find the number, mark it with the next serial number.

Pay attention—your time is limited. Perform very quickly but without errors. Further on you will find examples from the number pairs. Example 1.

X 16	44	15
89	94	66
40	13	43
65	85	51
47	49	12
38	36	26
35	38	14

On this page you were asked to search for number 1. Start with the left column[1] marked X and go through the other columns from top to bottom in the same order as they are written. Everytime you find the number 1 mark its serial

---

[1] In Hebrew the starting point is on the right column.

number on the pair of numbers where it appears. Attention! Perform quickly, but be careful not to mark a pair where the number does not appear. Be especially cautious not to skip over a number pair where it appears. Since time is limited you cannot check all targets, therefore work systematically from top to bottom, starting from the X. We shall pay you 5 Agora for each correct marking and deduct 5 Agora for each error. Now, for practice, perform the search in Example 1. After completing the search here, turn to the random display.

Example 2.

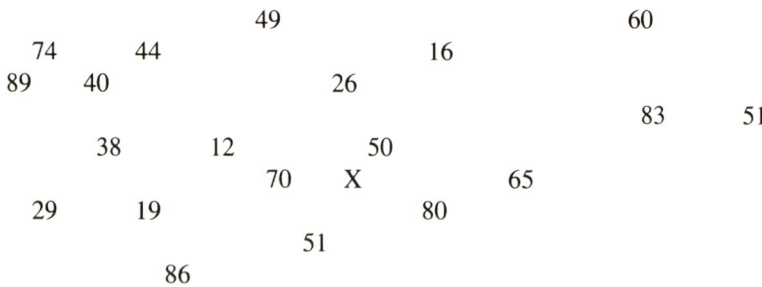

On this page you were asked to mark the number 0. Go through the number pairs and each time you find the number 0 mark its serial number on the pair of numbers in which it appears. Attention! Perform quickly, but be careful not to mark the wrong number. Because time is limited and the numbers are scattered on the page, we suggest you start searching from the middle of the page, marked with X. We shall pay you 5 Agora for each correct marking and deduct 5 Agora for each error. Now, for practice, perform the search in Example 2.

In addition to the above mentioned tasks, you will receive pages, on which the pairs of numbers are arranged in the same way as in Example 2. But you will be asked to look for pairs of numbers, which will be written on the center of the page. This given pair of numbers will appear three times on the page. Having found it, you will have to mark it each time with a serial number *1* (first), *2* (second), *3* (third).

We shall pay you 50 Agora for each marked target.

Later on you will receive pages of number pairs of the kind mentioned above, where you have to search for the number (or pairs of numbers) which is given on the page. Your time will be limited.

When the start signal is given, turn the page over and start to mark the given number with serial numbers. When the stop signal is given, stop searching, and if you are dealing with pages of columns like Example 1, underline the last pair of numbers you have reached in your search.

Immediately after this turn over to the next page which is a blank sheet of paper and wait. When the following start signal is given, turn over the blank sheet and start a new search. Be careful to turn over *one* page only each time.

If there are any questions, please ask now.

Don't turn over to the next page without being told to do so.

Appendix D

In this experiment you were asked to perform a number search task while you are expecting an electric shock.

1. Try to use the following scale to describe your feelings during the various stages of task performance.

    completely relaxed _____ very tense
    1   2   3   4   5   6   7

    (a) In the first session while searching for a one-digit number
    in an ordered display _____
    while performing a search for a one-digit number
    in a random display _____
    while performing a search for a pair of digits
    in a random display _____

    (b) In the second session while performing a search for a one-digit number
    in an ordered display _____
    while performing a search for a one-digit number
    in a random display _____
    while performing a search for a pair of digits
    in a random display _____

    (c) In the third session while performing a search for a one-digit number
    in an ordered display _____
    while performing a search for a one-digit number
    in a random display _____
    while performing a search for a pair of digits
    in a random display _____

2. Did performance improve from one session to the next? Check the correct answer:
   Yes_____ No_____
3. When did you succeed most in the number search task:
   (a) during the sessions _____ (b) while relaxing following termination of experiment _____
4. Did you succeed in task performance:
   (a) more than other people _____
   (b) less than other people _____
   (c) the same as other people _____ (Check the correct answer)
5. Which task did you like best?
   (a) one-digit number search in an ordered display _____
   (b) one-digit number search in a random display _____
   (c) pair of digits search in a random display _____
6. Which task did you perform best?
   (a) one-digit number search in an ordered display _____
   (b) one-digit number search in a random display _____
   (c) pair of digits search in a random display _____
7. As we mentioned before, sometimes people are able to judge the level of their fear. Do you think that task performance had any influence on your fear level? Check the correct answer:
   (a) My fear increased because of task performance _____
   (b) My fear did not change in spite of task performance _____
   (c) My fear decreased because of task performance _____
8. Do you think that fear had any influence on task performance?
   (a) Because of fear I performed better _____
   (b) Because of fear I performed worse _____
   (c) Fear did not have any influence on task performance _____
9. Suppose you did not have to perform the search. Would you have
   (a) reduced the shock intensity more _____
   (b) reduced the shock intensity less _____
   (c) the performance of the task did not influence the reduction of the shock intensity _____
10. What would you advise people in a similar situation? (Check the correct answer)
   (a) Forget the shock and perform the search task _____
   (b) Reduce the shock intensity, relax, and afterwards perform the search task. _____
   (c) First perform the search task and then reduce the shock intensity _____
   (d) Perform the search task and reduce the shock intensity at the same time. _____

Appendix E

MEANS, STANDARD DEVIATIONS AND ANALYSES OF VARIANCE OF TASK PERFORMANCE

TABLE A.1
Task A—Correct Responses

Groups	B.S.[1]	Session 1 A	Session 1 C	Session 2 A	Session 2 C	n	A.S.[2]	n
1 BA+AC	14.14 (3.13)	13.00 (4.06)	15.00 (2.04)	14.36 (3.59)	14.00 (3.37)	14	15.00 (3.79)	13
2 BA+AC		12.86 (3.30)	14.71 (3.34)	15.07 (3.65)	16.00 (3.35)	14	14.50 (2.07)	14
3 BA+AC			13.64 (1.91)		15.14 (1.83)	14	15.29 (3.34)	14

	Session 3 A_1	A_2	C_1	C_2	A.S.	n
1+2+3BC	12.95 (3.25)	13.10 (2.81)	15.71 (3.16)	14.10 (2.19)	15.29 (2.85)	21

	Trials 1	2	3	4	n
Group C	12.82 (2.92)	14.50 (2.93)	14.95 (2.93)	14.80 (2.98)	157

[1] B.S.—before stress.
[2] A.S.—after stress.

TABLE A.2
Task A—Speed

Groups	B.S.	Session 1		Session 2		n	A.S.	n
		A	C	A	C			
1 BA+AC	73.21 (14.71)	67.07 (19.02)	80.71 (10.56)	76.07 (19.87)	75.43 (14.40)	14	79.62 (20.68)	13
2 BA+AC		68.29 (15.42)	74.50 (15.74)	81.00 (18.98)	84.50 (14.24)	14	74.14 (11.07)	14
3 BA+AC			71.38 (9.71)		80.38 (13.12)	13	77.46 (15.40)	13

	Session 3					
	A_1	A_2	C_1	C_2	A.S.	n
1+2+3BC	71.05 (13.28)	71.48 (11.37)	82.95 (18.14)	72.33 (13.38)	81.33 (12.54)	21

	Trials				
	1	2	3	4	n
Group C	67.59 (15.76)	75.80 (16.45)	80.29 (16.18)	78.73 (16.85)	157

TABLE A.3
Task A—Errors

Groups	B.S.	Session 1		Session 2		n	A.S.	n
		A	C	A	C			
1 BA+AC	.29 (.73)	.71 (.91)	1.00 (1.41)	1.07 (.92)	.71 (1.14)	14	.85 (1.68)	13
2 BA+AC		.36 (.63)	.21 (.43)	.71 (1.38)	.79 (1.05)	13	.86 (1.10)	14
3 BA+AC			.46 (.88)		.77 (1.17)	13	.92 (1.50)	13

	Session 3					
	A_1	A_2	C_1	C_2	A.S.	n
1+2+3BC	.53 (.76)	.57 (.81)	.57 (.87)	.43 (.81)	.48 (.75)	21

	Trials				
	1	2	3	4	n
Group C	.81 (1.38)	.78 (1.15)	.94 (1.36)	.79 (1.29)	157

TABLE A.4
Task B—Correct Responses

		Session 1		Session 2				
Groups	B.S.	A	C	A	C	n	A.S.	n
1 BA+BC	13.86	14.79	15.29	17.00	17.21	14	16.62	13
	(3.37)	(3.85)	(4.07)	(3.68)	(3.56)		(4.46)	
2 BA+BC		10.21	13.07	13.64	15.64	14	16.64	14
		(3.36)	(4.03)	(3.73)	(4.33)		(4.62)	
3 BA+BC			12.23		14.92	13	16.23	13
			(3.68)		(3.38)		(3.42)	

			Session 3				
	A_1	A_2	C_1	C_2	n	A.S.	n
1+2+3AC	14.14	16.79	17.71	18.14	14	17.20	15
	(3.44)	(5.26)	(3.89)	(4.22)		(6.00)	

		Trials			
	1	2	3	4	n
Group C	13.11	16.59	18.42	18.67	138
	(4.65)	(5.34)	(5.16)	(5.06)	

TABLE A.5
Task C—Correct Responses

		Session 1		Session 2			
Groups	B.S.	A	C	A	C	A.S.	n
1 BC+AC	1.71	1.79	1.71	1.07	1.50	1.50	14
	(.99)	(.80)	(1.07)	(.83)	(.94)	(.85)	
2 BC+AC		1.71	1.79	1.14	1.36	1.43	14
		(.73)	(1.31)	(.95)	(.93)	(1.02)	
3 BC+AC			1.50		1.36	1.57	14
			(.94)		(.93)	(.94)	

			Session 3			
	A_1	A_2	C_1	C_2	A.S.	n
1+2+3BA	1.57	1.71	1.52	1.43	1.38	21
	(1.02)	(.96)	(.93)	(.81)	(1.02)	

		Trials			
	1	2	3	4	n
Group C	1.27	1.41	1.50	1.48	175
	(.90)	(.91)	(.95)	(.90)	

Analyses of Variance performed on performance measures

TASK A—CORRECT RESPONSES

TABLE A.6
Groups 1 and 2, Sessions 1 and 2, Warnings A and C

	df	MS	F	p
Groups	1	9.14	<1	
SwG	26	23.77		
Sessions	1	26.04	5.96	<.05
Groups × Sessions	1	17.28	3.95	
Sessions × SwG	26	4.37		
Warnings	1	34.32	2.87	
Groups × Warnings	1	2.29	<1	
Warnings × SwG	26	11.98		
Sessions × Warnings	1	18.89	3.37	
Groups × Sessions × Warnings	1	3.58	<1	
Sessions × Warnings × SwG	26	5.60		

TABLE A.7
Groups 2 and 3, Sessions 1 and 2, Warning C

	df	MS	F	p
Groups	1	13.01	1.18	
SwG	26	11.06		
Sessions	1	27.16	7.50	<.05
Groups × Sessions	1	0.16		
Sessions × SwG	26	3.62		

TABLE A.8
Groups 1 and C—First Four Trials

	df	MS	F	p
Groups	1	1.04	<1	
SwG	169	20.65		
Trials	3	25.12	5.16	<.005
Groups × Trials	3	17.60	3.61	<.05
Trials × SwG	507	4.87		

TABLE A.9
Groups 1 and C—Three Trials (without the First)

	df	MS	F	p
Groups	1	15.31	<1	
SwG	169	17.42		
Trials	2	20.10	4.37	<.05
Groups × Trials	2	8.07	1.75	
Trials × SwG	338	4.60		

TABLE A.10
Groups 2 and C—First Four Trials

	df	MS	F	p
Groups	1	7.92	<1	
SwG	169	21.37		
Trials	3	65.67	13.91	<.001
Groups × Trials	3	3.79	<1	
Trials × SwG	507	4.72		

TABLE A.11
Group C and Performance During Session 3

	df	MS	F	p
Groups	1	7.04	<1	
SwG	176	19.88		
Trials	3	79.03	16.26	<.001
Groups × Trials	3	16.72	3.46	<.05
Trials × SwG	528	4.86		

TASK A—SPEED

TABLE A.12
Groups 1 and 2, Sessions 1 and 2, Warnings A and C

	df	MS	F	p
Groups	1	141.75	<1	
SwG	26	670.25		
Sessions	1	1222.32	11.50	<.01
Groups × Sessions	1	631.75	5.94	<.05
Sessions × SwG	26	106.32		
Warnings	1	902.89	4.10	
Groups × Warnings	1	18.90	<1	
Warnings × SwG	26	220.18		
Sessions × Warnings	1	505.76	7.75	<.01
Groups × Sessions × Warnings	1	234.31	3.59	
Sessions × Warnings × SwG	26	65.25		

TABLE A.13
Groups 2 and 3, Sessions 1 and 2, Warning C

	df	MS	F	p
Groups	1	176.22	<1	
SwG	25	288.01		
Sessions	1	1223.13	16.48	<.001
Groups × Sessions	1	3.37	<1	
Sessions × SwG	25	74.20		

TABLE A.14
Groups 1 and C—First Four Trials

	df	MS	F	p
Groups	1	91.98	<1	
SwG	169	722.59		
Trials	3	1197.32	10.45	<.001
Groups × Trials	3	462.25	4.04	<.01
Trials × SwG	507	114.56		

TABLE A.15
Groups 1 and C—Three Trials (without the First)

	df	MS	F	p
Groups	1	515.66	<1	
SwG	169	613.21		
Trials	2	1091.52	8.36	<.001
Groups × Trials	2	278.64	2.69	
Trials × SwG	338	103.61		

TABLE A.16
Groups 2 and C—First Four Trials

	df	MS	F	p
Groups	1	111.10	<1	
SwG	169	731.00		
Trials	3	2028.07	18.30	<.001
Groups × Trials	3	117.11	1.06	
Trials × SwG	507	110.84		

TASK B—CORRECT RESPONSES

TABLE A.17
Groups 1 and 2, Sessions 1 and 2, Warnings A and C

	df	MS	F	p
Groups	1	240.14	6.12	<.05
SwG	26	39.25		
Sessions	1	180.04	21.67	<.001
Groups × Sessions	1	6.04	0.73	
Sessions × SwG	26	8.31		
Warnings	1	54.32	13.89	<.005
Groups × Warnings	1	30.04	7.68	<.05
Warnings × SwG	26	3.91		
Sessions × Warnings	1	2.29	<1	
Groups × Sessions × Warnings	1	0.57	<1	
Sessions × Warnings × SwG	26	7.35		

TABLE A.18
Groups 2 and 3, Sessions 1 and 2, Warning C

	df	MS	F	p
Groups	1	8.21	<1	
SwG	25	19.77		
Sessions	1	93.35	9.01	<.01
Groups × Sessions	1	0.05	<1	
Sessions × SwG	25	10.36		

TABLE A.19
Groups 1 and C—First Four Trials

	df	MS	F	p
Groups	1	108.75	2.07	
SwG	150	52.56		
Trials	3	178.20	11.67	<.001
Groups × Trials	3	33.19	2.17	
Trials × SwG	450	15.27		

TABLE A.20
Groups 2 and C—First Four Trials

	df	MS	F	p
Groups	1	643.45	12.08	<.001
SwG	150	53.28		
Trials	3	285.78	18.88	<.001
Groups × Trials	3	9.35	<1	

TABLE A.21
Groups C and Performance in Session 3

	df	MS	F	p
Groups	1	0.01	<1	
SwG	150	53.59		
Trials	3	241.08	15.65	<.001
Groups × Trials	3	7.97	<1	
Trials × SwG	450	15.40		

TASK C—CORRECT RESPONSES

TABLE A.22
Groups 1 and 2, Sessions 1 and 2, Warnings A and C

	df	MS	F	p
Groups	1	0.01	<1	
SwG	26	1.43		
Sessions	1	6.51	10.12	<.005
Groups × Sessions	1	0.01	<1	
Sessions × SwG	26	0.64		
Warnings	1	0.72	1.21	
Groups × Warnings	1	0.01	<1	
Warnings × SwG	26	0.60		
Sessions × Warnings	1	0.72	<1	
Groups × Sessions × Warnings	1	0.22	<1	
Sessions × Warnings × SwG	26	1.01		

TABLE A.23
Groups 2 and 3, Sessions 1 and 2, Warning C

	df	MS	F	p
Groups	1	0.29	<1	
SwG	26	0.84		
Sessions	1	1.14	<1	
Groups × Sessions	1	0.28	<1	
Sessions × SwG	26	1.33		

TABLE A.24
Groups 1 and C—First Four Trials

	df	MS	F	p
Groups	1	1.25	1.07	
SwG	187	1.16		
Trials	3	1.24	1.69	
Groups × Trials	3	1.96	2.69	<.05
Trials × SwG	561	0.73		

TABLE A.25
Groups 2 and C—First Four Trials

	df	MS	F	p
Groups	1	0.37	<1	
SwG	187	1.17		
Trials	3	0.72	<1	
Groups × Trials	3	1.96	2.65	<.05
Trials × SwG	561	0.74		

TABLE A.26
Group C and Performance During Session 3

	df	MS	F	p
Groups	1	1.52	1.32	
SwG	194	1.15		
Trials	3	0.28	<1	
Groups × Trials	3	0.64	<1	
Trials × SwG	582	0.73		

Appendix F

INSTRUCTIONS FOR INTOLERANCE OF AMBIGUITY TASK

I am going to show you a series of cards. The first card of the series always has just a few elements of a complete design on it; but each card gives you a few additional hints or cues as to what the final design or picture is going to be. Here is a sample. [Sample series of cards are shown to subject and fully explained; all questions pertaining to the cards are answered.]

Remember there is only one design or picture on each card; all the details belong to a complete design which is on the final card. Here is a list of . . . [professions, etc.]. One of these is the correct answer; that is, one is the final card of this series. You have 10 seconds to look at this list.

Now the object of the task is to see how soon you can organize the elements of a card into the complete design or picture. You may look at each card as long as you wish. Remember: The idea is to see how few cards you need to decide what it is going to be.

[After the first response was made] Now tell me, on each card, what you think it is going to be on the final card.

Appendix G

INSTRUCTIONS FOR RISK-TAKING TEST

Game Instructions

Part 1

We are now going to play a betting game. For this purpose we will use the roulette wheel and the chart in front of you. I shall soon explain how the betting is done. The betting will be repeated several times. During the first part of the game you will receive for each bet one chip which is the equivalent of 5 IL. Each time you will bet with 5 IL. After every bet we shall check if you have won or lost, and you will be paid whatever you have gained, or lose the 5 IL., respectively. After this you will get additional 5 IL. and bet again.

The money for the bets will be placed on the chart; more details will follow.

After this, one spins the wheel and throws the ball in. The hole in which the ball lands is the winning number. For winning bets, the following odds are paid:
(a) If you bet that the ball will fall on number 1–18, or 19–36, or black or red, or even or odd number, and you have won, you win your bet plus the same amount. For betting you put the money on the place on the chart which shows the kind of bet you have chosen.
(b) Placing your bet on numbers 1–12, 13–24, or 25–36, or on a vertical column of 12 numbers, you win your bet plus twice as much.
(c) Betting on six consecutive numbers, i.e., by placing the bet on the right or left line at the point of intersection of two numbers and the side line, you will get your bet plus 5 times as much.

(d) On four numbers in a square, i.e., by placing the bet on the point of intersection of the four numbers, you will get your money plus 8 times as much.
(e) On any three consecutive numbers within one horizontal row, i.e., by placing the bet on the left or right line at the side of the three numbers, you get your money plus 11 times as much.
(f) On any pair of adjacent numbers, i.e., by placing the bet on the line between any two contiguous squares, you get your money plus 17 times as much.
(g) Betting on one single number including 0, you will get your money plus 35 times as much.

If the winning number is 0, you will lose your money except if you have bet on 0.

It should be clear on the basis of the above that the chance to win gets smaller as the numbers you bet on are fewer. Thus, betting on 1–18, 19–36, black or red, even or odd, means a probability of ½ (or 50%) to win and ½ to lose. Betting on a column or a series of twelve numbers has a probability of ⅓ to win. Betting on six numbers has a probability of ⅙ to win and so on, and betting on one number has a probability of ¹⁄₃₆ to win.

Part 2

In this part of the game you will get 20 chips each time; each one is worth ½ IL., in total 10 IL. This time you may bet on red or black *only*, but the amount you bet is up to you, namely you can bet on any amount from ½ IL (1 chip) to 10 IL. (20 chips). After every bet we shall check if you have won or lost; if you have won you will get your money back and another additional amount of the same bet. If you have lost, you will lose the sum you have bet.

After this you will receive 20 additional chips and start a new game of betting on red or black.

References

Adorno, T. W., Frenkel-Brunswick, E., Levinson, D. J., & Sanford, R. N. *The authoritarian personality.* New York: Harper, 1950.

Anner, N. *The influence of different thinking tasks upon time estimation: An attempt to apply the cognitive theory of time estimation to processing of "internal information."* Unpublished master's thesis, The Hebrew University, Jerusalem, 1972.

Averill, J. R. Personal control over aversive stimuli and its relationship to stress. *Psychological Bulletin,* 1973, *80,* 286–303.

Averill, J. R., & Rosenn, M. Vigilant and nonvigilant coping strategies and psychophysiological stress reactions during the anticipation of electric shock. *Journal of Personality and Social Psychology,* 1972, *23,* 128–141.

Baddeley, A. D. Selective attention and performance in dangerous environments. *British Journal of Psychology,* 1972, *63,* 537–546.

Badia, P., & Harsh, J. Choosing between predictable and unpredictable shock conditions: Data and theory. *Psychological Bulletin,* 1979, *86,* 1107–1131.

Baker, G. W., and Chapman, D. W. (Eds.) *Man and society in disaster.* New York: Basic Books, 1962.

Becker, H., & Costello, C. Effects of graduated exposure. *Journal of Consulting and Clinical Psychology,* 1975, *43,* 478–484.

Ben-Zur, H., & Breznitz, S. The effect of time pressure on risky choice behavior. *Acta Psychologica,* 1981, *47,* 89–104.

Bergstroem, B. Differential effects of threat-induced stress on tracking performance. *Perceptual & Motor Skills,* 1970, *30,* 811–820.

Berlyne, D. *Conflict, arousal and curiosity.* New York: McGraw-Hill, 1960.

Brady, J. V. Ulcers in "executive" monkeys. *Scientific American,* 1958, *199*(4), 95–100.

Breznitz, S. *Influence of the time interval between threat with a frightening stimulus and its execution upon fear reaction in humans.* Unpublished doctoral dissertation, The Hebrew University, Jerusalem, 1965.

Breznitz, S. Incubation of threat: Duration of anticipation and false alarm as determinants of fear reaction to an unavoidable frightening event. *Journal of Experimental Research in Personality,* 1967, *2,* 173–180.

Breznitz, S. 'Incubation of threat' in a situation of conflicting expectations. *Psychological Reports,* 1968, *22,* 755–756.

Breznitz, S. A study of worrying. *British Journal of Social and Clinical Psychology,* 1971, *10,* 271–279.

Breznitz, S. The effect of frequency and pacing of warnings upon the fear reaction to a threatening event. *Research Report to the Ford Foundation,* 1972.

Breznitz, S. The seven kinds of denial. In S. Breznitz (Ed.), *Denial of stress.* New York: International Universities Press, 1982.

Broadbent, D. E. *Decision and stress.* London: Academic Press, 1971.

Chapman, D. W. A brief introduction to contemporary disaster research. In G. W. Baker & D. W. Chapman (Eds.), *Man and society in disaster.* New York: Basic Books, 1962.

Cofer, C. N., & Appley, H. M. *Motivation: Theory and research.* New York: Wiley, 1964.

Cousins, N. *Anatomy of an illness.* New York: Norton, 1979.

Cronbach, L. J., & Furby, L. How we should measure "change"—or should we? *Psychological Bulletin,* 1970, *74*(1), 68–80.

Crowne, D. P., & Marlowe, D. A. A new scale of social desirability independent of psychopathology. *Journal of Consulting Psychology*, 1960, *24*, 349–354.

Deane, G. E. Human heart rate responses during experimentally induced anxiety: Effects of instructions on acquisition. *Journal of Experimental Psychology*, 1966, *71*, 772–773.

Deese, J., & Hulse, S. H. *The psychology of learning*. New York: McGraw-Hill, 1967.

Dollard, J. Fear in battle. Washington, D.C.: *The Infantry Journal*, 1944.

Elliott, R. Tonic heart rate. *Journal of Personality and Social Psychology*, 1969, *12*, 211–218.

Elliott, R. Effects of uncertainty about the nature and advent of a noxious stimulus (shock) upon heart rate. *Journal of Personality and Social Psychology*, 1966, *3*, 353–356.

Elliott, R., Bankart, B., & Light, T. Differences in the motivational significance of heart rate and palmar conductance. *Journal of Personality and Social Psychology*, 1970, *14*, 166–172.

Epstein, S., & Clarke, S. Heart rate and skin conductance during experimentally induced anxiety: The effects of anticipated intensity of noxious stimulation and experience. *Journal of Experimental Psychology*, 1970, *84*, 105–112.

Epstein, S., & Fenz, W. Steepness of approach and avoidance gradients in humans as a fraction of experience. *Journal of Experimental Psychology*, 1965, *70*, 1–12.

Epstein, S., & Roupenian, A. Heart rate and skin conductance during experimentally induced anxiety: The effects of uncertainty about receiving a noxious stimulus. *Journal of Personality and Social Psychology*, 1970, *16*, 20–28.

Festinger, L. *A theory of cognitive dissonance*. Stanford, Ca.: Stanford University Press, 1957.

Flavell, J. H. *Cognitive development*. Englewood Cliffs, N.J.: Prentice-Hall, 1977.

Folkins, C. H. Temporal factors and the cognitive mediators of stress reaction. *Journal of Personality and Social Psychology*, 1970, *14*, 173–184.

Fraser, R., Leslie, I., & Phelps, D. Psychiatric effects of severe personal experiences during bombing. *Proceedings of the Royal Society of Medicines*, 1943, *36*, 119–123.

Gal, R., & Lazarus, R. S. The role of activity in anticipating and confronting stressful situations. *Journal of Human Stress*, 1975, *1*(4), 4–20.

Glover, E. Notes on the psychological effects of war conditions on the civil population: Part III, the blitz. *International Journal of Psychoanalysis*, 1942, *23*, 17–37.

Graham, F. K., & Clifton, R. K. Heart-rate change as a component of the orienting response. *Psychological Bulletin*, 1966, *65*, 305–320.

Green, D. M., & Swets, J. A. *Signal detection theory and psychophysics*. New York: Wiley, 1966.

Groves, P., & Thompson, R. Habituation: A dual-process theory. *Psychological Review*, 1970, *77*, 419–450.

Guttman, L. A basis for scaling qualitative data. *American Sociological Review*, 1944, *9*, 139–150.

Hammerton, M. H., & Tickner, A. H. An investigation into the effects of stress upon skilled performance. *Ergonomics*, 1969, *12*, 851–855.

Heider, F. *The psychology of interpersonal relations*. New York: Wiley, 1958.

Helson, H. Adaptation-level as a basis for a quantitative theory of frames of reference. *Psychological Review*, 1948, *55*, 297–313.

Hepner, A., & Cauthen, N. Effect of subject control and graduated exposure. *Journal of Consulting and Clinical Psychology*, 1975, *43*, 478–484.

Hersen, M. Self-assessment of fear. *Behavior Therapy*, 1973, *4*, 241–257.

Hess, A., & Breznitz, S. Termination of a stressful task reduces fear of an approaching shock. *Psychonomic Science*, 1971, *23*(4), 311–312.

Hodges, W. F., & Spielberger, C. D. The effects of threat of shock on heart rate for subjects who differ in manifest anxiety and fear of shock. *Psychophysiology*, 1966, *2*(4), 287–294.

Hodgson, R., & Rachman, S., II. Desynchrony in measures of fear. *Behavior Research and Therapy*, 1974, *12*, 319–326.

Horowitz, M. *Stress response syndromes*. New York: Aronson, 1976.

Inbar, M. Developmental and educational use of simulations: An example, the Community Response Game. *International Journal of Experimental Educational Research*, 1969, *6*, 5–44.

James, W. *The principles of psychology.* New York: Holt, 1890.
Janis, I. L. *Air war and emotional stress: Psychological studies of bombings and civilian defense.* New York: McGraw-Hill, 1951.
Janis, I. L. Problems of theory in the analysis of stress behavior. *Journal of Social Issues,* 1954, *10*(3), 12–25.
Janis, I. L. *Psychological stress.* New York: Wiley, 1958.
Janis, I. L. Psychological aspects of decisional conflicts. In M. Jones (Ed.), *Nebraska Symposium on Motivation* (Vol. 7). Lincoln: University of Nebraska Press, 1959.
Janis, I. L. Psychological effects of warnings. In G. W. Baker & D. W. Chapman (Eds.), *Man and society in disaster.* New York: Basic Books, 1962.
Janis, I. L. Stress inoculation as a means of preventing pathogenic denial. In S. Breznitz (Ed.), *Denial of stress.* New York: International Universities Press, 1982.
Jennings, R. J., Averill, J. R., Opton, E. M., & Lazarus, R. S. Some parameters of heart rate change. Perceptual versus motor tasks requirements, noxiousness and uncertainty. *Psychophipiology,* 1970, *7,* 194–212.
Kahneman, D. *Attention and effort.* Englewood Cliffs, N.J.: Prentice-Hall, 1973.
Katkin, E. S. Relationship between manifest anxiety and two indices of autonomic response to stress. *Journal of Personality and Social Psychology,* 1965, *2*(3), 324–333.
Katkin, E. S. The relationship between a measure of transitory anxiety and spontaneous autonomic activity. *Journal of Abnormal Psychology,* 1966, *71*(2), 142–146.
Keinan, G. *The effects of personality and training variables on the experienced stress and quality of performance in situations where physical integrity is threatened.* Unpublished doctoral dissertation, Tel Aviv University, 1979.
Kelley, H. H., Condry, J. C. Jr., Dahlke, A. E., & Hill, A. H. Collective behavior in a simulated panic situation. *Journal of Experimental Social Psychology,* 1965, *1,* 20–54.
Killian, L. M. *Evacuation of Panama City before Hurricane Florence.* Washington, D.C.: National Academy of Sciences—National Research Council, Committee on Disaster Studies, 1954.
Kim, J., & Kohout, F. J. Special topics in general linear models. In N. H. Nie, C. H. Hull, J. G. Jenkins, K. Steinbrenner, & D. H. Bent (Eds.), *Statistical package for the social sciences.* New York: McGraw-Hill, 1975.
Lacey, J. I., Kagan, J., Lacey, B. C., & Moss, H. A. The visceral level: Situational determinants and behavioral correlates of autonomic response patterns. In P. H. Knapp (Ed.), *Expression of the emotions in man.* New York: International Universities Press, 1963.
Lacey, J. I., & Lacey, B. C. The law of initial value in the longitudinal study of autonomic constitution: Reproducibility of autonomic responses and response patterns over a four-year interval. *Annual of the New York Academy of Science,* 1962, *98,* 1257–1290; 1322–1326.
Lader, M., & Marks, I. *Clinical anxiety.* London: Heinemann Medical, 1971.
Lang, P. Stimulus control, response control and desensitization of fear. In D. Levis (Ed.), *Learning approaches to therapeutic behaviour change.* Chicago: Aldine Press, 1970.
Lazarus, R. S. A laboratory approach to the dynamics of psychological stress. *American Psychologist,* 1964, *19,* 400–411.
Lazarus, R. S. *Psychological stress and the coping process.* New York: McGraw-Hill, 1966.
Lazarus, R. S. Psychological stress and the coping process. In Z. S. Lipowski, D. R. Lipsitt, & P. C. Whylrow (Eds.), *Psychosomatic medicine: Current trends and clinical applications.* New York: Oxford University Press, 1977.
Lazarus, R. S., Deese, J., & Osler, S. F. The effects of psychological stress upon performance. *Psychological Bulletin,* 1952, *49,* 293–317.
Leitenberg, H., Agras, S., Butz, R., & Wincze, J. Heart rate and behavioral change during treatment of phobia. *Journal of Abnormal Psychology,* 1971, *78,* 59–64.
Leventhal, H. Findings and theory in the study of fear communications. In L. Berkowitz (Ed.), *Advances in experimental social psychology* (Vol. 5). New York: Academic Press, 1970.
Liddle Hart, B. H. *Strategy.* New York: Praeger, 1962.

REFERENCES

Lipsitt, L. P., & Reese, H. W. *Child development.* Glenview, Ill.: Scott, Foresman, 1979.
Lundberg, U., Ekman, G., & Frankenhaeuser, M. Anticipation of electric shock: A psychophysical study. *Acta Psychologica,* 1971, *35,* 309–315.
MacCurdy, J. T. *The structure of morale.* New York: Macmillan, 1943.
Mackworth, J. F. *Vigilance and habituation.* London: Penguin Books, 1969.
Mansueto, C. S., & Desiderato, O. External vs. self-produced determinants of fear reaction after shock threat. *Journal of Experimental Research in Personality,* 1971, *5,* 30–36.
Martin, B. The assessment of anxiety by physiological behavioral measures. *Psychological Bulletin,* 1961, *58,* 234–255.
McCutcheon, B., & Adams, A. The physiological basis of implosive therapy. *Behavior Research and Therapy,* 1975, *13,* 93–100.
McGrath, J. E. Settings, measures and themes: An integrative review of some research on social-psychological factors in stress. In J. E. McGrath (Ed.), *Social and psychological factors in stress.* New York: Holt, Rinehart & Winston, 1970.
Meichenbaum, D. A self-instructional approach to stress management: A proposal for stress inoculating training. In C. D. Spielberger & I. G. Sarason (Eds.), *Stress and anxiety* (Vol. 1). New York: Wiley, 1975.
Meichenbaum, D. *Cognitive-behavior modification: An integrative approach.* New York: Plenum Press, 1977.
Michotte, A. *The perception of causality.* New York: Basic Books, 1963.
Mintz, A. Non-adaptive group behavior. *Journal of Abnormal and Social Psychology,* 1951, *46,* 150–159.
Monat, A., Averill, J. R., & Lazarus, R. S. Anticipatory stress and coping reactions under various conditions of uncertainty. *Journal of Personality and Social Psychology,* 1972, *24,* 237–253.
Moore, H. E. Some emotional concomitants of disaster. *Mutual Hygiene,* 1958, *42,* 45–50. (a)
Moore, H. E. *Tornadoes over Texas.* Austin: University of Texas Press, 1958. (b)
Mowrer, O. H. *Learning theory and personality dynamics.* New York: Ronald Press, 1950.
Mowrer, O. H. *Learning theory and behavior.* New York: Wiley, 1960.
Niemela, P. Heart rate response during anticipation of an electric shock of variable probability. *Scandinavian Journal of Psychology,* 1969, *10,* 232–242.
Nomikos, M. S., Opton, E. M., Averill, J. R., & Lazarus, R. S. Surprise versus suspense in the production of stress reaction. *Journal of Personality and Social Psychology,* 1968, *2,* 204–208.
Obrist, P. A. Cardiovascular differentiation of sensory stimuli. *Psychosomatic Medicine,* 1963, *25,* 450–458.
Opton, E. M., & Lazarus, R. S. Personality determinants of psychophysiological response to stress: A theoretical analysis and an experiment. *Journal of Personality and Social Psychology,* 1967, *6,* 291–303.
Ornstein, R. E. *On the experience of time.* Harmondsworth: Penguin Books, 1969.
Petry, H. M., & Desiderato, O. Changes in heart rate, muscle activity and anxiety level following shock threat. *Psychophysiology,* 1978, *15,* 398–402.
Piaget, J. Piaget's theory. In P. H. Mussen (Ed.), *Carmichael's manual of child psychology* (Vol. 1, 3rd ed.). New York: Wiley, 1970.
Powell, J. W., & Rayner, J. Progress notes. *Disaster investigation July 1, 1951–June 30, 1952.* Edgewood, Md.: Army Chemical Center, Chemical Corps Medical Laboratories, 1952.
Prather, D. C. The effects of trial and error or errorless training on the efficiency of learning a perceptual-motor skill and performance under transfer and stress. *Dissertation Abstracts,* 1969, *30*(6-A), 2385.
Proceedings of the regional seminar on community preparedness and disaster prevention. New York: United Nations, 1978.
Rachman, S. J. *Fear and courage.* San Francisco: Freeman, 1978.
Ross, L. The intuitive psychologist and his shortcomings: Distortions in the attribution process. In

L. Berkowitz (Ed.), *Advances in experimental social psychology*. New York: Academic Press, 1977.

Rotter, J. B. Generalized expectancies for internal versus external control of reinforcement. *Psychological Monographs,* 1966, *80*(1, Whole No. 609).

Ruff, G. E., & Korchin, S. J. Adaptive stress behavior. In M. H. Appley & R. Trumbull (Eds.), *Psychological stress*. New York: Appleton-Century-Crofts, 1967.

Schachter, S., & Singer, J. E. Cognitive social and physiological determinants of emotional state. *Psychological Review,* 1962, *69,* 379–399.

Seligman, M. E. P. Phobias and preparedness. *Behavior Therapy,* 1971, *2,* 307–320.

Seligman, M. E. P. *Helplessness*. San Francisco: Freeman, 1975.

Seligman, M. E. P., & Groves, D. Non-transient learned helplessness. *Psychonomic Science,* 1970, *19,* 191–192.

Selye, H. *The stress of life*. New York: McGraw-Hill, 1956.

Selye, H. The evolution of the stress concept. *American Scientist,* 1973, *61,* 692–699.

Selye, H. *Stress in health and disease*. Woburn, Mass.: Butterworth, 1976.

Shaffer, L. *Psychological studies of anxiety reactions to combat* (USAAF Aviation Psychology Research Report No. 14). Washington, D.C.: U.S. Government Printing Office, 1947.

Skinner, B. F. *Science and human behavior*. New York: Macmillan, 1953.

Slovic, P. Assessment of risk taking behavior. *Psychological Bulletin,* 1964, *61,* 220–233.

Slovic, P., Fischoff, B., & Lichtenstein, S. Rating the risks. *Environment,* 1979, *21*(3), 14–39.

Slovic, P., Fishoff, B., & Lichtenstein, S. Perceived risk. In R. C. Schwing & W. A. Abers, Jr. (Eds.), *Societal risk assessment: How safe is safe enough?* New York: Plenum Press, 1980.

Slovic, P., & Lichtenstein, S. Comparison of Bayesian and regression approaches to the study of information processing in judgment. *Organizational Behavior and Human Performance,* 1971, *6,* 649–744.

Smelser, N. J. *Theory of collective behavior*. New York: Free Press, 1963.

Smock, C. D. The influence of psychological stress on the "Intolerance of Ambiguity." *Journal of Abnormal and Social Psychology,* 1955, *50,* 177–182.

Solomon, R. N., & Wynne, L. C. Traumatic avoidance learning: The principle of anxiety conservation and partial irreversibility. *Psychological Review,* 1954, *61,* 353–385.

Spence, K. W. Behavior theory and conditioning. New Haven, Conn.: Yale University Press, 1956.

Spielberger, C. D. Anxiety: State–trait–process. In C. D. Spielberger & I. G. Sarason (Eds.), *Stress and anxiety* (Vol. 1). New York: Wiley, 1975.

Starr, C. Social benefits versus technological risk. *Science,* 1969, *165,* 1232–1238.

Szpiler, J. A., & Epstein, S. Availability of an avoidance response as related to autonomic arousal. *Journal of Abnormal Psychology,* 1976, *85*(1), 73–82.

Terris, W., & Rahhal, D. K. Generalized resistance to the effects of psychological stressors. *Journal of Personality and Social Psychology,* 1969, *13,* 93–97.

Tversky, A., & Kahneman, D. The belief in the "law of small numbers." *Psychological Bulletin,* 1971, *76,* 105–110.

Tversky, A., & Kahneman, D. Availability: A heuristic for judging frequency and probability. *Cognitive Psychology,* 1973, *5,* 207–232.

Tversky, A., & Kahneman, D. Judgment under uncertainty: Heuristics and biases. *Science,* 1974, *185,* 1124–1131.

Vossel, G., & Laux, L. The impact of stress experience on heart rate and task performance in the presence of a novel stressor. *Biological Psychology,* 1978, *6,* 193–201.

Wachtel, P. C. Conceptions of broad and narrow attention. *Psychological Bulletin,* 1967, *68,* 417–429.

Wallace, A. F. C. *Tornado in Worcester: An exploratory study of individual and community behavior in an extreme situation* (Disaster Study No. 3). Washington, D.C.: National Academy of Sciences—National Research Council, 1956.

Welford, A. T. *Fundamentals of skill.* London: Methuen, 1968.
Welford, A. T. *Skilled performance: Perceptual and motor skills.* Glenview, Ill.: Scott, Foresman, 1976.
Whittow, J. *Disasters.* London: Allen Lane, 1980.
Winer, B. J. *Statistical principles in experimental design.* New York: McGraw-Hill, 1971.
Withey, S. B. Reaction to uncertain threat. In G. W. Baker & D. W. Chapman (Eds.), *Man and society in disaster.* New York: Basic Books, 1962.
Wolfenstein, M. *Disaster: A psychological essay.* Glencoe, Ill.: Free Press, 1957.

Author Index

Numbers in *italics* denote pages with complete bibliographic information.

A

Adams, A., 177, *256*
Adorno, T. W., 175, *253*
Agras, S., 177, *255*
Anner, N., 43, 57, *253*
Appley, H. M., 131, 132, *253*
Averill, J. R., 6, 25, 26, 30, 63, 78, *253, 256*

B

Baddeley, A. D., 132, *253*
Badia, P., 2, *253*
Baker, G. W., 78, *253*
Bankart, B., 29, *254*
Becker, H., 177, *253*
Ben-Zur, H., 167, *253*
Bergstroem, B., 132, *253*
Berlyne, D., 25, 63, *253*
Brady, J. V., 112, *253*
Breznitz, S., 5, 28, 30, 32, 35, 39, 40, 42, 48, 57, 94, 122, 167, 174, 197, *253, 254*
Broadbent, D. E., 132, *253*
Butz, R., 177, *255*

C

Campbell, T., 1
Cauthen, N., 177, *254*
Chapman, D. W., 3, 78, *253*
Clark, S., 33, *254*
Clifton, R. K., 39, *254*
Cofer, C. N., 131, 132, *253*
Condry, J. C., Jr., 6, *255*
Costello, C., 177, *253*
Cousins, N., 21, *253*
Cronbach, L. J., 208, *253*
Crowne, D. P., 162, *254*

D

Dahlke, A. E., 6, *255*
Deane, G. E., 39, *254*
Deese, J., 132, 143, *254, 255*
Desiderato, O., 6, 30, 31, 33, 39, *256*
Dollard, J., 159, *254*

E

Ekman, G., 32, *256*
Elliott, R., 29, 32, 33, 39, *254*
Epstein, S., 25, 29, 33, 49, 63, 186, *254, 257*

F

Fenz, W., 186, *254*
Festinger, L., 108, 125, 196, 214, *254*
Fischoff, B., 5, 100, *257*

259

260 AUTHOR INDEX

Flavell, J. H., 115, *254*
Folkins, C. H., 6, 29, *254*
Frankenhaeuser, M., 32, *256*
Fraser, R., 126, *254*
Frenkel-Brunswick, E., 175, *253*
Furby, L., 208, *253*

G

Gal, R., 130, 147, *254*
Glover, E., 126, *254*
Graham, F. K., 39, *254*
Green, D. M., 10, *254*
Groves, D., 5, *257*
Groves, P., 201, *254*
Guttman, L., 84, *254*

H

Hammerton, M. H., 132, *254*
Harsh, J., 2, *253*
Heider, F., 16, *254*
Helson, H., 26, *254*
Hepner, A., 177, *254*
Hersen, M., 177, *254*
Hess, A., 30, *254*
Hill, A. H., 6, *255*
Hodges, W. F., 39, *254*
Hodgson, R., 178, 184, *254*
Horowitz, M., 78, *254*
Hulse, S. H., 143, *254*

I

Inbar, M., 128, *254*

J

James, W., 79, *255*
Janis, I. L., 3, 26, 124, 125, 126, 197, 200, *255*
Jennings, 25, 63, *255*

K

Kagan, J., 39, 147, *255*
Kahneman, D., 5, 16, 25, 106, 132, *255*, *257*
Katkin, E. S., 49, *255*
Keinan, G., 131, *255*
Kelley, H. H., 6, *255*
Killian, L. M., 125, *255*

Kim, J., 74, *255*
Kohout, F. J., 74, *255*
Korchin, S. J., 132, *257*

L

Lacey, B. C., 39, 49, 147, *255*
Lacey, J. I., 39, 49, 147, *255*
Lader, M., 177, *255*
Lang, P., 178, *255*
Launier, R., *255*
Laux, L., 131, *257*
Lazarus, R. S., 3, 4, 6, 25, 26, 39, 63, 78, 122, 130, 132, 147, 160, *254*, *255*, *256*
Leitenberg, H., 177, *255*
Leslie, I., 126, *254*
Leventhal, H., 79, 197, *256*
Levinson, D. J., 175, *253*
Lichtenstein, S., 5, 25, 100, *257*
Liddle Hart, B. H., *256*
Light, T., 29, *254*
Lipsitt, L. P., 115, *256*
Lundberg, U., 32, *256*

M

MacCurdy, J. T., 126, *256*
Mackworth, J. F., 201, *256*
Mansueto, C. S., 6, 30, 33, *256*
Marks, I., 177, *255*
Marlowe, D. A., 162, *254*
Martin, B., 39, *256*
McCutcheon, B., 177, *256*
McGrath, J. E., 131, *256*
Meichenbaum, D., 94, *256*
Michotte, A., 16, *256*
Mintz, A., 6, *256*
Monat, A., 25, 31, 33, 63, 67, 68, 78, 91, 92, *256*
Moore, H. E., 126, *256*
Moss, H. A., 39, 147, *255*
Mowrer, O. H., 79, 195, 198, *256*

N

Niemela, P., 25, 63, *256*
Nomikos, M. S., 6, 29, *256*

O

Obrist, P. A., 39, *256*
Opton, E. M., 6, 25, 39, 63, *255*, *256*

Ornstein, R. E., 56, 150, *256*
Osler, S. F., 132, *255*

P

Petry, H. M., 31, 33, 39, *256*
Phelps, D., 126, *254*
Piaget, J., 115, *256*
Powell, J. W., 3, *256*
Prather, D. C., 132, *256*

R

Rachman, S. J., 177, 178, 184, 185, 195, 201, *254, 257*
Rahhal, D. K., 131, *257*
Rayner, J., 3, *256*
Reese, H. W., 115, *256*
Rosenn, M., 30, *253*
Ross, L., 16, *257*
Rotter, J. B., 162, *257*
Roupenian, A., 25, 29, 33, 63, *254*
Ruff, G. E., 132, *257*

S

Sanford, R. N., 175, *253*
Schachter, S., 122, *257*
Seligman, M. E. P., 5, 100, 174, 202, *257*
Selye, H., 21, *257*
Shaffer, L., 159, *257*
Singer, J. E., 122, *257*
Skinner, B. F., 72, *257*

Slovic, P., 5, 25, 100, 162, *257*
Smelser, N. J., 6, *257*
Smock, C. D., 162, 163, *257*
Solomon, R. N., 195, *257*
Spence, K. W., 162, *257*
Spielberger, C. D., 39, 32, 161, *254, 257*
Starr, C., 100, *257*
Swets, J. A., 10, *254*
Szpiler, J. A., 49, *257*

T

Terris, W., 131, *257*
Thompson, R., 201, *254*
Tickner, A. H., 132, *254*
Tversky, A., 5, 16, 25, 106, *257*

V

Vossel, G., 131, *257*

W

Wachtel, P. C., 132, *257*
Wallace, A. F. C., 3, *258*
Wincze, J., 177, *255*
Welford, A. T., 132, *258*
Whittow, J., 229, *258*
Winer, B. J., 121, 138, *258*
Withey, S. B., 3, 4, *258*
Wolfenstein, M., 126, *258*
Wynne, L. C., 195, *257*

Subject Index

A

Accidents, 20
Ambiguity, 2, 26
  intolerance of, 162, 163–164
American Psychological Association, 43
Anticipation, 2, 3, 37–38, 128
Anxiety, 1, 161–162
Avoidance behavior, distinction between protective behavior and, 195–198

B

Behavior, protective, *see* Protective behavior

C

Clock paradigm, 34
Conditioning paradigm, 34
Control, locus of, 161, 162, 173
Coping, 2, 5, 6
  active, 6
Credibility of warning systems, 11–13, 16, 19
  attempts to restore by explaining causes of false alarms, 114–127
  initial, law of, 206–214, 216
  near miss experiences and, 126–127
  toward a theory of, 204–218
Cynical dangers, 17–22, 197, 219, 230

D

Danger
  fear of, versus fear of fear, 198–200
  probability of the, 32–33
Danger of orientation, task orientation versus, 129–133
Dangers
  cynical, 17–22, 197, 219, 230
  naive, 17–22, 219, 229
Death, 1, 6, 233
Desynchrony, 178–194, 200, 203
  false alarm effect and, 184–194
Disasters
  industrial, 7
  military, 7, 230–231
  natural, 7–8, 18, 229–230
Discrete warnings paradigm, 33–38

E

Effectiveness of warning systems, 11
Extinction, false alarm effect and, 200–203

F

False alarm effect, 9–16
  as instrument for achieving surprise, 14–16
  behavioral measures of the, 17–102
  desynchrony and, 184–194

263

False alarm effect (*continued*)
  extinction and, 200–203
  habituation and, 200–203
  indexes of the, 39
  pacing of warnings and the, 40–60
  probability of threat and the, 61–76
  protective behavior and the, 77–102
  selecting individuals resistant to, 225–226
  sequential, 187–188
  testing, 51–53
  training against, 226
False alarms
  as reinforcer, 191–193
  defense against, 219–233
    institutional support in, 227
    social norms in, 226–227
  explaining causes of, in attempt to restore credibility of warning systems, 114–127
  positive aspects of, 217
  reasons for, 116
False promises, psychology of, 217–218
Fear
  of fear, fear of danger versus, 198–200
  protective behavior and, 94–98
Fear reaction, 1, 5, 27–39, 169–174
  analysis of, 177–194
  effect of probability of threat on, 63–76
  effects of task performance on, 143
  pacings of warnings and, 40–60

H

Habituation, false alarm effect and, 200–203
Health, warning systems in area of, 232–233
Helplessness, 5, 6, 27, 112, 173–174
Hurricanes, 9–10, 13, 14, 125

I

Imminence, 34
Immune system, 7
Incubation of threat, 5–6
Individual differences
  false alarm situation and, 160–176
  in the false alarm effect, 174–176
Industrial disasters, 7
Information-management subsystems, 8
  corrective measures by, 223–225
  preventive measures by, 220–223

Initial credibility, law of, 206–214, 216
Institutional support in defense against false alarms, 227–233
Interwarning similarity, law of, 214–217

J

Just noticeable difference, 32

L

Law of initial credibility, 206–214, 216
Law of interwarning similarity, 214–217
Locus of control, 161, 162, 173

M

Military disasters, 7, 230–231
Minimization of regret, principle of, 213

N

Naive dangers, 17–22, 219, 229
Natural disasters, 7–8, 18, 229–230
Near miss experiences, 124–127

P

Pacing of warnings, and the false alarm effect, 40–60
"Palliation," coping by, 6
Panic behavior, 6
Performance, task, *see* Task performance
Personality differences, role in false alarm situation, 160–176
Post-Experimental Questionnaire, 234–235
Probability of the danger, 32–33
Probability of threat, and the false alarm effect, 61–76
Promises, false, psychology of, 217–218
Protective behavior
  defined, 196
  distinction between avoidance behavior and, 195–198
  false alarm effect and, 72–102
  fear and, 94–98
  in the absence of threat, 193–194
  individual differences and, 165–168
  training of, 154–159
  under time pressure, 103–113

R

Reality testing, 199
Regret, minimization of, principle of, 213
Research method, 23-29
Risk taking, 162, 164

S

Sensitivity of warning systems, 10, 13-14
Social desirability, 161, 162
Social norms, and defense against false alarm effect, 226-227
Stress, psychological, 3
Surprise, 2, 10, 14, 219
  achieving, false alarm effect as instrument for, 14-16

T

Task orientation, versus danger orientation, 129-133
Task performance, 128-154
  effect of protective behavior training on, 155-158
  effects on fear reaction, 143
  training and, 133-154
Threat
  absence of protective behavior in, 193-194
  appraisal of, 4
  as a psychological variable, 3-4
  basic, 27-38
  defined, 4
  incubation of, 5-6
  parameters of, 5-6, 25-38
  probability of, and the false alarm effect, 61-76
  reactions, typology of, 100-102
  relaxation from, study of, 48
  "Time-locked" condition, 34
  "Time-unknown" condition, 34
Training
  against the false alarm effect, 226
  protective behavior, 154-159
  task performance and, 133-154
Tropical storms, 9-10, 13

U

Uncertainty, 2
  temporal, 33-35

W

Warning systems, 1-8
  biological, 7
  credibility of, see Credibility of warning systems
  effectiveness of, 11
  false alarm effect on, 9-16
  functional, 6-8
  information flow in, 11-12
  sensitivity of, 10, 13-14
  pacing of, and the false alarm effect, 40-60
Worry, 5, 122, 174

Y

Yerkes-Dodson Law, 131

BF
789
.F29
B73
1984